Complete

Literature in English

for Cambridge IGCSE® & O Level

Second Edition

Mark Pedroz

Oxford excellence for Cambridge IGCSE® & O Level

OXFORD
UNIVERSITY PRESS

OXFORD
UNIVERSITY PRESS

Great Clarendon Street, Oxford, OX2 6DP, United Kingdom

Oxford University Press is a department of the University of Oxford.
It furthers the University's objective of excellence in research,
scholarship, and education by publishing worldwide. Oxford is a
registered trade mark of Oxford University Press in the UK and in
certain other countries

British Library Cataloguing in Publication Data
Data available

978-0-19-842500-7

5 7 9 10 8 6 4

Paper used in the production of this book is a natural, recyclable product
made from wood grown in sustainable forests. The manufacturing
process conforms to the environmental regulations of the country of
origin.

Printed in India by Multivista Global Pvt. Ltd.,

Acknowledgements
We are grateful to the authors and publishers for use of extracts from
their titles and in particular for the following:
Alan Bennett: The History Boys: A Play, pp 54-6 © Alan Bennett. Faber & Faber,
2004. Reproduced by permission of Faber & Faber Ltd and Farrar, Straus and
Giroux. Sujata Bhatt: 'A Different History' from Collected Poems. Reproduced
by permission of Carcanet Press Limited. John Cassidy: 'Sons, Departing'
from Night Cries, Bloodaxe, 1982. Reproduced by permission of the author.
Gillian Clarke: 'Lament'' from Collected Poems, Carcanet Press Limited, 1996.
Reproduced by permission. Allen Curnow: COLLECTED POEMS, edited by
Elizabeth Caffin and Terry Sturm, published in 2017 by Auckland University
Press. Copyright Tim Curnow. Reproduced by permission. Emily Dickinson:
THE POEMS OF EMILY DICKINSON, edited by Thomas H. Johnson, Cambridge,
Mass.: The Belknap Press of Harvard University Press, Copyright © 1951, 1955
by the President and Fellows of Harvard College. Copyright © renewed 1979,
1983 by the President and Fellows of Harvard College. Copyright © 1914,
1918, 1919, 1924, 1929, 1930, 1932, 1935, 1937, 1942, by Martha Dickinson
Bianchi. Copyright © 1952, 1957, 1958, 1963, 1965, by Mary L. Hampson.
Graham Greene: 'The Destructors' from Collected Short Stories, published
by Penguin Books. Reproduced by permission of David Higham Associates.
Seamus Heaney: 16 lines (as specified) from 'Digging', from OPENED GROUND:
SELECTED POEMS 1966-1996 Reproduced by permission of Farrar, Straus and
Giroux and Death of a Naturalist, 1966 Reproduced by permission of Faber
and Faber Ltd. Henry James: Washington Square, edited by le Fanu (1982) 471
words from pp.37-38. Reproduced by permission of Oxford University Press,
www.oup.com. Philip Larkin: 'Coming' (complete poem) from THE COMPLETE
POEMS OF PHILIP LARKIN, edited by Archie Burnett. Copyright © 2012 by
The Estate of Philip Larkin. Introduction copyright © 2012 by Archie Burnett.
Reprinted by permission of Farrar, Straus and Giroux and Faber and Faber
Ltd. Harper Lee: Excerpt from pp. 321-2 from To Kill a Mockingbird, published
by William Heinemann, 1960. Copyright © 1960, renewed 1988 by Harper
Lee. Reprinted by permission of HarperCollins Publishers and The Random
House Group Limited. George Orwell: Nineteen Eighty-Four (Copyright ©
George Orwell, 1949) by permission of Bill Hamilton as the Literary Executor
of the Estate of the Late Sonia Brownell Orwell, Houghton Mifflin Harcourt
Publishing Company and Penguin Books Limited. All rights reserved. R. K.
Narayan: A Horse and Two Goats, Copyright © 1970 by R. K. Narayan. Used by
permission of The Wallace Literary Agency. Carol Rumens: 'Carpet-weavers,
Morocco'. © Carol Rumens. Reproduced by permission of the author. William
Shakespeare: Oxford School Shakespeare: Romeo and Juliet (2008), edited by
Gill, 339 words. By permission of Oxford University Press. George Bernard
Shaw: Extracts from Pygmalion, The Society of Authors, on behalf of the
Bernard Shaw Estate. Reproduced by permission. Carol Shields: Excerpt(s) from
THE STONE DIARIES, copyright © 1993 by Carol Shields. Used by permission
of The Carol Shields Literary Trust and Viking Books, an imprint of Penguin
Publishing Group, a division of Penguin Random House LLC. All rights reserved.
Any third party use of this material, outside of this publication, is prohibited.
Interested parties must apply directly to Penguin Random House LLC for
permission. Ahdaf Soueif: Sandpiper, Copyright © Ahdaf Soueif, 1994, used by
permission of The Wylie Agency (UK) Limited. Sylvia Townsend Warner: 'Road
1940' from Selected Poems, Carcanet Press Limited, January 1996. Reproduced
by permission. P. G. Wodehouse: The Custody of the Pumpkin published by
The Random House Group 1924. Copyright © P. G. Wodehouse. Reproduced
by permission of the estate of the author c/o Rogers, Coleridge & White Ltd, 20
Powis Mews, London W11 1JN.

Cover: Chatpong Kunakornkasem/Shutterstock

Artworks: Q2A Media and Phoenix Photosetting

Photos: p7 (T): SuperStock/Getty Images; **p7 (B):** Ramin Talaie/Corbis/Getty
Images; **p8 (R):** Alvin Langdon Coburn/George Eastman House/Getty Images;
p8 (L): Dylan Martinez/Reuters; **p14:** Masks designed by Jocelyn Herbert for
The Oresteia (1981), photographer: Sandra Lousada; **p15:** Geraint Lewis /
Alamy Stock Photo; **p16:** RGR Collection/Alamy Stock Photo; **p18:** Snap Stills/
REX/Shutterstock; **p21:** Warner Brothers/Getty Images; **p25:** Tony Larkin/REX/
Shutterstock; **p31:** Sylvain Gaboury/Patrick McMullan via Getty Images; **p32:**
King's Own Royal Regiment Museum, Lancaster; **p37 (TL):** British Library /
Robana/REX/Shutterstock; **p37 (TM):** Buyenlarge/Archive Photos/Getty Images;
p37 (TR): Granger Historical Picture Archive / Alamy Stock Photo; **p37 (B):**
REX/Shutterstock; **p39:** General Photographic Agency/Hulton Archive/Getty
Images; **p43:** Elizabeth Whiting & Associates/Alamy Stock Photo; **p44:** Dustin
Dennis/Shutterstock; **p46 (B):** Design Pics Inc/Alamy Stock Photo; **p46 (T):**
Guildhall Library & Art Gallery/Heritage Images/Getty Images; **p51:** Czesznak
Zsolt/Shutterstock; **p52:** National Geographic Creative / Alamy Stock Photo;
p55 (T): Oxford University Press ANZ; **p55 (B):** ONSLOW AUCTIONS LIMITED/
Mary Evans Picture Library; **p56:** Neil Holmes/VisitBritain/Getty Images;
p59: Hulton-Deutsch/Hulton-Deutsch Collection/Corbis/Getty Images; **p67:**
Carl Mydans/The LIFE Picture Collection/Getty Images; **p72:** Purestock/Getty
Images; **p73:** Wim Claes/Shutterstock; **p74:** Viorika/iStockphoto; **p77 (TR):**
John Frost Newspapers/Alamy Stock Photo; **p77 (BL):** Entertainment Pictures/
Alamy Stock Photo; **p80:** Everett Collection Inc/Alamy Stock Photo; **p82:**
Moviestore/REX/Shutterstock; **p83:** Everett Collection Inc/Alamy Stock Photo;
p88: AF Archive/Alamy Stock Photo; **p95:** Chris Mellor/Lonely Planet Images/
Getty Images; **p101:** Insights/Universal Images Group/Getty Images; **p102(T):**
Moviestore Collection/REX/Shutterstock; **p102(B):** Moviestore Collection/
REX/Shutterstock; **p103:** Robbie Jack/Corbis/Getty Images; **p106:** ITV/REX/
Shutterstock; **p110:** Robbie Jack/Corbis Entertainment/Getty Images; **p118:**
Hulton Archive/Getty Images; **p125:** Hulton Deutsch/ Corbis Historical/
Getty Images; **p138:** Geraint Lewis/REX/Shutterstock; **p142:** Popperfoto/
Getty Images; **p145:** Donald Cooper/REX/Shutterstock; **p147:** Jupiterimages/
Stockbyte/Getty Images; **p148:** Hi-Story/Alamy Stock Photo; **p149:** Granger
Historical Picture Archive/Alamy Stock Photo; **p153:** Julian Pottage/Alamy
Stock Photo; **p156:** Classic Image / Alamy Stock Photo; **p157:** AF archive/
Alamy Stock Photo; **p160:** Ekspansio/iStockphoto; **p161:** Moviestore
collection Ltd/Alamy Stock Photo; **p163:** The Print Collector/Print Collector/
Getty Images; **p168:** ITV/REX/Shutterstock; **p174:** Universal History Archive/
Getty Images; **p180:** Daniel Farson/Picture Post/Getty Images; p185: Universal/
Kobal/REX/Shutterstock; **p191:** Mark O'Flaherty/Alamy Stock Photo; **p195:**
Bettmann/Getty Images; **p199:** Visage/Stockbyte/Getty Images; **p200:**
PhotosIndia.com/Getty Images; **p202:** Hulton-Deutsch Collection/CORBIS/
Corbis/Getty Images; **p204:** Baker Alhashki/Shutterstock; **p207:** Everett
Historical/Shutterstock; **p210:** Ann Ronan Pictures/Print Collector/Getty
Images; **p211:** Tiger-Star/PantherMedia; **p213:** Snap Stills/REX/Shutterstock;
p218: Simon Stirrup/Alamy Stock Photo; **p220:** Parkerphotography/Alamy
Stock Photo; **p222:** Image Source/Alamy Stock Photo;

Contents

Access your support website at:
www.oxfordsecondary.com/9780198425007

What's on the website?

English Literature for Cambridge IGCSE® is supported by a website packed full of additional material specially written to support your learning. Everything in the book and on the website has been designed to help you develop your skills and achieve your very best.

Extra units

Two extra units designed to stretch your skills and approach assessment with confidence. Unit 5 is an extension unit which tackles unseen texts and extended essay writing. Unit 6 has lots of revision advice to use as you prepare for the assessment.

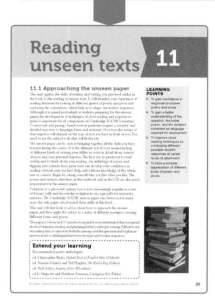

Worksheets

A wide range of activities to cement your understanding and develop your close reading skills. Some relate to specific texts but many can be used to analyse any text you study.

Glossary

A comprehensive revision tool that unpacks the vocabulary and carefully explains tricky terms.

Exam-style questions

These questions, written in the style of exam questions, will help you develop all the skills you need.

Setting off as a literature student

Introduction

Congratulations. You have just begun a voyage of discovery as you begin your **Cambridge Literature in English** course. Up to now you have probably studied a single subject called 'English' or 'literacy' and you have developed your skills in reading (both for specific purposes and for pleasure), writing, speaking, and listening. Your Cambridge IGCSE or O Level studies will continue to develop all of those skills, but in order to prepare you for the challenges of further study, you are now likely to be studying for two subjects, 'Language' and '**Literature**'.

This handbook will help you to prepare for Cambridge Literature in English by developing your skills in the **close reading** of different kinds of fictional text and improving your critical writing. It cannot replace the preparation of the set texts that you will work on with your teacher, but it gives you examples of how to improve your response to literature and develop your skills to higher levels. You will be introduced to texts in the three genres of drama, prose, and poetry, and to ways of analysing them and writing about them. There will be plenty of activity-based learning, with suggestions of activities you can try, in pairs and in groups, in order to develop your understanding, and there will be a range of extension tasks, both in the book and on the website, for further study and revision work.

How to use this book

The first three units are introductory and build on what you already know about English, working on your reading and writing skills and developing your understanding of how literature texts work. Students and teachers can use different parts of this unit in the early stages of the course in order to develop appreciation of genre, structure, and form. There is also an introduction to texts in their historical and cultural contexts.

Unit 4 is central to the course. It explores ways of studying and interpreting set texts through more detailed analysis of the conventions of each genre. Examples are drawn from some of the Cambridge Literature in English set texts, from past or future syllabuses.

KEY TERMS

Cambridge Literature in English = this textbook prepares you for both Cambridge IGCSE and O Level Literature in English.

literature = writing across the genres of poetry, prose, and drama. Not all literature needs to be fiction. Literature texts are those in which language and the imagination play an especially important role.

close reading = analysis of the words and effects writers use and how they make an impact on their readers.

The website includes two additional units. Unit 5 is an extension unit. It further develops your ability through more challenging coursework tasks, revision activities, and a whole chapter on the unseen paper, using past questions to develop an understanding of genre, form, and style.

Unit 6 is a final revision unit with exam-style questions and suggestions about how to answer them, revision advice, and tips for developing exam technique.

Activity-based learning

This will follow the principles of **assessment for learning** by encouraging a range of self-directed activities for students, allowing you to explore the meaning of texts, and work creatively to develop personal responses to the language and ideas used by writers. Each unit includes activities under the following headings.

LEARNING POINTS

These set out the objectives for each unit, chapter or section. They provide a clear definition of what you will be learning and which skills you will be practising.

Think ahead

These are activities that explore the world of the text, involving research into culture and background, genre and convention, ideas and themes, and the relationship between a text and its context. They will encourage you to engage with the world of the text before looking in detail at the words.

Check your understanding

These questions aim to achieve basic understanding of how the text works. They can be used as written activities or opportunities for whole-class discussion.

Pair and share

These are opportunities to discuss your response to a text with a partner or as part of a group. They are intended to extend and develop your understanding. You may find that different views and opinions are also possible!

The website includes two units to allow you to extend your learning.

Viewpoints

These are more extended activities in groups, which allow the development of personal response through drama, debate, and structured discussion. Working together to make meaning from texts, you should be able to develop your understanding of how characters and situations are presented by the writers.

Extend your learning

These activities go beyond the surface to explore ideas and attitudes through language, and encourage you to look back on your reading with deeper understanding of words, the writer's choices, and their effect on the reader.

Language links

Through both reading and writing activities there will be opportunities to link your literature work with the skills you are developing in your English language course. There will also be opportunities to write creatively in response to what you have read.

Looking back

You will be encouraged to check what you have learned and to assess the ways in which you have developed your skills as a student of literature by reviewing what you have learned in the current unit and how it builds on skills you have learned earlier in the course.

Practice questions

These questions follow a format similar to those used by Cambridge Literature in English exams, with advice on how to improve your answers. Some questions are identified as past paper questions from the Cambridge IGCSE or O Level. All other questions have been written by the author. You will find some 'student-style responses', with helpful comments on their strengths and weaknesses.

Throughout this handbook you will find additional information, and suggestions in boxes on the right-hand side of the page, including advice about how to plan and time your answers and glossary terms.

Where this icon occurs, there will be an opportunity to extend activities by referring to the website for text extracts, more worksheets, and more exam-style questions. These will help you to practise your essay writing skills and demonstrate your understanding of the texts.

Individual responsibility for your learning and the development of your ideas will be emphasized throughout: this book will not tell you the answers but it will help you to ask yourself the right questions.

What is literature?

1.1 The Cambridge syllabus

Literature has been described as the best that has been thought and said. Above all the Cambridge syllabus has the aim of encouraging you to 'enjoy the experience of reading literature'. Literature texts have often stood the test of time. They appeal to very different cultures. At university, the study of literature allows you to study a huge range of texts and explore different ways of reading them. At school, your teachers will introduce you to various texts, some chosen by them and others set for examination, in order to introduce the key skills for success in this subject. These are:

- close reading—analysing the effects that writers use in order to make an impact on their readers
- reading in depth—tackling substantial whole texts in order to look at meaning beyond the surface narrative
- writing critically—exploring and evaluating a range of ideas and opinions, and coming to conclusions of your own about them
- writing discursively—learning to argue, finding evidence to support your views, and making an informed personal response to a text.

While language study teaches you a range of practical skills, literature study is more theoretical. Assessment focuses on the way in which students communicate their own response to texts through their essays. Studying literature teaches you to be sensitive to different people and what interests them, to be alert to the ways in which writers express themselves, and to ensure that your own ideas are well supported by close observation of language and form. These are all transferable skills and will be useful to you in your future studies.

Literature assessment objectives

Now have a look at the assessment objectives (AOs) for the Literature in English course.

AO1	Show detailed knowledge of the content of literary texts in the three main forms (drama, poetry, and prose)
AO2	Understand the meanings of literary texts and their contexts, and explore texts beyond surface meanings to show deeper awareness of ideas and attitudes
AO3	Recognize and appreciate ways in which writers use language, structure and form to create and shape meanings and effects
AO4	Communicate a sensitive and informed personal response to literary texts

LEARNING POINTS

- ▶ To understand the nature of literature as a subject
- ▶ To appreciate the Cambridge Literature in English syllabus assessment objectives

Cambridge O Level Literature in English divides AO3 in two:

AO3   Recognize and appreciate ways in which writers use language

AO4   Recognize and appreciate ways in which writers achieve their effects (e.g. structure, plot, characterization, dramatic tension, rhythm, setting and mood)

This helpfully defines language, structure and form but does not affect the way your work is assessed, which is the same as Cambridge IGCSE. AO5 for O Level is the same as AO4 for IGCSE.

Clearly all these objectives ask you to take a responsible and responsive approach to the reading you are asked to do. You will need to read and think about the books! However, for your understanding to go **beyond the surface** and for your **personal response** to be truly sensitive to the text you will need further qualities. They are:

- confidence in tackling the writer's use of language and ideas
- engagement in the close reading and interpretation of a text
- an innovative and individual approach—your own response should be both truly personal and relevant to the question.

It is the purpose of this book to encourage those further skills, so that your response becomes personal, developed, and critical.

Thinking about assessment

Your teachers will set you various tasks to test your knowledge and understanding of your literature texts. Throughout this book and on the website you will find practice essay questions, in the style of the Cambridge Literature in English exams but written by the author. You will also find some examples of past paper questions. Initially, you will be given plenty of help in structuring and answering practice questions through bullet points and essay plans. Chapters 5 and 6 and online chapters 10 and 12 give guidance on how to make your essays more sophisticated.

Throughout the textbook, you are encouraged to assess your own work and those of others, as well as working with your teachers to improve your grades. You will not be achieving high marks right away but you should see yourself improving throughout the course.

Structure of the course

Cambridge IGCSE Literature in English has two syllabus codes: 0475 and 0992. These syllabuses are identical. One is grade A*–G for international students, and the other is graded 9–1 for UK schools. We do not refer to grades or mark schemes in this textbook, but concentrate on key skills. You will see examples of stronger and weaker work.

There are three different routes through the IGCSE syllabuses as shown below:

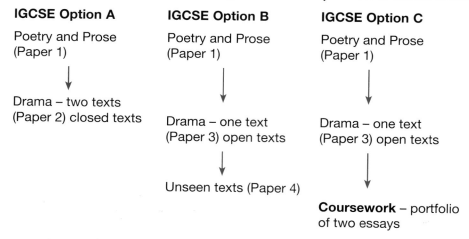

IGCSE Option A

Poetry and Prose
(Paper 1)

↓

Drama – two texts
(Paper 2) closed texts

IGCSE Option B

Poetry and Prose
(Paper 1)

↓

Drama – one text
(Paper 3) open texts

↓

Unseen texts (Paper 4)

IGCSE Option C

Poetry and Prose
(Paper 1)

↓

Drama – one text
(Paper 3) open texts

↓

Coursework – portfolio
of two essays

KEY TERMS

coursework = work completed during the course, assessed by your teacher, and moderated both within the school and by Cambridge. The process of moderation is to ensure that students given the same mark have achieved the same standard. Any of the longer essays you write could be submitted as coursework. See online chapter 10 for more advice on assembling a coursework folder.

The syllabus for O Level is identical to Option A in IGCSE, but you can study either one or two plays, as shown below:

O Level

Poetry and Prose (Paper 1)

↓

Drama – one or two texts (Paper 2)

The route you take will depend on your teachers' choices. Paper 1 is the same for all of them. If you take O Level, you must do Option A, but you may study either one or two drama texts. The drama texts and questions are identical for Paper 2 and Paper 3.

Your teachers will decide which texts you study, especially for coursework. The unseen paper tests your response to poetry and prose texts which you have not read before. The other exams all have a choice of passage-based or discursive essay questions. However, all examinations require close and detailed study of the three genres or forms of Literature in English: poetry, prose and drama. Each genre requires different skills, and this textbook develops those skills, beginning with drama, and using passages from current and past set texts.

You and your teachers can decide in which order to study texts and genres. This book is designed progressively, aiming to develop your reading skills over two or three years through close appreciation of different forms of writing. On the website, you can extend your studies with chapters on writing long essays, reading and writing about unseen literature, and preparing for examination.

Understanding genre

Literature began with poetry. These were songs and stories recited by bards or storytellers around the fire in ancient days which then became written texts. They were composed in a form of verse to make them easier to remember: lines have set patterns of rhythm and sound.

✎ Check your understanding

Draw up three columns headed prose, poetry, and drama in your exercise book or on paper. Think about the texts you have already studied or know about. Which column do they belong in?

Note: Texts chosen for study in this syllabus must have been originally written in English. Cambridge offer another syllabus called 'World Literature' which includes texts in translation.

Lyrics (songs based around emotional experiences) and epics (longer narrative or story) were the first poems to become established as parts of world literature. Before long, actors supplemented the recitals of bards, whether by adopting the parts of characters (called personae or more literally 'masks', as most early drama involved the wearing of masks) or by forming part of a chorus. This was the beginning of drama. Early drama was often in verse too: it helped the actors to remember their parts through structures of rhythm, repetition, and sound effect. Actors wore different masks for the different forms of tragedy and comedy.

However, sometimes both drama and stories were told in prose, keeping more closely to the language, rhythms, and rules of everyday speech.

How did English literature develop?

It is worth knowing that English literature is not really very old: the language itself comes from a fusion of the languages of the Anglo-Saxons and the Norman French, both heavily influenced by the Viking Norse, and really only becomes recognizable as English from about 1200 CE. The form of the novel is even more recent (indeed the name means 'new'), as prose only became the most common genre for writing a narrative from around 1700 CE. It was the process of colonization and trade during the following years which established English as such a dominant world language: readers of English took their literature all over the world, and the world contributed its stories to what we now call 'English'. This course book will take an international approach to our appreciation of literature, appropriate to Cambridge Literature in English which is studied all over the globe.

The poet Ezra Pound said that 'Literature is news that stays news', in other words, it comes out of the society that produced it and always begins as something novel, but over time different readers agree that there is still plenty to learn and understand in these texts long after they have been written. Literature scholars talk about a canon of texts which have remained a part of current thought or culture, and which students might expect to study. However, the texts which make up that canon keep changing, and they probably tell us more about the society we live in than the society that originally produced those texts.

When Shakespeare, for example, wrote his plays (although not his poems) he was probably more concerned about filling the theatres of which he was a shareholder. He probably did not imagine he was writing texts which would become canonical. He seems to have been fairly careless about how his plays were written down. Others collected his plays and studied them after his death. Many modern writers have rather mixed feelings about finding their works on school syllabuses, especially while they are still alive and writing!

English literature moved around the globe and now includes work from writers such as the Indian novelist Anita Desai

First collection of Shakespeare's works

🗨 Pair and share

With a partner create a mind map to explore what you understand by the study of 'English'. How does it divide into studies in language and literature? How do we decide the skills we need to demonstrate and develop in each? What makes up a syllabus for each subject? How did English get a 'literature'? Which books have you read which you would call 'literature'?

'Literature is news that stays news.'
Ezra Pound

1.2 How do modern writers see the craft of writing?

Digital communication is rapidly changing the way we think about writing and literature, and you might want to think about what 'English literature' will look like at the end of the twenty-first century.

However, for an example of the ways in which writers saw the craft of literature in the twentieth century, there are few better examples than the poem which follows by Seamus Heaney called 'Digging', which headed his first published volume of poetry in 1966.

Many readers find poetry quite difficult at first. Remember that poetry comes out of song, and needs to be read, or at least 'heard' aloud. Listen for the sounds and 'music' of the poem and reflect on what it makes you feel. A famous poet said that 'poetry communicates before it is understood'. A second reading can push your understanding further: focus on the images, or pictures, the poet creates and how they tell a story.

In this poem the poet tells us that his father is a farmer, seen here planting potatoes, and his grandfather used to cut 'turfs', squares of peat used for heating. Both are traditional activities in the countryside of Ireland. The poet, however, has returned from university and wants to live life as a writer (he later won the Nobel Prize for Literature).

'Digging' by Seamus Heaney (1966)

Between my finger and my thumb
The squat pen rests; snug as a gun.

Under my window, a clean rasping sound
When the spade sinks into gravelly ground:
My father, digging. I look down

Till his straining rump among the flowerbeds
Bends low, comes up twenty years away
Stooping in rhythm through potato drills
Where he was digging.

8

The coarse boot nestled on the lug, the shaft
Against the inside knee was levered firmly.
He rooted out all tops, buried the bright edge deep
To scatter new potatoes that we picked
Loving their cool hardness in our hands.

By God, the old man could handle a spade.
Just like his old man.

My grandfather cut more turf in a day
Than any other man on Toner's bog.
Once I carried him milk in a bottle
Corked sloppily with paper. He straightened up

To drink it, then fell to right away
Nicking and slicing neatly, heaving sods
Over his shoulder, going down and down
For the good turf. Digging.

The cold smell of potato mould, the squelch and slap
Of soggy peat, the curt cuts of an edge
Through living roots awaken in my head.
But I've no spade to follow men like them.

Between my finger and my thumb
the squat pen rests.
I'll dig with it.

✎ Check your understanding

1. The poet uses a lot of hard or harsh sounds. List as many words as you can find that sound harsh. Why do these sounds suit the masculine activity of digging?

2. The poem is made up of a series of images, beginning with the poet looking out of his window then working back through his memory, through family legends, and stories. The poem tells a story across three generations. Organize your notes chronologically to explain:

   a. what the poet sees now

   b. how his father worked 20 years before

   c. how his grandfather worked before that.

3. Clearly what the poet is going to do is very different, but he tells us that he will 'dig' with his pen. In what ways might writing poetry be similar to digging? Think about the regular rhythms of work, the hard effort, and finding or planting something precious. How does the poet justify his choice of work?

4. When the poet talks about 'living roots' he is perhaps describing the stories of his family, as well as digging through the soil. How has his writing helped to convey those roots to you?

5. The end of the poem is very similar to the start, but it is also different. Why do you think the image of a spade has replaced that of a gun? Write down the effect of that change on you. This will help you to evaluate or interpret the poem.

💬 Pair and share

How can we turn the poem into a drama? Form a group of three: poet, father, and grandfather. The father and grandfather are worried about what the boy will do with his life after university. What are the questions they have? Why doesn't he want to be a farmer or dig for peat turfs? Discuss the ways in which they might argue or interact.

When writing a script, remember that audiences need to be introduced to each character and their interests. (It helps to give them a name!) It is often easier to start a scene with just two characters and then introduce a third. Give characters some longer speeches in order to explain their points of view and show them telling stories or passing on memories.

Perform your scene to your classmates. Has writing and performing the poem as drama helped you to understand it better? Has it developed your own understanding of the characters, or has it made the poem less intimate and personal?

Extend your learning

Now try turning the poem into a novel. Will you tell the story in the first person or the third person? First try drafting the boy's diary, showing us his ideas as he thinks them through.

This probably does not look very different from the poem. Do you still have a strong sense of the characters and the realism of the situation which you created in your play?

You need to capture the drama of the moment when the boy tells his family what he intends to do, and, like in the play, you may want to use dialogue. However, a novel needs description to capture the realism of the moment and it needs to get inside the minds of the central characters and communicate some of their thoughts. You can do this in the third person just as effectively as in the first person, so now use the third person to give the young writer's thoughts: a novel does not need to sound like a diary.

Re-write your diary or journal entry as a novel, in the third person, but giving the thoughts as well as the spoken words of the characters.

What have you discovered about how prose communicates? How is it different from drama?

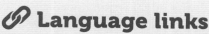 Language links

Heaney uses the **extended metaphor** of digging to pay homage to what his father and grandfather did and to explore what he will do in his adult life. He makes his poem out of a slideshow of images or pictures which are briefly but memorably described.

Do you have an idea of the activity that will define your future life? If you don't, perhaps looking at what your ancestors did will help you to think about this, even if it is your intention to rebel against their model, just as Heaney does, and explore a different kind of life.

Use Heaney's style of writing which does not need a set and regular pattern of rhyme or rhythm to write a poem of your own, based on a sequence of images. You might like to illustrate your poem with images. Think about the ways in which sound effects, the contrast of long and short lines, and different kinds of punctuation (pauses) can make your writing more memorable.

Compare your ideas with a friend. Concentrate on the lines which your partner agrees work best. Your poem does not need to be very long, provided it works.

1.3 Making meaning

We now live in a global culture. Not only do sons choose very different lives from their fathers, but English has become a world language, spoken by over a quarter of the world's population. That means it is not always easy to understand one another. Reading literature is about the art of **interpretation**, making sense and meaning out of the language of others. This is a very useful skill, but it isn't always easy, and in our diverse world, people don't always understand one another.

Look at this extract from a short story written by R.K. Narayan in 1970. 'A Horse and Two Goats' describes an encounter between a very old, very poor Indian man called Muni and a rich American. Muni only has two words of English, 'yes' and 'no', and so doesn't realize that the American wants to buy the statue of a horse which he is sitting under. Indeed Muni thinks he may want to question him about a murder. Muni is speaking Tamil in reply to the American's English.

'A Horse and Two Goats' by R.K. Narayan (1970)

Muni felt totally confused but decided the best thing would be to make an attempt to get away from this place. He tried to edge out, saying, 'Must go home,' and turned to go. The other seized his shoulder and said desperately, 'Is there no one, absolutely no one here, to translate for me?' He looked up and down the road, which was deserted in this hot afternoon; a sudden gust of wind churned up the dust and dead leaves on the roadside into a ghostly column and propelled it towards the mountain road. The stranger almost pinioned Muni's back to the statue and asked, 'Isn't this statue yours? Why don't you sell it to me?'

The old man now understood the reference to the horse, thought for a second, and said in his own language, 'I was an urchin this high when I heard my grandfather explain this horse and warrior, and my grandfather himself was this high when he heard his grandfather, whose grandfather…'

The other man interrupted him with, 'I don't want to seem to have stopped here for nothing. I will offer you a good price for this,' he said, indicating the horse. He had concluded without the least doubt that Muni owned this mud horse. Perhaps he guessed by the way he sat at its pedestal, like other souvenir-sellers in this country presiding over their wares.

Muni followed the man's eyes and pointing fingers and dimly understood the subject matter and, feeling relieved that the theme of the mutilated body had been abandoned at least for the time being, said again, enthusiastically, 'I was this high when my grandfather told me about this horse and the warrior, and my grandfather was this high when he himself…' and he was getting into a deeper bog of reminiscence each time he tried to indicate the antiquity of the statue.

The Tamil that Muni spoke was stimulating even as pure sound, and the foreigner listened with fascination. 'I wish I had my tape-recorder here,' he said, assuming the pleasantest expression. 'Your language sounds wonderful. I get a kick out of every word you utter, here' – he indicated his ears – 'but you don't have to waste your breath in sales talk. I appreciate the article. You don't have to explain its points.'

✎ Check your understanding

1. List the words which suggest how frustrated the American is by his inability to understand Muni.

2. Which words tell you how isolated this place is?

3. What is the importance of the horse to Muni?

4. What sort of value does the American place on the horse?

5. What does the American like about Muni's language?

6. What does he fail to understand?

The American cannot appreciate that Muni does not own the mud horse, or that it is part of a very old culture which he does not understand, even though he does respond to its beauty (and wants to take it home). For the American, everything has a price, and it is a price which will be welcome to Muni as he is very poor, although Muni thinks the American is offering him a hundred rupees for his two goats.

As the story goes on, Muni tries to explain that the horse represents 'Kalki' who will come at the end of the world to trample down bad men, and then tells stories about god, avatars, and the plays he used to take part in. The American gets out a large wad of money.

You can see that the meaning of the story goes beyond a language barrier. The American does not just fail to understand the literal meaning of Muni's words but he also can't imagine the values and traditions of a culture much older than his own. These are also 'lost in translation' and there is no one there to interpret them to him. As a reader, we see that making meaning is about interpretation at a deeper level; we need to go beyond literal meanings and understand the kind of world a story comes from, or tells us about. The meaning of an object or a text needs to be connected to the community and culture that produced it.

Pair and share

Cultural understanding is often about values and traditions, not just about money or the acquisition of knowledge.

1. What does your own culture value especially highly?

2. Are there stories you know which support those values?

3. Which myths and traditions should visitors be aware of in order to understand your culture?

Extend your understanding

Different generations and different cultures have different ideas of values and traditions. How do stories preserve traditions for future generations? Write a review of a play you have seen or a story you have read that has told you something about the values and culture of the past. Try to answer the following questions.

1. Who was the story about?

2. What were the values or ideas which it presented?

3. How did it make you think about them?

4. What was the impact of the story on you and what do you remember best about it?

You will now see that interpreting the language and meaning of a story is about understanding ideas and attitudes as well as words.

Looking back

Do you now feel that you have a better idea of what a literature course involves? Here are some questions and activities for you to discuss and write about.

1. Give your own definition of the subject you are studying and its different parts. Explain the kind of literature you most enjoy and why. Remember your teachers may have different ideas about what they want you to study!

2. What are the skills that teachers are looking to reward in this subject?

3. How do poetry, prose and drama differ in form and effect? Which is the most private form

and which the most public? Which is the most concentrated and which did you find easiest to write?

4. How does interpretation relate to the meaning of a text? What is meant by going beyond the literal meaning?

5. Why is cultural understanding important alongside an appreciation of language if we are to appreciate literature?

You are now ready to progress to the second unit, where we will explore the skills of reading across these three genres in more detail.

Developing reading skills

The forms of literature

The next two units are designed as an introduction before you begin the detailed study of your set texts. They introduce the features of the three genres you will be studying. They explore ways of linking texts through their structure and choice of subject in order to develop a critical and comparative response to literature.

We will look at the choices writers make about the form and structure of their texts, addressing assessment objective 3. We will explore comedy, the short story, and war poetry.

The texts chosen will introduce you to some short texts from the past, showing some of the traditions of literature in English. You will not need to read these texts in the same close detail as you will your set texts (although some of the texts used here could be your set texts) but by exploring form and structure you will appreciate some of the history and traditions of each genre, while also moving forward in time to consider more contemporary texts.

In this unit, we want you to understand the conventions and forms of texts. This approach to the structure of texts should help you to look at plot and character in new ways. You will also begin to practise close reading and ways of making your response both personal and informed. Units 3 and 4 will develop these skills further.

LEARNING POINTS

▶ To explore in more depth and understand the ways in which readers respond to the three genres of drama, prose, and poetry

▶ To appreciate ways in which language, structure, and form shape our response

▶ To begin to identify writers' effects

▶ To appreciate how texts are influenced by culture and historical context

Reading drama

How did drama evolve?

As we saw in chapter 1, ancient literature consisted of lyrical and epic poetry, recited out loud. **Lyrical** poetry was usually like a song with a single speaking voice, expressing emotions, and accompanied by a stringed instrument, like a lyre. **Epic** poetry told

Masked Greek chorus

long stories about the gods and men, with many adventures, battles, and confrontations. There were lots of characters making speeches and many changes of scene or situation, so the poems were divided into books.

Drama emerged out of epic poetry: a theatre audience wanted to hear more about the characters and their stories, and to see these performed. **Drama** introduces a second voice, so that there is **dialogue** between the characters. It introduces more debate, as we can hear and see different viewpoints, and identify with different characters, depending on how they are played. Instead of being told a story, it is presented to us. We, as the audience, can make our own sense of it. While early dramas had a **chorus** to help the audience to make meaning out of the story, we are now used to dramas where we make meaning ourselves. Live theatre is an event, with a sense of performance and with intervals, allowing us to discuss our reaction to characters and events. Most film and television actors began their careers in, and enjoy, live theatre. They like the element of risk and they like the more immediate reactions that a live audience can give.

To write about drama, you will need to imagine the texts on stage. Think about how they could come to life, and how an audience would react to the words. Try to link your reaction to the text of the play. 'The text' refers to the words the actors are given and also the directions which suggest how a scene could be staged.

Ancient drama involved actors in masks. Masks remind us that we are watching a play, and the faces would often make clear if the play was tragedy or comedy. In the European tradition, costume replaced the mask: in medieval times, and in Shakespeare's theatre, costume told audiences a lot

LEARNING POINTS

▶ To appreciate distinct features of dramatic form, especially dialogue

▶ To look at a range of texts from the past and how they can come to life through staging and performance

▶ To look at setting, characterization, and conflict

▶ To explore some of the conventions of comedy, for example, status anxiety and misunderstanding

▶ To look at and question the traditional 'happy ending'

KEY TERMS

lyric = a traditional form of poem, which is song-like and expresses a single, but often complex, emotion.

epic = an extended and heroic poem, often containing mythological characters.

drama = text designed for performance.

dialogue = any situation where two or more people are speaking. Dialogue helps to dramatize prose and bring the characters to life.

chorus = in drama, characters who work together, often commenting on the action of a play.

about a character. Drama in the English tradition has also enjoyed combining elements of **tragedy** and **comedy**: there are serious elements in comedy, and comic scenes in tragedies. These can add extra levels of irony as we shall see.

Part of the pleasure of theatre has always come from watching larger-than-life characters, in elaborate costumes, behaving in ways that are much more exaggerated than real life, who we can laugh at, but also understand. Comedy in literature often involves the complications of love, and sometimes also depends on the comedy of class, bringing characters from different parts of society together in a clash of cultures.

We will look at three theatre texts. All of them are comedies and involve people acting outrageously. What do we find funny about this and why?

We will also explore some of the **conventions** of drama. It is much easier to analyse drama when you are aware of how writers make choices about:

- character
- situation and setting
- **contrast** and conflict
- problems and plot development
- social comedy and conventions involving status
- use of exaggeration and the **surreal** (larger than life) in comedy
- misunderstanding and its consequences, especially plot complication ('**farce**')
- the convention of the happy ending.

One of the building blocks of drama is **duologue**—a dialogue involving just two characters, as opposed to the **monologue** in which only one character speaks. All the texts we will be looking at involve arguments or quarrels. What do we learn about the two characters from their conversation and confrontation?

Mark Rylance in a production of Shakespeare's *Twelfth Night*. In Shakespeare's theatre female roles were played by men. Some modern productions follow this convention.

KEY TERMS

tragedy = a serious and often disturbing play which usually ends in death.

comedy = a play that is funny and usually ends happily.

convention = the ways in which texts are written to meet reader or audience expectations.

contrast = a striking difference.

surreal = a situation which is beyond the real, taking us into a different way of looking at the 'real' world.

farce = especially exaggerated comedy, which relies heavily on stage conventions.

duologue = a dialogue involving just two characters.

monologue = one character speaking and telling the audience their thoughts.

Think ahead

Find out the definition of the following terms:

1. drawing-room comedy
2. duologue
3. Gorgon (a mythological beast)
4. earnest (as an adjective)
5. pun
6. irony
7. ward (a legal term)
8. epigram
9. snobbery
10. Victorian

Share your definitions with your classmates.

 See Worksheet 1 on the website for an activity on comedy and tragedy.

2.1 Introducing characters: the double act

In *The Importance of Being Earnest* Jack Worthing has just proposed to his girlfriend, Gwendolen, who says that she loves him because his name is Ernest. However, this isn't his real name—it is just the name he uses when he visits London from the country, where he uses his real name, Jack. In the country he pretends to be very mature and respectable, especially in front of his niece, Cecily, but says he needs to go up to London regularly to help his wicked brother, Ernest. He has also spoken to Lady Bracknell, Gwendolen's mother, and the aunt of Ernest's best friend, Algernon, and revealed to her that his surname, Worthing, is also made up. He was found in a handbag in the cloakroom of Victoria station by a rich gentleman who adopted him. Lady Bracknell is appalled: she cannot allow her daughter to marry someone who grew up in a handbag!

Rupert Everett as Algernon and Colin Firth as Jack in a film adaptation of *The Importance of Being Earnest*

The Importance of Being Earnest by Oscar Wilde (1895)

Algernon Didn't it go off all right, old boy? You don't mean to say Gwendolen refused you? I know it is a way she has. She is always refusing people. I think it is most ill-natured of her.

Jack Oh, Gwendolen is as right as a trivet. As far as she is concerned, we are engaged. Her mother is perfectly unbearable. Never met such a Gorgon … I don't really know what a Gorgon is like, but I am quite sure that Lady Bracknell is one. In any case, she is a monster, without being a myth, which is rather unfair … I beg your pardon, Algy, I suppose I shouldn't talk about your own aunt in that way before you.

Algernon My dear boy, I love hearing my relations abused. It is the only thing that makes me put up with them at all. Relations are simply a tedious pack of people, who haven't got the remotest knowledge of how to live, nor the smallest instinct about when to die.

Jack O, that is nonsense!

Algernon It isn't!

Jack Well, I won't argue about the matter. You always want to argue about things.

Algernon That is exactly what things were originally made for.

Jack Upon my word, if I thought that I'd shoot myself … (*A pause.*) You don't think there is any chance of Gwendolen becoming like her mother in about a hundred and fifty years, do you, Algy?

Algernon All women become like their mothers. That is their tragedy. No man does. That's his.

Jack Is that clever?

Algernon It is perfectly phrased! And quite as true as any observation in civilized life should be.

Jack I am sick to death of cleverness. Everybody is clever nowadays. You can't go anywhere without meeting clever people. The thing has become an absolute public nuisance. I wish to goodness we had a few fools left.

Algernon We have.

Jack I should extremely like to meet them. What do they talk about?

Algernon The fools? Oh! About the clever people, of course.

Jack What fools!

🗨 Pair and share

1. Which lines do you find shocking?
2. Who do you think is cleverer: Algernon or Jack?
3. Who do we laugh with and who do we laugh at?
4. What are the qualities that make Algernon and Jack attractive and interesting characters?

Comedy is often about 'fooling', that is, playing characters who are a bit larger than life, either cleverer than we really are or less clever. Have a go at performing this duologue together, exaggerating the characters. How funny can you make them?

Check your understanding

Comedy involves exaggeration, featuring outrageous characters who are allowed to say shocking things. In England at the time the play was written, marriage was about your social status and relations were important, not only for status but for the money they might leave you when they died. When he is in the country, Jack lives a very conventional life which he finds boring. In London with Algernon he can go to parties and say witty and outrageous things.

Write or discuss answers to the following questions.

1. Why would Algernon not have been surprised if Gwendolen had turned Jack down?
2. What does that suggest about attitudes to marriage and proposals at that time?
3. Why does Jack call Lady Bracknell a Gorgon?
4. Why does Algernon wish his relations knew when to die?
5. Why is Jack so worried about Gwendolen becoming like her mother?
6. How does Algernon turn this into an **epigram**?
7. Why does Algernon like Jack's epigram about fools and clever people?
8. Who do they think are 'fools'?

Extend your learning

We have seen that double acts provide witty characters who can compete with each other in saying outrageous things. This gives us epigrams, witty sayings you could apply to other situations in life:

- … she is a monster, without being a myth, which is rather unfair …
- Jack: You always want to argue about things. Algernon: That is exactly what things were originally made for.
- All women become like their mothers. That is their tragedy. No man does. That's his.

Writing essays in English literature about the texts you study involves choosing the right quotations and saying something interesting about how they work. As you know, this play is about relatives and relationships, about battles of wit, and about inheritance. Commenting on a quotation is a three-stage process, sometimes called the PEA technique, that you need to practise.

- Make a *point* (P) about how the quotation illustrates the impact of an aspect of the text or the character on the audience. (Use the hints in the previous paragraph.)
- Use the quotation as *evidence* (E).
- *Analyse* (A) how the language shows a characteristic of the language of the play, in the last case contrast, or to use a more classical term, **antithesis**.

Viewpoints

You can see that a lot of the comedy of this scene comes from characterization. The writer has created two characters who are friends but very different from one another. They contrast very effectively.

1. Who do you find more likeable?
2. Why do you think Algernon felt 'Ernest' the right name for Jack and said 'You are the most earnest-looking character I ever met in my life'?
3. Why does Jack need a friend like Algernon, and why does Algernon need Jack?
4. Can you think of other famous pairs of characters, comic like Laurel and Hardy or 'straight' (that is, serious) like Holmes and Watson? List as many as you can. These are called double acts.
5. How do they contrast? Funny and serious? Clever and foolish (or gullible)?

 See Worksheet 3 on the website for an activity on double acts.

Developing the situation

Analysis helps us to look at how writers use language, but we should also look at their choices of form and structure. The playwright has used two contrasting characters to amuse the audience but also to develop his plot while keeping us entertained.

We have established that in this play the 'town', London, is a place where Jack can be outrageous and have a different name and identity. However, if he is to get married to Gwendolen, whom he loves, he will need her mother's approval. He needs relatives so that he can establish who he really is. This gives us a situation.

There is a further plot complication or problem. Complications help comic plots: they lead to further confusion and misunderstanding (always funny) and involve all the characters in the action that follows. Look at the next passage and how it shows further developments, both of situation and character. It shows the developing contrast between the town and the country.

In the country, Jack has a young ward, the daughter of the rich man who found him, Cecily. She thinks Jack is a very serious person. When Jack gets bored of being serious, he uses an invented friend called 'Bunbury' who lives in town and is always getting in trouble which requires Jack's help (and money), rather like the real life Algernon. Of course, when he gets to London, Jack becomes Ernest, as we have seen, allowing him to live a double life. Algernon rather likes the sound of the innocent young Cecily.

The Importance of Being Earnest by Oscar Wilde (1895)

Algernon   By the way, did you tell Gwendolen the truth about your being Ernest in town and Jack in the country?

Jack   *(in a very patronizing manner)* My dear fellow, the truth isn't quite the sort of thing one tells, to a nice, sweet, refined girl. What extraordinary ideas you have about the way to behave to a woman!

Algernon   The only way to behave to a woman is to make love to her, if she is pretty, and to some one else, if she is plain.

Jack   Oh, that is nonsense.

Algernon   What about your brother? What about the profligate Ernest?

Jack   Oh, before the end of the week I shall have got rid of him. I'll say he died in Paris of apoplexy. Lots of people die of apoplexy, quite suddenly, don't they?

Algernon   Yes, but it's hereditary, my dear fellow. It's a sort of thing that runs in families. You had better say a severe chill.

Jack   You are sure a severe chill isn't hereditary, or anything of that kind?

Reese Witherspoon as Cecily

Algernon	Of course it isn't!
Jack	Very well then. My poor brother Ernest is carried off suddenly, in Paris, by a severe chill. That gets rid of him.
Algernon	But I thought you said that … Miss Cardew was a little too much interested in your poor brother Ernest. Won't she feel his loss a good deal?
Jack	Oh, that is all right. Cecily is not a silly romantic girl, I am glad to say. She has got a capital appetite, goes for long walks, and pays no attention at all to her lessons.
Algernon	I would rather like to see Cecily.
Jack	I will take very good care you never do. She is excessively pretty, and she is only just eighteen.
Algernon	Have you told Gwendolen yet that you have an excessively pretty ward who is only just eighteen?
Jack	Oh! One doesn't blurt these things out to people. Cecily and Gwendolen are perfectly certain to be extremely great friends. I'll bet you anything you like that half an hour after they have met, they will be calling each other sister.
Algernon	Women only do that when they have called each other a lot of other things first.

Check your understanding

Wilde called this play 'a trivial play for serious people' and added that its philosophy was that 'we should take all the trivial things of life seriously, and all the serious things of life with sincere and studied triviality'. In other words silly things (like eating lots of cucumber sandwiches or crumpets) are treated very seriously, but the play makes lots of jokes about serious things such as marriage. What do Jack and Algernon have to say about the following?

1. Telling the truth
2. The way to behave towards women
3. Death and illness
4. Education and learning
5. Looking after young people
6. How women behave towards each other

Pair and share

Using the PEA technique you learned in the previous section, find the most outrageous epigram in this extract and comment on what makes it funny and memorable. Do you agree on what it is?

 See Worksheet 2 on the website for an activity on the conventions of comedy.

Viewpoints

1. Do you find the attitudes of Algernon and Jack funny or disturbing?
2. Why doesn't Jack like to tell the truth?
3. What attitude do they seem to have towards women?

Create a table with two columns. Under the headings 'witty' and 'shocking' find quotations to give evidence of their attitudes.

Extend your learning

Whatever the underlying attitudes of the two young men, this scene certainly advances the plot and adds extra complications.

- What does it reveal about Algernon's interest in Cecily?
- What kind of man does Cecily think 'Ernest' must be?
- What qualities do 'Bunbury', 'Ernest' and Algernon all have in common?

In a few moments, Jack will give his address in the country over the telephone. Why do you think that Algernon takes good care to write it down and what is he planning? Write a brief sketch of what happens next.

You can see why we call the storyline in a play or novel the **plot**. Writers need to construct a map of the characters and how they are going to combine them. How will they pair them up or contrast them? How will they reveal their hidden secrets and connections (the process of revelation)? How will they handle different locations? How will they add complications and twists? How will they bring all these elements together to achieve a climax?

These are the ways we will develop our understanding of the structure of texts. The purpose of a good first act or first chapter is to set things up.

The contrast between town and country is clearly a very important part of setting in the text. Setting is often a form of **symbolism**, in other words different places stand for different attitudes or ways of life. Compare and contrast town and country attitudes in the duologue.

Drama comes out of a clash of cultures and attitudes. How might they conflict in the next act?

The passage reveals underlying attitudes to marriage, the role of women, and the class system at the time the play was written. In 1895 Queen Victoria ruled over Britain and its Empire, and was called Empress of India. To attack the attitudes of society was subversive; marriage underpinned the values of class and **status**.

To extend your understanding, explore Victorian attitudes in other texts you have read, and read Oscar Wilde's novel *The Picture of Dorian Gray* or his play *The Ideal Husband*. How did marriage underpin the class system?

For comparison, have a look at P.G. Wodehouse's story 'The Custody of the Pumpkin', which we will be exploring further in chapter 3.

Compare:

- attitudes to marriage
- attitudes to class and status
- how Algernon and Jack and the Honourable Freddie all use slang.

2.2 Status and problems

Think ahead

Group activity

Actors often play status games to establish the ways in which their characters relate to each other. For example, you could walk silently around the room after having been assigned numbers from 1 (low status) to 4 (high status) and without talking guess which number applies to each person you meet. Is it a higher number than your own? Or a lower one? Or are you at the same level?

Clearly Algernon has higher status than Jack as he is cleverer and wittier (and has relations). But in the country Jack

KEY TERMS

plot = the scheme of events in a work of fiction.

symbolism = when writers use symbols; the use of an object or person to represent or 'stand for' something else.

status = relative importance of people in society, or in a drama.

stage directions = instructions telling the actors when to move, and sometimes how to say their lines.

has higher status than Algernon: he has more money, is more mature, and has a stable situation in life. Britain in the nineteenth century was very class-conscious: money and status mattered a lot, and people were afraid of losing status, or not having a secure identity. We now call this status anxiety.

▶ Are there similar concerns about social status in your country?

▶ Does it matter what car you have (or even if you have a car)?

▶ Does it matter where you live, where you go to school, or how you speak?

These things can be serious as well as trivial, but comedy makes fun of them all. Nowadays, social class may be less important, and you are judged less by who your relatives are, but appearances still matter a great deal. People employ image consultants to tell them how to make the right impression.

Social attitudes did not change greatly in Britain until after the Second World War, hence the success of Shaw's play *Pygmalion* which showed a flower girl Eliza Doolittle learning to pass herself off as a duchess by studying how to change her accent. The most comic moment in the play—which shocked audiences at the time—comes when she says 'Not bloody likely' at the end of a polite tea party. The professor teaching her, Professor Higgins, realizes that he also need to work on the register and content of her speech, and all goes well at the smart ball they attend. Indeed the professor's former pupil thinks she is a foreign princess as she speaks English far too well to be a native! The play was adapted into a musical entitled *My Fair Lady*.

However, then comes the problem of what will happen next. We have seen how comedy comes out of contrasts, misunderstandings, mistakes, and exaggerations. Sometimes comedy comes close to being shocking, outrageous, or disturbing. What happens when the joking is over and characters need to face real life? Shaw asks this more serious question too. Colonel Pickering is the Professor's friend, (another double act) who had made a bet with him that he could not do it.

Audrey Hepburn as Eliza in *My Fair Lady*

Pygmalion by George Bernard Shaw (1914)

PICKERING. Anyhow, it was a great success: an immense success. I was quite frightened once or twice because Eliza was doing it so well. You see, lots of the real people can't do it at all: they're such fools that they think style comes by nature to people in their position; and so they never learn. There's always something professional about doing a thing superlatively well.

HIGGINS. Yes: that's what drives me mad: the silly people don't know their own silly business. [*Rising*] However, it's over and done with; and now I can go to bed at last without dreading tomorrow.

Eliza's beauty becomes murderous.

PICKERING. I think I shall turn in too. Still, it's been a great occasion: a triumph for you. Good-night. [*He goes*].

HIGGINS [*following him*] Good-night. [*Over his shoulder, at the door*] Put out the lights, Eliza; and tell Mrs. Pearce not to make coffee for me in the morning: I'll take tea. [*He goes out*].

Eliza tries to control herself and feel indifferent as she rises and walks across to the hearth to switch off the lights. By the time she gets there she is on the point of screaming. She sits down in Higgins's chair and holds on hard to the arms. Finally she gives way and flings herself furiously on the floor raging.

HIGGINS [*in despairing wrath outside*] What the devil have I done with my slippers? [*He appears at the door*].

LIZA [*snatching up the slippers, and hurling them at him one after the other with all her force*] There are your slippers. And there. Take your slippers; and may you never have a day's luck with them!

HIGGINS [*astounded*] What on earth—! [*He comes to her*]. What's the matter? Get up. [*He pulls her up*]. Anything wrong?

LIZA [*breathless*] Nothing wrong—with YOU. I've won your bet for you, haven't I? That's enough for you. *I* don't matter, I suppose.

HIGGINS. YOU won my bet! You! Presumptuous insect! *I* won it. What did you throw those slippers at me for?

LIZA. Because I wanted to smash your face. I'd like to kill you, you selfish brute. Why didn't you leave me where you picked me out of—in the gutter? You thank God it's all over, and that now you can throw me back again there, do you? [*She crisps her fingers, frantically*].

HIGGINS [*looking at her in cool wonder*] The creature IS nervous, after all.

LIZA [*gives a suffocated scream of fury, and instinctively darts her nails at his face*]!!

HIGGINS [*catching her wrists*] Ah! would you? Claws in, you cat. How dare you show your temper to me? Sit down and be quiet. [*He throws her roughly into the easy-chair*].

LIZA [*crushed by superior strength and weight*] What's to become of me? What's to become of me?

HIGGINS. How the devil do I know what's to become of you? What does it matter what becomes of you?

LIZA. You don't care. I know you don't care. You wouldn't care if I was dead. I'm nothing to you—not so much as them slippers.

HIGGINS [*thundering*] THOSE slippers.

LIZA [*with bitter submission*] Those slippers. I didn't think it made any difference now.

A pause. Eliza hopeless and crushed. Higgins a little uneasy.

✎ Check your understanding

1. What has Higgins said to Pickering that has upset Eliza so much?
2. How does Shaw show you how angry she is?
3. Why was Higgins asking about his slippers so provocative?
4. Why is the fight so shocking?
5. What is Eliza's status in society now?
6. Who is in charge in this duologue and why?
7. Who gets the most sympathy from you?

Pair and share

The emotions of this scene are certainly very different from the witty conversation of Algernon and Jack. Eliza's emotions are much more raw, her anxieties about her status much more genuine. Now Higgins has won his bet is she a lady or only a servant?

The fight between the two characters is a dramatic way of showing conflict, the kind of clash of emotions and ideas which creates tension and has a powerful impact on the audience.

How does Shaw show his actors how they should communicate this tension? He uses **stage directions** to indicate both movement and how lines should be spoken. He shows Eliza's concern about her status by showing her on the floor beneath Higgins, and then rising up to claw at his face, before being thrown into a chair.

When writing about drama, stage directions as well as the characters' words need analysis, as sometimes characters express themselves as much through gestures and tone as through the words they use. In pairs, complete the table to examine Eliza's feelings.

Quotation	Comment
Eliza's beauty becomes murderous.	This shows her emotions are becoming violent.
flings herself furiously on the floor raging.	Shaw's language demonstrates how physically she feels her anger and despair.
hurling them at him one after the other with all her force.	The word 'hurling' powerfully conveys Eliza's energy and fury.
breathless	
She crisps her fingers, frantically	
gives a suffocated scream of fury	
instinctively darts her nails at his face	
crushed by superior strength and weight	
with bitter submission	Shows Eliza giving in to Higgins's intellect as well as his strength, but the word 'bitter' shows that she is resentful at the way he bullies her.
Eliza hopeless and crushed.	

Is Higgins really unfeeling and a 'selfish brute'? Can you find clues in the stage directions to suggest he is more emotional than he likes to pretend? Explore the effect of the stage directions given for him.

Quotation	Comment
in despairing wrath outside	
astounded	
He pulls her up	
looking at her in cool wonder	
He throws her roughly into the easy-chair	
thundering	
Higgins a little uneasy	

Act out the duologue as a pair, giving plenty of expression to these stage directions.

Viewpoints

The audience's response

This drama is moving towards its climax, with the problems and consequences of the initial plot emerging and becoming more complicated. Eliza has managed to achieve a new status through changing her voice, but now asks 'What's to become of me?' Higgins's reply implies that he thinks status doesn't matter, but do his words and behaviour suggest this? The scene ends with more questions than answers.

Shaw asks for 'a pause', so the scene ends with dramatic tension. The audience need to think about what they are seeing, and not just find it amusing.

Let's evaluate the evidence. Is Higgins a brute and a bully, or someone who challenges the conventions of society (an awkward revolutionary)? What evidence can you and your partner find? Create a table to record you findings like the one below.

Brute and bully	Awkward revolutionary
Throws her roughly	*a little uneasy*

Shaw shows Higgins's pride in what he can achieve:

> *HIGGINS. YOU won my bet! You! Presumptuous insect! I won it. What did you throw those slippers at me for?*

How does the language here show Higgins's lack of interest in Eliza as a person? Analyse the use of sarcasm, imagery, and questions here. Does he show her any respect? Why not?

Higgins is a professor and his main interest in language is academic. He seems to think that image and language matter more than feelings. This makes him witty and a good comic character. However, an audience will notice powerful emotions emerge here, and they are not just comic, but based on serious questions.

Is it possible to change people's identity by changing their image?

Debate this question, drawing examples from the modern world.

Extend your learning

Drama can combine both comic and serious elements. A tragedy can have comic scenes, especially in Shakespeare, and comedy can address serious questions about life.

How has Shaw made sure the characters are well-matched in this scene? Look at more of this scene from the play to explore the ways in which Eliza eventually achieves a kind of victory in her quarrel with Higgins, by making him reveal real emotions.

1. Do real emotions belong in comedy?

2. What happens when an audience stops laughing and starts to think?

Higgins wants to see Eliza as a kind of animal he can experiment and play with: he calls her 'insect', 'cat', and 'creature'. How human do you find him?

Write two paragraphs of character notes for an actor playing Higgins to bring out his contradictions. Using the quotations above, bring out his dark side and his more human side.

Writing techniques

Teachers often ask you questions about the impact of a scene and the writing on an audience. This is sometimes called **dramatic effectiveness**. You will need to use quotations and evidence in order to explore, analyse, and evaluate the way in which a live audience would react to what it sees and hears.

✎ Practice question

Looking back at the scene from *Pygmalion* and the evidence you have gathered, write a short essay (400–500 words) in answer to the following question:

> *How does Shaw make this confrontation a powerful and revealing moment for an audience?*

Remember to refer to details of language and their effect, and to concentrate on *how* the audience respond, rather than just retell *what* happens. Look at the situation, the characters, and what is **revealed** about them, deeper attitudes and suggestions, and the way the action builds to a **climax**, followed by a dramatic pause.

KEY TERMS

dramatic effectiveness = how well a scene works in live performance; the effect on the audience.

revealed = this term is often used to encourage students to go beyond the surface meaning and look at deeper attitudes, especially what words tell us about characters.

climax = the moment audiences and readers will see as the high point to which everything has been building up.

2.3 Quarrels

Think ahead

Our next text also involves a quarrel, this time between a pair of lovers. This is taken from Shakespeare's *A Midsummer Night's Dream*. If you study a Shakespeare text as part of your Cambridge Literature in English course, it is important not to be put off his plays by the verse and the language of his day. He became famous as a writer of comedy, and he uses many of the same conventions of comedy as other writers.

A pair of lovers in *A Midsummer Night's Dream*

A Midsummer Night's Dream shows many of the elements of traditional drama we have explored already:

▶ pairs of characters

▶ a situation caused by marriage conventions

▶ the problems caused by love

▶ status and money often determining marriage rather than love

▶ comedy caused by misunderstandings

▶ a surreal element, taking us beyond a completely realistic situation

▶ conflict leading to tension, quarrels, and insults

▶ exaggeration and larger-than-life characters

▶ outrageous language and behaviour

▶ a setting which allows these qualities to be seen.

Read the brief synopsis of the situation which follows and identify these elements.

Sketch out in your notes the love triangle before the fairies intervene: who is in love with whom, and who is left out of the triangle with no one to love her? How has this changed after the fairies' interference?

Lysander and Hermia are in love and have run off into the forest outside Athens because Hermia's father has insisted that she must marry Demetrius, who comes from a richer family. Demetrius used to love Hermia's best friend, Helena, and, convinced he is in love with Hermia, follows the lovers into the forest. He is followed by Helena, although he keeps telling her he hates her. They all get lost and fall asleep, at which point the fairies in the forest intervene to try to sort things out with a love potion. Unfortunately Puck, the fairy given this task, has given the potion to the wrong man: now Lysander is in love with Helena and hates Hermia. Helena assumes he is joking and that he and Hermia are making fun of her. Oberon, king of the fairies, now gives the love juice to Demetrius, but he has not yet given the antidote to Lysander. Puck (who enjoys mischief) is now watching the fun … (and so are we). Note that words and phrases that may be unfamiliar to you are explained to the right of the extract.

A Midsummer Night's Dream by William Shakespeare (circa 1594)

LYSANDER

> Helen, I love thee; by my life I do;
> I swear by that which I will lose for thee
> To prove him false that says I love thee not.

to prove him false = *prove him a liar*

DEMETRIUS

> I say I love thee more than he can do.

LYSANDER

> If thou say so, withdraw, and prove it too.

withdraw and prove it too = *come and fight me (they have swords)*

DEMETRIUS

> Quick, come,--

HERMIA

> Lysander, whereto tends all this?

whereto tends all this? = *what does this all mean?*

LYSANDER

> Away, you Ethiope!

Away, you Ethiope = *refers to Hermia's dark hair and complexion*

DEMETRIUS

> No, no, sir:--he will
> Seem to break loose; take on as you would follow:
> But yet come not. You are a tame man; go!

take on as you would follow = *match your words to deeds and fight*

LYSANDER

> Hang off, thou cat, thou burr: vile thing, let loose,
> Or I will shake thee from me like a serpent.
>
> Out, loathed medicine! hated potion, hence!

thou burr = *you sticky plant*

HERMIA

> Why are you grown so rude? What change is this,
> Sweet love?

LYSANDER

Thy love! Out, tawny Tartar, out!
Out, loathed medicine! O hated potion, hence!

HERMIA

Do you not jest?

HELENA

Yes, sooth; and so do you.

LYSANDER

Demetrius, I will keep my word with thee.

DEMETRIUS

I would I had your bond; for I perceive
A weak bond holds you; I'll not trust your word.

LYSANDER

What! should I hurt her, strike her, kill her dead?
Although I hate her, I'll not harm her so.

HERMIA

What! can you do me greater harm than hate?
Hate me! wherefore? O me! what news, my love?
Am not I Hermia? Are not you Lysander?
I am as fair now as I was erewhile.
Since night you lov'd me; yet since night you left me:
Why then, you left me,--O, the gods forbid!--
In earnest, shall I say?

LYSANDER

Ay, by my life;
And never did desire to see thee more.
Therefore be out of hope, of question, doubt,
Be certain, nothing truer; 'tis no jest
That I do hate thee and love Helena.

HERMIA

O me! you juggler! you cankerblossom!
You thief of love! What! have you come by night,
And stol'n my love's heart from him?

HELENA

Fine, i' faith!
Have you no modesty, no maiden shame,
No touch of bashfulness? What! will you tear
Impatient answers from my gentle tongue?
Fie, fie! you counterfeit, you puppet, you!

HERMIA

Puppet! why so? Ay, that way goes the game.

Out, tawny Tartar = another reference to Hermia's dark complexion

Do you not jest? = are you joking?

A weak bond holds you = you don't keep your promises

Therefore be out of hope = give up, have no more hopes about me

you cankerblossom = you insect ruining the flower of love

you counterfeit = you fake

Now I perceive that she hath made compare
Between our statures; she hath urg'd her height;
And with her personage, her tall personage,
Her height, forsooth, she hath prevail'd with him.--
And are you grown so high in his esteem
Because I am so dwarfish and so low?
How low am I, thou painted maypole? speak;
How low am I? I am not yet so low
But that my nails can reach unto thine eyes.

HELENA

I pray you, though you mock me, gentlemen,
Let her not hurt me. I was never curst;
I have no gift at all in shrewishness;
I am a right maid for my cowardice;
Let her not strike me. You perhaps may think,
Because she is something lower than myself,
That I can match her.

HERMIA

                    Lower! hark, again.

HELENA

Good Hermia, do not be so bitter with me.
I evermore did love you, Hermia;
Did ever keep your counsels; never wrong'd you;
Save that, in love unto Demetrius,
I told him of your stealth unto this wood:
He follow'd you; for love I follow'd him;
But he hath chid me hence, and threaten'd me
To strike me, spurn me, nay, to kill me too:
And now, so you will let me quiet go,
To Athens will I bear my folly back,
And follow you no farther. Let me go:
You see how simple and how fond I am.

HERMIA

Why, get you gone: who is't that hinders you?

HELENA

A foolish heart that I leave here behind.

HERMIA

What! with Lysander?

HELENA

                    With Demetrius.

LYSANDER

Be not afraid; she shall not harm thee, Helena.

thou painted maypole = *you tall, gaudy pole for dancing around in spring*

shrewishness = *being a difficult woman*

keep your counsels = *kept your secrets*

your stealth unto this wood = *how you crept away secretly to the wood*

he hath chid me hence = *he drove me away with insults*

spurn me = *reject me*

will I bear my folly back = *I will take all my silly ideas (of love) with me*

DEMETRIUS

    No, sir, she shall not, though you take her part.

HELENA

    O, when she's angry, she is keen and shrewd:
    She was a vixen when she went to school;
    And, though she be but little, she is fierce.

She was a vixen = *she was like a cunning, aggressive female fox*

HERMIA

    Little again! nothing but low and little!--
    Why will you suffer her to flout me thus?
    Let me come to her.

LYSANDER

        Get you gone, you dwarf;
    You minimus, of hind'ring knot-grass made;
    You bead, you acorn.

minimus = *thing of insignificant size*

of hind'ring knot-grass made = *made of an annoying weed*

DEMETRIUS

        You are too officious
    In her behalf that scorns your services.
    Let her alone: speak not of Helena;
    Take not her part; for if thou dost intend
    Never so little show of love to her,
    Thou shalt aby it.

You are too officious = *you are trying too hard to impress someone who isn't interested in you (that is, Helena)*

Thou shalt aby it = *you will pay for it (in a fight)*

LYSANDER

        Now she holds me not;
    Now follow, if thou dar'st, to try whose right,
    Of thine or mine, is most in Helena.

to try whose right = *to fight over the right (to Helena)*

DEMETRIUS

    Follow! nay, I'll go with thee, cheek by jowl.

cheek by jowl = *close behind*

[Exeunt LYSANDER and DEMETRIUS.]

HERMIA

    You, mistress, all this coil is 'long of you:
    Nay, go not back.

all this coil is 'long of you = *this trouble is all your fault*

HELENA

        I will not trust you, I;
    Nor longer stay in your curst company.
    Your hands than mine are quicker for a fray;
    My legs are longer though, to run away.

quicker for a fray = *quicker to fight*

[Exit.]

HERMIA

    I am amaz'd, and know not what to say.

[Exit, pursuing HELENA.]

Did you work out the following pattern?

- Lysander loves Hermia who loves him back
- Demetrius loves Hermia but she doesn't love him
- Helena loves Demetrius but he doesn't love her
- No one loves Helena

This becomes the following.

- Helena loves Demetrius but he doesn't love her
- Demetrius loves Hermia but she doesn't love him
- Hermia loves Lysander but he doesn't love her
- Lysander loves Helena but she doesn't believe him

And finally we get this.

- Helena loves Demetrius and he loves her but she doesn't believe him
- Lysander loves Helena but she doesn't believe him
- Hermia loves Lysander but he doesn't love her
- No one loves Hermia

The fairies, like the audience, are watching the lovers' quarrels. As the boys both love Helena (when they used to both be in love with Hermia), they are rude to Hermia. However, Helena thinks that all three are just pretending in order to make fun of her. Why do we find this so amusing? We don't just enjoy the teasing and the insults; there is also something amusing about observing other people who are in love and making fools of themselves. Puck, the mischievous fairy who has accidentally caused these problems, says 'Lord, what fools these mortals be!'

✎ Check your understanding

Have some fun collecting the insults hurled at Hermia and Helena.

Create a table to list the insults used about each of the girls. We have given you a few below to start you off. Notice that Hermia is insulted by both Lysander and Helena, and that Helena even insults herself.

The jokes revolve around the fact that Hermia is short and dark, and Helena is tall and fair. Hermia tends to get angry while Helena is more self-pitying.

About Hermia	About Helena
you Ethiope	thou painted maypole
thou cat, thou burr	you juggler! you cankerblossom
you dwarf; You minimus	how simple and how fond

Viewpoints

Discuss and debate the following questions.

1. 'What change is this?' Everyone used to love Hermia, and Helena was rejected. What do you think Hermia has learned in this scene about what it feels like to be rejected?

2. Does the audience simply laugh at this scene or is there something uncomfortable in what it tells us about love?

3. What happened to Hermia and Helena's friendship once rivalry in love came along?

4. How does this scene resemble a bad dream?

One way to address these questions is to write an **empathy response**, to imagine you are the character writing down her thoughts, as in a diary.

You are Hermia waking up after this bad dream. Write your thoughts about imagining all your friends had turned against you.

Language links

Empathic responses help you to find the 'voice' of a character, which is also good practice for the reading paper in First Language English.

Pair and share

We have seen the different ways in which characters contrast, develop, and come into conflict. We have looked at tensions between characters, and how arguments over status create drama. We have seen how duologues and pairs of characters can create powerful drama through double acts. How do the dramatists we have studied in this chapter, all masters of the craft of writing, bring these problems to a **resolution**? Discuss these questions with a partner.

Pair and share

One of you is Hermia and the other Helena. Serve up the insults you listed to play insult tennis. Which insults return service and which are an ace? Ask your teacher to play the role of umpire as you throw them at each other. Helena (thanks to Lysander) probably has more weapons.

Now prepare a performance of this scene. Begin by dividing into pairs of 'boys' and 'girls'.

How will the audience react to the outrageous things you say to each other?

KEY TERMS

empathy response = sometimes called 'empathic response', this is an opportunity to write the character's thoughts at a particular moment in the text (see chapter 5).

resolution = an ending which sorts out problems and differences, and brings everything together, also called 'closure'.

2.4 Happy endings?

We will now explore the different ways of concluding comedies. The traditional ending for a comedy is to find a way to get virtually the entire cast on stage, sort out all the misunderstandings through a series of happy (and often unlikely) coincidences and marry off the young (and even the not-so-young) couples. Everyone joins in to celebrate the marriages. Can you spot the similarities to the conventions of romantic comedy in films today?

Act 3 of *The Importance of Being Earnest* with most of the cast on stage

A traditional ending: bringing everyone together

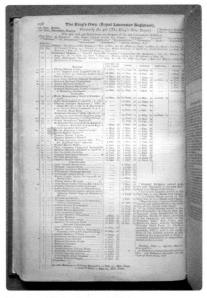

Book of lists from 1890s

Jack discovers that he is in fact Algernon's brother (and, incidentally, Gwendolen's cousin and Lady Bracknell's nephew). Algernon gets to marry Cecily because he really is Jack's wicked friend—indeed his brother (even if he is not called Ernest). All that is needed is to find out Jack's real name (which oddly enough no one, not even Lady Bracknell, can remember).

The Importance of Being Earnest by Oscar Wilde (1895) (final scene)

Jack. The Army Lists of the last forty years are here. These delightful records should have been my constant study. [*Rushes to bookcase and tears the books out.*] M. Generals … Mallam, Maxbohm, Magley, what ghastly names they have—Markby, Migsby, Mobbs, Moncrieff! Lieutenant 1840, Captain, Lieutenant-Colonel, Colonel, General 1869, Christian names, Ernest John. [*Puts book very quietly down and speaks quite calmly.*] I always told you, Gwendolen, my name was Ernest, didn't I? Well, it is Ernest after all. I mean it naturally is Ernest.

Lady Bracknell. Yes, I remember now that the General was called Ernest, I knew I had some particular reason for disliking the name.

Gwendolen. Ernest! My own Ernest! I felt from the first that you could have no other name!

Jack. Gwendolen, it is a terrible thing for a man to find out suddenly that all his life he has been speaking nothing but the truth. Can you forgive me?

Gwendolen. I can. For I feel that you are sure to change.

Jack. My own one!

Chasuble. [*To Miss Prism.*] Laetitia! [*Embraces her.*]

Miss Prism. [*Enthusiastically.*] Frederick! At last!

Algernon. Cecily! [*Embraces her.*] At last!

Jack. Gwendolen! [*Embraces her.*] At last!

Lady Bracknell. My nephew, you seem to be displaying signs of triviality.

Jack. On the contrary, Aunt Augusta, I've now realised for the first time in my life the vital Importance of Being Earnest.

Viewpoints

Do comedies really need happy endings? Where are the suggestions in this scene that Wilde might be saying something more serious about the things we take seriously and the things we laugh at?

In pairs, script an interview with Oscar Wilde after the first performance of this play and ask him some serious questions about what he meant by the title of the play, its action, and its ending. Do you think he will give serious answers?

✎ Check your understanding

1. How do the Army Lists introduce some (rather unlikely) realism into the play?
2. How does the writer use names to bring characters together in a happy ending?
3. Do we believe that names are really so important?
4. What does Jack suggest about the relationship between names and being serious or telling the truth?
5. Why is Gwendolen's comment 'I feel that you are sure to change' very revealing?

Another kind of ending: the epilogue

When the 'mechanicals' put on a play for Duke Theseus in *A Midsummer Night's Dream*, he tells them not to bother with an **epilogue** (the last words of the play) 'for your play needs no excuse'. However, Shakespeare decides to end this play with a traditional epilogue, in which one actor addresses the audience directly, once the other characters have left the stage to prepare for their weddings.

KEY TERMS

epilogue = the last words of a literary text, especially a play, after the action is over. An epilogue may be spoken by a named character, or by one of the actors, stepping out of role. These used to be much more common in the past (as were prologues, at the beginning of the play) and were not necessarily written by the author.

Shakespeare gives the last word to the mischievous fairy, Puck, who tells the audience that the actors are really 'shadows' and the whole play only a 'dream'. He asks for their pardon and applause, and daringly promises a better play next time.

A Midsummer Night's Dream by William Shakespeare (circa 1594)

PUCK

If we shadows have offended,
Think but this, and all is mended,
That you have but slumber'd here
While these visions did appear.
And this weak and idle theme,
No more yielding but a dream,
Gentles, do not reprehend;
If you pardon, we will mend.
And, as I am an honest Puck,
If we have unearned luck
Now to 'scape the serpent's tongue,
We will make amends ere long;
Else the Puck a liar call:
So, good night unto you all.
Give me your hands, if we be friends,
And Robin shall restore amends.

Gentles = ladies and gentlemen
reprehend = tell off
to 'scape the serpent's tongue = to escape being hissed off the stage
We will make amends = we will come up with something better next time
restore amends = bring everything to a happy ending

🗨 Pair and share

Discuss these questions.

1. Why do you think Shakespeare gives Puck, the spirit of mischief, the last word?

2. Why does he want the audience to treat the play like a dream?

3. Does he really think he has written a bad play?

4. Why does Puck get to say he has?

5. How will applause (clapping your hands) make it better?

6. Does this help you to understand the nature of comedy?

Puck says that the play is, literally, 'claptrap'—just a piece of amusement. Compare this with Wilde's comment that *The Importance of Being Earnest* was 'a trivial play for serious people'. Do the writers mean this? Why do the writers of comedies draw attention to ways in which they are not realistic?

Controversial endings

Extend your learning

You have an opportunity here to evaluate and review what you have learned in this chapter. This task gives you an extended piece of text and an opportunity to look back, compare, and come to your own judgment. You are given less help with this task, as you can use the skills that you developed earlier in the chapter.

Controversially, *Pygmalion* does not have an entirely conventional happy ending. Liza and Higgins will not marry—instead she will marry a young boy called Freddy. The film and musical have slightly different endings. Shaw felt he needed to write an essay to justify his chosen ending. He condemned 'the ragshop in which Romance keeps its stock of "happy endings" to misfit all stories' and wanted to write an ending which was realistic.

However, he struggled with the final lines of the play and several versions exist.

1. Why do you think producers would have preferred to bring the two main characters together?

2. Why do you think the writer resists this idea?

3. What does this tell you about the differences between the social conventions of comedy and those of realism (that is, drama based on real life)?

You now have a chance to evaluate Shaw's ending for yourself.

Annotate your copy of this scene (from the CD-ROM). Explore the impact of the language and the stage directions.

Eliza is now ready for the wedding with which a comedy traditionally ends. However, it isn't the wedding we expected—instead Eliza's father, a dustman, is getting married at the end of the play because he has (accidentally) become a rich celebrity. Freddy, who loves Eliza, is from a higher class than Eliza, but he is not rich, and he certainly isn't as clever as Eliza or Professor Higgins. However, the audience's main interest is in how the relationship between Eliza and Higgins will end. Look out for the change in status in this scene.

Pygmalion by George Bernard Shaw (1914) (final scene)

LIZA. Freddy loves me: that makes him king enough for me. I don't want him to work: he wasn't brought up to it as I was. I'll go and be a teacher.

HIGGINS. What'll you teach, in heaven's name?

LIZA. What you taught me. I'll teach phonetics.

HIGGINS. Ha! Ha! Ha!

LIZA. I'll offer myself as an assistant to that hairy-faced Hungarian.

HIGGINS [*rising in a fury*] What! That impostor! that humbug! that toadying ignoramus! Teach him my methods! my discoveries! You take one step in his direction and I'll wring your neck. [*He lays hands on her*]. Do you hear?

LIZA [*defiantly non-resistant*] Wring away. What do I care? I knew you'd strike me some day. [*He lets her go, stamping with rage at having forgotten himself, and recoils so hastily that he stumbles back into his seat on the ottoman*]. Aha! Now I know how to deal with you. What a fool I was not to think of it before! You can't take away the knowledge you gave me. You said I had a finer ear than you. And I can be civil and kind to people, which is more than you can. Aha! That's done you, Henry Higgins, it has. Now I don't care that [*snapping her fingers*] for your bullying and your big talk. I'll advertize it in the papers that your duchess is only a flower girl that you taught, and that she'll teach anybody to be a duchess just the same in six months for a thousand guineas. Oh, when I think of myself crawling under your feet and being trampled on and called names, when all the time I had only to lift up my finger to be as good as you, I could just kick myself.

HIGGINS [*wondering at her*] You damned impudent slut, you! But it's better than snivelling; better than fetching slippers and finding spectacles, isn't it? [*Rising*] By George, Eliza, I said I'd make a woman of you; and I have. I like you like this.

LIZA. Yes: you turn round and make up to me now that I'm not afraid of you, and can do without you.

HIGGINS. Of course I do, you little fool. Five minutes ago you were like a millstone round my neck. Now you're a tower of strength: a consort battleship. You and I and Pickering will be three old bachelors together instead of only two men and a silly girl.

Mrs. Higgins returns, dressed for the wedding. Eliza instantly becomes cool and elegant.

MRS. HIGGINS. The carriage is waiting, Eliza. Are you ready?

LIZA. Quite. Is the Professor coming?

MRS. HIGGINS. Certainly not. He can't behave himself in church. He makes remarks out loud all the time on the clergyman's pronunciation.

LIZA. Then I shall not see you again, Professor. Good-bye. [*She goes to the door*].

MRS. HIGGINS [*coming to Higgins*] Good-bye, dear.

HIGGINS. Good-bye, mother. [*He is about to kiss her, when he recollects something*]. Oh, by the way, Eliza, order a ham and a Stilton cheese, will you? And buy me a pair of reindeer gloves, number eights, and a tie to match that new suit of mine. You can choose the colour. [*His cheerful, careless, vigorous voice shows that he is incorrigible*].

LIZA. [*disdainfully*] Number eights are too small for you if you want them lined with lamb's wool. You have three new ties that you have forgotten in the drawer of your washstand. Colonel Pickering prefers double Gloucester to Stilton; and you don't notice the difference. I telephoned Mrs Pearce this morning not to forget the ham. What you are to do without me I cannot imagine. [*She sweeps out*].

MRS. HIGGINS. I'm afraid you've spoiled that girl, Henry. I should be uneasy about you and her if she were less fond of Colonel Pickering.

HIGGINS. Pickering! Nonsense: she's going to marry Freddy. Ha ha! Freddy! Freddy!! Ha ha ha ha ha!!!!! [*He roars with laughter as the play ends*]

Instead of a happy ending, we see that the pupil has turned the tables on her teacher.

✎ Check your understanding

1. What does Eliza say which makes Higgins so angry?
2. How will Eliza set herself up as a teacher of phonetics (the sounds of languages, the professor's subject)?
3. Why does Higgins now find Eliza admirable?
4. Why does Shaw bring in Mrs Higgins to say that Higgins always behaves badly in church?
5. How does Higgins show that he is sure Eliza will come back after her father's wedding?
6. How does Eliza show him that he will now struggle to cope without her?
7. Do you think she will come back?

💬 Pair and share

Form a group of three to perform this scene.

Look together at the stage directions.

● How does Shaw make this scene dramatically effective?

● How do various actions support the words of the characters?

● How does he indicate the tone with which the actors speak?

Now make the scene as dramatic and full of contrasts of tone as you can.

Practice question

This kind of question asks you to analyse the writer's methods ('how') and techniques ('writing') and to evaluate Shaw's purpose. Remember to think about the effect on the audience. Think about the decisions he has made about the final scene, his stage directions, and his choice of words:

How successfully does Shaw's writing in this scene show that Eliza is now a more powerful character than Higgins?

Write 300–400 words.

Note that although there will be no bullet points to help you in the drama paper, there is guidance in the unseen paper in the form of bullet points. Use the questions here to structure your response.

1. How do the stage directions in this scene show you how much stronger Eliza is now?

2. How has Eliza's status changed? Why has she developed more than Higgins?

3. What do you think Shaw might be suggesting to his audience about the changing relationships between different classes and between men and women?

4. Where does Eliza show her understanding of how the modern world works?

5. How would the audience react to such a powerful portrayal of Eliza and to her rejection of a traditional 'happy ending' with Higgins?

For more advice about writing critical essays, look ahead to chapter 6.

 **Viewpoints**

Does this work well as an alternative to the happy ending that Shaw's audience might have expected? Do you agree that a marriage between Eliza and Higgins would never work? Why not? Why have those who have **adapted** the play wanted to soften the ending?

Looking back

We have explored the ways in which drama is structured and the effect of its form on the audience. We have also suggested that dramatic form changes in response to changes in society.

Write notes in response to the following questions.

1. What kind of characters interest and intrigue an audience most?

2. Why is a contrast a successful way of developing drama?

3. What makes conflict between characters, whether serious or comic, so dramatically effective?

4. What is the traditional way of resolving conflicts in comedy?

5. Why might the more realistic writers of recent times have wanted to quarrel with this tradition?

We will explore dramatic form and its effect on the audience in more detail in chapter 7.

Reading prose texts

3.1 Prose: the novel and short story

'Prose' may not be a term you use very often, but literary texts that are not written in verse are usually called 'prose texts'. Shakespeare's dramas are written in a mixture of verse (like the poetry used by the quarreling friends and lovers in *A Midsummer Night's Dream*) and prose (used by the 'rude mechanicals', the ordinary workers, when they are not trying to act).

Prose really means anything that is not written in verse. When this is explained in Molière's comedy *Le Bourgeois Gentilhomme* to the middle-class gentleman of the title, Monsieur Jourdain, he is amazed to discover that 'I have been speaking prose all my life and did not know it'. By 'prose texts', English literature teachers usually mean novels and short stories.

The novel is, in fact, one of the most recent of literary forms: as we have seen, imaginative literary texts were originally devised to be performed aloud, sung or acted before an audience. In the history of literature, prose only becomes a genre for storytelling once more people can read, books have become much cheaper to produce, and as a result many more people have access to texts.

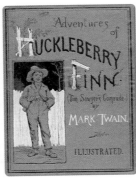

Covers of some prose texts

Today, prose is the literary form we are most familiar with. We read books and stories privately for their plot, for interesting characters, and to take us into an imaginary world different from our own. What is called 'genre fiction', for example, detective stories, thrillers, fantasy novels, romances, Gothic stories, and adventure, is especially popular. These kinds of books are often adapted into films and television series. We are less used to reading prose texts aloud, together, or performing or analysing them, although you have probably done all of these activities in your English classes.

LEARNING POINTS

▶ To develop appreciation of the forms of literature by looking at prose

▶ To explore writers' choices of structure, viewpoint, and characterization through the short story

▶ To appreciate the importance of developments such as conflict and confrontation in identifying key moments in a short story

▶ To explore different forms of closure, including the use of irony and symbolism

▶ To develop further the ways in which our understanding of texts is shaped by their historical and cultural context

Stories about characters such as Sherlock Holmes are often turned into television series

The set prose text is probably the biggest challenge of your Cambridge Literature in English course. It involves the detailed study of quite a long text, written for adults not children, with complex characters and a plot (in film usually called the 'storyline'). There is a lot to read, even more that you can analyse, and difficult choices to make about what you should concentrate on. One option in the prose section is to study ten short stories. This is not necessarily an easier option: you have more characters and plots to learn, a variety of different styles and contexts to master, and no single storyline to help you through the text. However, you can learn a lot about how prose works through the short story.

In this chapter, we will explore how three writers begin, develop, and conclude their short stories. You can use this chapter as an introduction to the study of the language and structures of prose, or you can apply the same reading skills to the set stories you are studying. There are further suggestions about how to do this in the boxes called 'Extend your Learning: other stories'.

Think ahead

When writing a story where is the best place to start?

What are the advantages and disadvantages of beginning your story:

▶ at the beginning

▶ somewhere in the middle and then include a flashback

▶ at the end and then explain how you got there?

What decisions do you need to make before you start?

You need to answer the questions: Where? When? Who? What? How? Why? But not necessarily in that order.

Who is going to tell your story? Consider the advantages and disadvantages of:

▶ a first-person narrative by one of the characters, inside the story and involved in its action

▶ an objective narrator telling the story in the third person, and viewing the action from the outside

▶ a narrator telling the story in the third person but able to enter the minds of the characters and explain their thoughts and viewpoints.

The choice of **viewpoint** is crucial when beginning a story.

KEY TERMS

viewpoint = the person from whose point of view we 'see' the events of the story. This might be a narrator looking at events from outside the story or one of the characters.

characters = characters are people invented by the writer to have a particular effect on the reader. Characterization is the way writers use characters.

 **Language links**

Think about the decisions you have made in your own narrative writing. How have you achieved a striking opening? How have you introduced **characters**, setting, and situation?

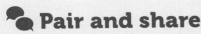

Pair and share

With your partner, discuss the kind of books and stories you like.

1. What are the names of your favourite books?
2. Where are they set?
3. Who are your favourite characters?
4. What kind of action is involved?
5. What are the funniest moments?
6. Which are the most exciting?
7. Do you prefer happy or sad endings?
8. What do the writers do to get your attention in the first pages?

Viewpoints

The essential building blocks of prose writing are:

- action
- **dialogue**
- **description**.

Which do you think is the most important and which is the least important? Why are all three necessary? What is the purpose of description?

Write down three essential purposes for description in writing stories.

What is the function of detail in description and how does it help you to visualize the story?

Think ahead

In chapter 2, we explored the ways in which class and social attitudes towards the end of the nineteenth century influenced comedy and drama. We explored tension, the clash of characters, and the ways in which drama handles conflict (quarrels and fights) and resolution (different kinds of ending).

The first three short stories in this chapter all show generations clashing.

▶ Why might different generations have different attitudes and ways of speaking?

▶ What are the slang words you use that your parents and teachers don't understand?

▶ How do your attitudes differ from theirs?

▶ Who has a better understanding of the way the world is changing?

▶ Which attitudes of older people are you most critical of?

3.2 Opening a short story

Many short stories begin with description which gradually introduces a character. Thomas Hardy begins his short story 'The Son's Veto' with a long descriptive passage which plunges into the middle of the story. A mother and son are described, but we will only find out their names, the nature of their relationship, and how the mother came to be married and living in London later in the story. At first, the woman is described from the outside, but towards the end of this extract, the writer decides to change his viewpoint and to tell us her thoughts. Hardy is using a technique of gradual revelation: the reader becomes more informed about the characters in the story than the characters are themselves, but only in stages.

'The Son's Veto' by Thomas Hardy (1894)

To the eyes of a man viewing it from behind, the nut-brown hair was a wonder and a mystery. Under the black beaver hat, surmounted by its tuft of black feathers, the long locks, braided and twisted and coiled like the rushes of a basket, composed a rare, if somewhat barbaric, example of ingenious art. One could understand such weavings and coilings being wrought to last intact for a year, or even a calendar month; but that they should be all demolished regularly at bedtime, after a single day of permanence, seemed a reckless waste of successful fabrication.

And she had done it all herself, poor thing. She had no maid, and it was almost the only accomplishment she could boast of. Hence the unstinted pains.

She was a young invalid lady – not so very much of an invalid – sitting in a wheeled chair, which had been pulled up in the front part of a green enclosure, close to a bandstand, where a concert was going on, during a warm June afternoon. It had place in one of the minor parks or private gardens that are to be found in the suburbs of London, and was the effort of a local association to raise money for some charity. There are worlds within worlds in the great city, and though nobody outside the immediate district had ever heard of the charity, or the band, or the garden, the enclosure was filled with an interested audience sufficiently informed on all these.

As the strains proceeded many of the listeners observed the chaired lady, whose back hair, by reason of her prominent position, so challenged inspection. Her face was not easily discernible, but the aforesaid cunning tress-weavings, the white ear and poll, and the curve of a cheek which was neither flaccid nor sallow, were signals that led to the expectation of good beauty in front. Such expectations are not infrequently disappointed as soon as the disclosure comes; and in the present case, when the lady, by a turn of the head, at length revealed herself, she was not so handsome as the people behind her had supposed, and even hoped – they did not know why.

For one thing (alas! the commonness of this complaint), she was less young than they had fancied her to be. Yet attractive her face unquestionably was, and not at all sickly. The revelation of its details came each time she turned to talk to a boy of twelve or thirteen who stood beside her, and the shape of whose hat and jacket implied that he belonged to a well-known public school. The immediate bystanders could hear that he called her 'Mother.'

When the end of the recital was reached, and the audience withdrew, many chose to find their way out by passing at her elbow. Almost all turned their heads to take a full and near look at the interesting woman, who remained stationary in the chair till the way should be clear enough for her to be wheeled out without obstruction. As if she expected their glances, and did not mind gratifying their curiosity, she met the eyes of several of her observers by lifting her own, showing these to be soft, brown, and affectionate orbs, a little plaintive in their regard.

She was conducted out of the gardens, and passed along the pavement till she disappeared from view, the schoolboy walking beside her. To inquiries made by some persons who watched her away, the answer came that she was the second wife of the incumbent of a neighbouring parish, and that she was lame. She was generally believed to be a woman with a story – an innocent one, but a story of some sort or other.

In conversing with her on their way home the boy who walked at her elbow said that he hoped his father had not missed them.

'He have been so comfortable these last few hours that I am sure he cannot have missed us,' she replied.

'*Has*, dear mother – not *have*!' exclaimed the public-school boy, with an impatient fastidiousness that was almost harsh. 'Surely you know that by this time!'

His mother hastily adopted the correction, and did not resent his making it, or retaliate, as she might well have done, by bidding him to wipe that crumby mouth of his, whose condition had been caused by surreptitious attempts to eat a piece of cake without taking it out of the pocket wherein it lay concealed. After this the pretty woman and the boy went onward in silence.

That question of grammar bore upon her history, and she fell into reverie, of a somewhat sad kind to all appearance. It might have been assumed that she was wondering if she had done wisely in shaping her life as she had shaped it, to bring out such a result as this.

Check your understanding

1. What is it that makes the woman's coiled hair 'a wonder and a mystery'?
2. What does the narrator know that a casual observer would not?
3. What do these facts reveal about the woman's class and status?
4. Why might people watching her find her fascinating?
5. And why might they also be disappointed?
6. What picture does Hardy give of people and attitudes in this part of London?
7. What is revealing about the boy's uniform and the way he addresses his mother?
8. What do the woman's eyes reveal about her temperament?
9. What does the boy's correction of his mother's grammar show?
10. How does her grammar relate to her past life or 'history'?

Pair and share

Create a table and collect quotations that show some of the characteristics of the woman in the story, who is called Sophie. We have given a few below to start you off. Hardy's language is difficult, so you may need a dictionary to help you.

Quotation	What it reveals about Sophie
a reckless waste of successful fabrication	She has nothing else to do but keep up her appearance which is slightly fake – 'fabrication'
unstinted pains	
challenged inspection	
attractive her face unquestionably was, and not at all sickly	
did not mind gratifying their curiosity	
affectionate orbs, a little plaintive in their regard	
generally believed to be a woman with a story	
did not resent his making it, or attempt to retaliate	
reverie, of a somewhat sad kind to all appearance	

1. How does Hardy manage to suggest that although Sophie's life has been successful in terms of raising her social status, it is not really a happy one?
2. Why might the attitude of her son, Randolph, make this unhappiness greater?

Viewpoints

Should we feel sorry for Sophie, or do we think she has made her own destiny ('shaping her life as she had shaped it')? Use the questions below to assemble your own notes.

Consider the evidence.

1. What makes her seem self-pitying and attention-seeking?

2. Which details make us feel sorry for her and the life she now lives?

There is evidence to make us feel sorry for her as well as think she has created her own situation because Hardy wants us to be interested and not to have made up our minds yet. The description and the snippet of dialogue between Sophie and Randolph make us want to find out more. They have interested us in the whole plot and how it develops.

3. Is the description of her hair a symbol or metaphor?

4. What else seems a 'reckless waste' and 'fabrication'?

5. How has Sophie's change of status affected the relationship she has with her son?

6. Because he was born into a higher class, he already seems to look down on her, in more than one way. Which is the key quotation which shows his attitude towards her?

Extend your learning

Hardy has deliberately chosen to give us a picture of Sophie from the outside, to make us judge her. Look back over the evidence, and then write a **character sketch** of Sophie. What questions does the reader ask about her? What is her status in society and what are her feelings?

Write about 300 words in answer to this question:

How does Hardy's language make her appear mysterious and gradually reveal her unhappiness?

KEY TERM

character sketch = description of how the writer has described and presented a character, using quotations as evidence.

Extend your learning: other stories

Compare the ways in which other characters are presented to us, such as Roderick Usher in 'The Fall of the House of Usher' or the Narrator's mother in 'On Her Knees'. Consider this question and respond either in an individual essay or group presentation:

How does your chosen story introduce us to a character and to her/his social context?

3.3 Developing character and situation

The next extract shows how writers use details of character and situation to develop their plots further.

**Think ahead**

Like Sophie Twycott in 'The Son's Veto', Lord Emsworth prefers the countryside. What images do you have of 'an English country gentleman' or an 'aristocrat'? Why might they make good comic characters if you exaggerate their characteristics?

Between the wars, England was still a very class-conscious society, but America offered new money and new attitudes.

P.G. Wodehouse's novels are set in an exaggerated and fantastic version of England between the wars and make fun of class-conscious society, eccentric aristocrats, and their clever and cunning servants. In 'The Custody of the Pumpkin', the Earl of Emsworth, owner of Blandings Castle, has, through his new telescope, spotted his party-loving second son, the Honourable Freddie, with a young lady called Aggie. He is horrified to hear they are engaged, and even more horrified to hear that Aggie is American and 'a sort of cousin' of his own gardener, Angus McAllister. Lord Emsworth wants Freddie to marry a rich girl, so he won't have to support him any longer. He therefore dismisses McAllister from his job at Blandings.

English country house

'The Custody of the Pumpkin' by P.G. Wodehouse (1935)

The importance of this pumpkin in the Earl of Emsworth's life requires, perhaps, a word of explanation. Every ancient family in England has some little gap in its scroll of honour, and that of Lord Emsworth was no exception. For generations back his ancestors had been doing notable deeds; they had sent out from Blandings Castle statesmen and warriors, governors and leaders of the people: but they had not – in the opinion of the present holder of the title – achieved a full hand. However splendid the family record might appear at first sight, the fact remained that no Earl of Emsworth had ever won a first prize for pumpkins at the Shrewsbury Show. For roses, yes. For tulips, true. For spring onions, granted. But not for pumpkins; and Lord Emsworth felt it deeply.

For many a summer past he had been striving indefatigably to remove this blot on the family escutcheon, only to see his hopes go tumbling down. But this year at last victory had seemed in sight, for there had been vouchsafed to Blandings a competitor of such amazing parts that his lordship, who had watched it grow practically from a pip, could not envisage failure. Surely, he told himself as he gazed on its golden roundness, even Sir Gregory Parsloe-Parsloe, of Matchingham Hall, winner for three successive years, would never be able to produce anything to challenge this superb vegetable.

And it was this supreme pumpkin whose welfare he feared he had jeopardized by dismissing Angus McAllister. For Angus was its official trainer. He understood the pumpkin. Indeed, in his reserved Scottish way, he even seemed to love it. With Angus gone, what would the harvest be?

Such were the meditations of Lord Emsworth as he reviewed the position of affairs. And though, as the days went by, he tried to tell himself that Angus McAllister was not the only man in the world who understood pumpkins, and that he had every confidence, the most complete and unswerving confidence, in Robert Barker, recently Angus's second-in-command, now promoted to the post of head-gardener and custodian of the Blandings Hope, he knew that this was but shallow bravado. When you are a pumpkin owner with a big winner in your stable, you judge men by hard standards, and every day it became plainer that Robert Barker was only a makeshift. Within a week Lord Emsworth was pining for Angus McAllister.

It might be purely imagination, but to his excited fancy the pumpkin seemed to be pining for Angus too. It appeared to be drooping and losing weight. Lord Emsworth could not rid himself of the horrible idea that it was shrinking. And on the tenth night after McAllister's departure he dreamed a strange dream. He had gone with King George to show his Gracious Majesty the pumpkin, promising him the treat of a lifetime; and when they arrived, there in the corner of the frame was a shrivelled thing the size of a pea. He woke, sweating, with his Sovereign's disappointed screams ringing in his ears; and Pride gave its last quiver and collapsed. To reinstate Angus would be a surrender, but it must be done.

Pair and share

Collect the adjectives and phrases that Lord Emsworth uses to describe the pumpkin, both in paragraphs two and three, and in paragraph five. How do they reveal the extent of Lord Emsworth's obsession?

A pumpkin

 Check your understanding

1. What were Lord Emsworth's ancestors famous for?

2. What is the only fame he is interested in?

3. Who is his enemy in the competition?

4. Why has dismissing McAllister caused him a problem?

5. What makes the dream so terrifying for Lord Emsworth?

6. Why is reinstating McAllister a 'surrender'?

Extend your learning

Although this passage is told in the third person, it clearly recreates Lord Emsworth's point of view. How does his language reveal his attitudes? Not only is he obsessed with the prize pumpkin (which is odd enough) but his language is very old-fashioned. Use your dictionary to establish the meaning of some of the odder words in this story.

Lord Emsworth's vocabulary	Modern English equivalent
achieved a full hand	Won everything possible
striving indefatigably	
blot on the family escutcheon	
but shallow bravado	
to his excited fancy	
his Gracious Majesty	
Pride gave its last quiver	
to reinstate Angus would be a surrender	

His language uses old-fashioned vocabulary, and he is also fond of imagery. Can you find metaphors and personification in his language?

Viewpoints

Is Lord Emsworth charmingly old-fashioned, eccentric, and funny? Or deeply sad, out of touch, and mad?

You decide.

1. Which is the better way to view Lord Emsworth?
2. What does the writer want you to think about him?

Write a paragraph supporting each point of view. Make sure you use quotations from the text as evidence to support your view.

Looking at the evidence, what do you think was Wodehouse's opinion of Lord Emsworth?

Extend your learning: other stories

Consider important developments or turning points in stories which reveal a lot about characters. You might choose La Guma's 'The Lemon Orchard' or MacLaverty's 'Secrets'. Choose a short passage (no more than a page) which shows this turning point. Answer this question either as an individual essay or a group presentation:

How does the language of this passage reveal more about a character and her/his thoughts and feelings at a crucial moment in the story?

3.4 Endings

As we have seen, happy endings are a convention in comedy, however unlikely they may seem. However, in the short story endings are often very much more open, and they can come rather abruptly, leaving you to decide what the story was about. The term for this is **closure**. Lord Emsworth is given a happy ending: Freddie marries a rich girl and is off his hands, and he beats Sir Gregory Parsloe-Parsloe with his immensely superior pumpkin, thanks to McAllister. However, nothing ends happily for Sophie in 'The Son's Veto', as her son forbids her a second chance at happiness, showing the power of class snobbery.

KEY TERM

closure = the way a text ends; sometimes we say that a text 'resists closure' because it does not end neatly, and problems are not resolved.

 **Think ahead**

Graham Greene's 'The Destructors' was written soon after the Second World War, when London and other major cities were still full of bomb sites.

Draw a timeline showing key world events between 1945 and 1954. The internet is a good resource for finding out what these key events were. Refer to websites such as www.bbc.co.uk/history/british/ or www.britishempire.co.uk/timeline/20century.htm.

Focus on the events that might have made British people feel their world was being transformed or destroyed. In particular look at:

▶ the end of the Second World War
▶ the end of the British Empire
▶ the Cold War with the USSR.

A view of London bombed in the Second World War

The gang of young boys who give this short story its title enjoy mischief. While Mr Thomas, or 'Old Misery', is away over the bank holiday, they get into his old house, one of the few left standing around the bomb site and held up by wooden props, and systematically demolish it, led by T. who has assumed leadership through this plan. Even the complication of Old Misery's early return makes no difference. They lock him in his own outdoor 'loo' (a slang word for toilet).

A house near a bomb site

'The Destructors' by Graham Greene (1954)

Mike had gone home to bed, but the rest stayed. The question of leadership no longer concerned the gang. With nails, chisels, screwdrivers, anything that was sharp and penetrating, they moved around the inner walls worrying at the mortar between the bricks. They started too high, and it was Blackie who hit on the damp course and realized the work could be halved if they weakened the joints immediately above. It was a long, tiring, unamusing job, but at last it was finished. The gutted house stood there balanced on a few inches of mortar between the damp course and the bricks.

There remained the most dangerous task of all, out in the open at the edge of the bomb-site. Summers was sent to watch the road for passers-by, and Mr Thomas, sitting on the loo, heard clearly now the sound of sawing. It no longer came from the house, and that a little reassured him. He felt less concerned. Perhaps the other noises too had no significance.

A voice spoke to him through the hole. 'Mr Thomas.'

'Let me out,' Mr Thomas said sternly.

'Here's a blanket,' the voice said, and a long grey sausage was worked through the hole and fell in swathes over Mr Thomas's head.

'There's nothing personal,' the voice said. 'We want you to be comfortable tonight.'

'Tonight,' Mr Thomas repeated incredulously.

'Catch,' the voice said. 'Penny buns – we've buttered them, and sausage-rolls. We don't want you to starve, Mr Thomas.' Mr Thomas pleaded desperately. 'A joke's a joke, boy. Let me out and I won't say a thing. I've got rheumatics. I got to sleep comfortable.'

'You wouldn't be comfortable, not in your house, you wouldn't. Not now.'

'What do you mean, boy?' But the footsteps receded. There was only the silence of night: no sound of sawing. Mr Thomas tried one more yell, but he was daunted and rebuked by the silence – a long way off an owl hooted and made away again on its muffled flight through the soundless world.

At seven next morning the driver came to fetch his lorry. He climbed into the seat and tried to start the engine. He was vaguely aware of a voice shouting, but it didn't concern him. At last the engine responded and he backed the lorry until it touched the great wooden shore that supported Mr Thomas's house. That way he could drive right out and down the street without reversing. The lorry moved forward, was momentarily checked as though something were pulling it from behind, and then went on to the sound of a long rumbling crash. The driver was astonished to see bricks bouncing ahead of him, while stones hit the roof of his cab. He put on his brakes. When he climbed out the whole landscape had suddenly altered. There was no house beside the car-park, only a hill of rubble. He went round and examined the back of his lorry for damage, and found a rope tied there that was still twisted at the other end round part of a wooden strut.

The driver again became aware of somebody shouting. It came from the wooden erection which was the nearest thing to a house in that desolation of broken brick. The driver climbed the smashed wall and unlocked the door. Mr Thomas came out of the loo. He was wearing a grey blanket to which flakes of pastry adhered. He gave a sobbing cry. 'My house,' he said. 'Where's my house?'

'Search me,' the driver said. His eye lit on the remains of a bath and what had once been a dresser and he began to laugh. There wasn't anything left anywhere.

'How dare you laugh,' Mr Thomas said. 'It was my house. My house.'

'I'm sorry,' the driver said, making heroic efforts, but when he remembered the sudden check of his lorry, the crash of bricks falling, he became convulsed again. One moment the house had stood there with such dignity between the bomb-sites like a man in a top hat, and then, bang, crash, there wasn't anything left – not anything. He said, 'I'm sorry. I can't help it, Mr Thomas. There's nothing personal, but you got to admit it's funny.'

Check your understanding

Greene chooses to alternate description and dialogue in this passage.

1. How do the descriptions of the boys demolishing the house show their hard work as 'destructors'?
2. How does the detail of the dialogue reveal Mr Thomas's low status in comparison with that of the boys?
3. Why does the writer show the fall of Mr Thomas's house from the lorry driver's point of view?
4. Why do you think the boys are not there?
5. Which details show the violence and completeness of the 'desolation'?
6. How does the dialogue show the different points of view of Mr Thomas and the driver?
7. Why does the driver laugh? Is he right to laugh?
8. Is this a happy ending? Or an open ending?

Extend your learning

Irony is used by writers when they, and the readers, know things that the characters do not. We often read the details of stories differently once we know the ending. Looking more closely at language, aware of what will happen next, comment on the effects of the following phrases:

a. 'they moved around the inner walls worrying at the mortar between the bricks'
b. 'it was a long, tiring, unamusing job'
c. 'We want you to be comfortable tonight.'
d. 'A joke's a joke, boy.'
e. 'You wouldn't be comfortable, not in your house, you wouldn't. Not now.'
f. 'He was vaguely aware of a voice shouting'
g. 'the sound of a long rumbling crash'
h. 'the whole landscape had suddenly altered'
i. 'the nearest thing to a house in that desolation of broken brick'

j. 'How dare you laugh'

k. 'he became convulsed again'

Symbolism is the use of an extended metaphor to construct a story beneath the surface story. The word 'house' occurs more often than any other in this extract.

1. What might the house stand for or symbolize? (Remember that it is very old, and was left behind when others around it were destroyed by the war.)

2. Could it stand for Britain itself?

3. If so, who are the boys, and who is the lorry driver?

The style in this passage changes. Most of the language is plain and straightforward, especially compared to Lord Emsworth's old-fashioned language. However, the writer adds some poetic touches (similar to language we will explore in chapter 4).

Look at the use of **personification**:

'he was daunted and rebuked by the silence – a long way off an owl hooted and made away again on its muffled flight through the soundless world'.

4. How does this passage contrast the sounds of the human world with the silence of the night?

5. Why do you think Greene chose to mention the sound of a bird of prey?

Explore the significance of the final **simile**:

'the house had stood there with such dignity between the bomb-sites like a man in a top hat, and then, bang, crash, there wasn't anything left – not anything'.

6. What does the top hat image contribute to the reader's ideas about the house?

7. What is the effect of the repetition?

Extend your learning: other stories

Does the ending of your studied short story fit the mood and purpose of the story? Is it inevitable, or does it come as a shock? Consider the tragic but inevitable endings of 'The Fall of the House of Usher' or 'The Lemon Orchard'; the twists at the ends of 'Secrets' and 'On Her Knees'; or the bitter-sweet and ironic conclusion of 'There Will Come Soft Rains'. Explore the effect on the reader, and what the ending makes you think about. This will help you to develop a personal response, based on the details of the writing. Either as an individual essay or a group presentation, answer the following question:

How does the writing make the ending of this short story so effective?

3.5 Structure of the short story

We have looked at the structure of the short story through three examples. All these stories involve older people clashing with younger people and their attitudes.

We have explored how writers use:

*   setting when opening their stories
*   gradual revelation of character and situation
*   use of a character's viewpoint
*   the irony and symbolism implied by a story's ending.

You can use these structural ideas, and some of those in the previous chapter on drama, to look at other short stories.

On the next page we give you some headings that you can use to organize your notes with questions you could ask for each.

 See Worksheet 3 on the website for further help with the structure of short stories.

KEY TERMS

personification = a particular form of metaphor; ideas or objects are given human characteristics and treated as if they were a person.

simile = an explicit comparison using 'like' or 'as'.

SITUATION and CHARACTERS

1. Who are the characters from different generations and why do they clash?
2. What are their different interests?
3. Why are their motivations different?

CONFLICT

1. Why do those differences begin to cause problems?
2. What happens as the story develops which shows that the generations are going to clash?
3. What has brought out the difference in their interests, attitudes and way of thinking and speaking?

CONFRONTATION

Problems can lead to more arguments before there is a solution or resolution.

1. How have developments in the story brought on a battle between two different characters and ways of speaking as well as thinking?
2. Where do characters confront each other in a dramatic way?

CONTRAST

What are the differences between:

1. their appearances
2. the ways they speak
3. the ways they react to things
4. things they say or are said about them?

PROBLEM

Writers of short stories often introduce an additional problem about halfway through the story in order to complicate the plot further.

Can you find an example? How is it linked to the original conflict?

SOLUTION or RESOLUTION

1. Is the problem solved?
2. How has the writer chosen to end the story?
3. What does the reader think about at the end?
4. Are we happy with the ending or disturbed by it?
5. Does the writer have a particular bias or point of view which he or she wants you to share?
6. Do characters resolve their problems at all?
7. What is the difference between a comic (happy) ending and a tragic (sad) one?
8. Does the ending involve irony or symbolism?

Extend your learning

Refer to the story you are studying and answer these questions.

1. Identify the key pages where characters are introduced and where their differences become obvious.
2. How does the writer's use of language show differences between characters? Collect quotations which illustrate the difference between characters.
3. Where do additional problems complicate the action? Plot the action of your story and make a note of the page where the 'problem' develops.

How has the writer made this a dramatic moment?

4. Look for dialogue which reveals the difference between characters in a striking way. This is clear towards the end of 'The Son's Veto', or when the mother and son talk about money in 'On Her Knees'.
5. Do the differences between characters lead to a confrontation? Or are they left unresolved? For different reasons, there is no clear resolution in 'There Will Come Soft Rains' or 'Secrets'. This is left for us to work out from the symbolism of the language.

3.6 English literature becomes world literature

Think ahead

After 1945, with the United Kingdom in decline economically and politically, the story of 'English' becomes less connected with the story of England, and more about the English language as something that connects (and sometimes divides) people from many different cultures all over the world. We saw this in chapter 1 when we looked at 'A Horse and Two Goats'. Many twentieth-century texts explore America and the American dream of independence, or the process of independence and rediscovery of identity in **post-colonial** cultures after 1945.

The English language bound these many different cultures together, but has had to diversify in order to respect different identities. The increase in the number of people not born in the British Isles who speak English has changed the nature of 'English' language and literature, just as it has changed notions of culture and identity. Inter-marriage between members of very different communities and people has also influenced how individuals express their sense of who they are. We can read this in their language and stories: many novels and stories now explore the experience of migration and multiculturalism. You might read 'The Third and Final Continent' by Jhumpa Lahiri or Anita Desai's novel *Fasting, Feasting*.

Statue of Liberty

Gate of India

KEY TERM

post-colonial = referring to the literature which came after the break-up of the British Empire, and other colonial structures.

In the title story of Ahdaf Soueif's *Sandpiper*, a young writer from Britain reflects on her eight years of marriage to her husband, and her experience of living in his homeland of Egypt. She reflects on her visit to another part of Africa, how she fell in love, and on the image of her daughter Lucy, playing by their beach house near Alexandria. Her marriage has become difficult, as this quotation shows.

A sandpiper

'Sandpiper' by Ahdaf Soueif (1994)

I suppose I should have seen it coming. My foreignness, which had been so charming, began to irritate him. My inability to remember names, to follow the minutiae of politics, my struggles with his language, my need to be protected from the sun, the mosquitoes, the salads, the drinking water. He was back home, and he needed someone he could simply be at home with, at home. It took perhaps a year. His heart was broken in two, mine was simply broken.

✎ Check your understanding

1. What is the effect of the lists in the third sentence?

2. What has the narrator found so difficult about life in Egypt?

3. How has her husband reacted?

4. How does the use of pronouns bring out the rift between the unnamed narrator and her unnamed husband?

5. How does the writer bring out the importance of 'home' for the husband?

6. By contrast what seem to be the feelings of the narrator?

7. Why does it help to know that a sandpiper is a migratory bird, found all over the world? Who is the sandpiper in this story?

Before reading this, you need to know that the narrator has just told, in flashback, the story of how she was nearly killed when the aircraft she was travelling in when visiting Nigeria had to crash land. Soon afterwards, she married her husband.

'Sandpiper' by Ahdaf Soueif (1994)

And in that moment, not only my head, but all of me, my whole being, seemed to tilt into a blank, an empty radiance, but lucid. Then three giant thoughts. One was of him – his name, over and over again. The other was of the children I would never have. The third was that the pattern was now complete: this is what my life amounted to.

When we did not die, that first thought: his name, his name, his name became a talisman, for in extremity, hadn't all that was not him been wiped out of my life? My life, which once again stretched out before me, shimmering with possibilities, was meant to merge with his.

I finished the french plait and Lucy chose a blue clasp to secure its end. Before I let her run out I smoothed some after-sun on her face. Her skin is nut-brown, except just next to her ears where it fades to a pale cream gleaming with golden down. I put my lips to her neck. 'My Lucy, Lucia, *Lambah*,' I murmured as I kissed her and let her go. Lucy. My treasure, my trap.

Now, when I walk to the sea, to the edge of this continent where I live, where I almost died, where I wait for my daughter to grow away from me, I see different things from those I saw that summer six years ago. The last of the foam is swallowed bubbling into the sand, to sink down and rejoin the sea at an invisible subterranean level. With each ebb of green water the sand loses part of itself to the sea, with each flow another part is flung back to be reclaimed once again by the beach. That narrow stretch of sand knows nothing in the world better than it does the white waves that whip it, caress it, collapse onto it, vanish into it. The white foam knows nothing better than those sands which wait for it, rise to it, and suck it in. But what do the waves know of the massed, hot, still sands of the desert just twenty, no, ten feet beyond the scalloped edge? And what does the beach know of the depths, the cold, the currents just there, there – do you see it? – where the water turns a deeper blue.

💡 Viewpoints

The world has become a smaller place, bringing about new cultural exchanges but also more difficulties. The mysterious and open nature of the way this story ends leaves you, as the reader, with plenty to think about and work out for yourself. We are not directly told what will happen next, although we know plenty about the past. Perhaps this makes this kind of writing especially true to life. You will need to debate the meaning of the ending with a partner.

How do you interpret the imagery of sea, sand and desert in these powerful final paragraphs of the story?

An empty beach in north Africa

✎ Check your understanding

1. In the first paragraph, the narrator is still looking back at the moment when she thought she was going to die. What three things did she think of?

2. When she survives, how does the pattern of her thoughts show what mattered most to her at the time?

3. How do repetition and the form of her sentences show this?

4. What do you think she means by a 'talisman'?

5. How did she understand the pattern of life at the time when she realized she would not die?

6. How has the pattern of her life developed since?

7. Why do you think she pays special attention to her daughter when she is thinking in this way?

8. Why is the description of Lucy's skin colour significant here?

9. Why does she call her daughter 'My treasure, my trap'?

10. How does the beginning of the final paragraph bring together the narrator's thoughts about Africa, her daughter, and her marriage?

Pair and share

Compare your answers with a partner. You will need to work together to make sense of the final paragraph. One of you should look at the imagery of the sea and the foam of the waves. The other should explore the imagery that describes the sand or desert. Together you will work out what the description of the two coming together, or clashing, might symbolize.

First, use the quotation and comment technique to explore the meaning of each individual image. You will need to go beyond the surface meaning and look at what is suggested. Some answers have been done for you in the table below.

The sea	
I walk to the sea … where I wait for my daughter to grow away from me	Suggests a link between the sea and freedom, growing away from home
The last of the foam is swallowed bubbling into the sand …	
… to sink down and rejoin the sea at an invisible subterranean level …	Suggests the waves will never become part of the land, they will eventually rejoin the sea
The white foam knows nothing better than those sands which wait for it, rise to it and suck it in.	
But what do the waves know of the massed, hot, still sands of the desert …	
… the depths … where the water turns a deeper blue.	
The desert sands	
With each ebb of green water the sand loses part of itself to the sea …	
… another part is flung back to be reclaimed once again by the beach.	Suggests that the sand always returns to the land
That narrow stretch of sand knows nothing in the world better than it does the white waves that whip it, caress it, collapse onto it, vanish into it.	Suggests the relationship between sands and seas is sometimes gentle, sometimes violent, and that the sands absorb the water
… what does the beach know of the depths, the cold, the currents just there …	

Share your answers and discuss the following questions.

1. Have you noticed a pattern?
2. What kind of relationship is described?
3. Where do both sand and sea really belong?
4. How do the final questions move beyond the beach where the two meet and explore their very different worlds and senses?
5. How do these images contrast?
6. Which people in the marriage might sand and sea correspond to, and why?
7. What is ironic about this use of symbolism of sand and sea, considering coastal erosion?
8. What is suggested about the past and future of the marriage?

Practice question

You will need to look back at the complete passage and your notes so far. Write 300–400 words. Use the bullet points which follow the question to give structure to your response.

How does Soueif's writing portray the thoughts and feelings of the narrator and make this a powerful ending to her story?

To help you to answer, you might consider:

- the narrator's thoughts about the feelings which encouraged her to marry
- what she feels about her daughter now
- how her language expresses her thoughts about being a foreigner in Africa
- how the writer's choice of metaphors and expression show the nature of her marriage now
- what the reader feels about the way this story ends, and the way it expresses the narrator's deeper thoughts.

When you have written your answer, work with your teacher or a partner to assess your writing. Have you produced a developed response to the writing? Have you explored the 'deeper implications'? Have you provided well-selected textual support? Are you working towards 'critical understanding'?

💡 Viewpoints

You should now be able to answer the question you were asked earlier about how to interpret the final paragraph. As we have seen, making meaning goes far beyond the literal meaning of the words, and requires you to explore metaphor and imagery. The meaning of the story is also shaped by its viewpoint: we only hear the wife's account of her marriage. To make your response personal, relate your observations about language to the way you understand and interpret character and situation, as you have learned previously.

How have you come to understand her thoughts and feelings? Do you sympathize with her? What do you think will happen next?

Extend your learning: other stories

Explore the kind of culture created in the short stories you are studying, such as Crane's 'The Open Boat', Wharton's 'The Moving Finger', McGahern's 'The Stoat', Grace's 'The Journey' or Frame's 'The Bath'. Write an individual essay or make a group presentation to answer the following question:

How does the writing in your short story present a character's response to the world they live in?

In your response, consider the structure of the story, the language of its descriptions and how action and dialogue reveal character and attitudes.

Looking back

1. What have you learned about the importance of establishing interesting characters and situations?

2. How do problems, clashes, and conflicts contribute to the complexity of short stories?

3. How does viewpoint influence the reader's degree of sympathy?

4. Why are good endings often so mysterious or ambiguous?

5. Can you apply a similar structure to novels you have read or studied?

We will explore the structure and language of prose fiction in more detail in chapter 8.

Reading poetry

The poetry of war

Think ahead

War is a powerful and emotive subject. It is also one of the traditional subjects of poetry, going back to early epics like Homer's *Iliad* or *Beowulf*, which made fighting and heroic action part of their narrative. Modern warfare brings even greater destruction and fewer opportunities for heroic action: soldiers often seem victims of a system beyond their control. Today, poets use verse to commemorate loss or to express a protest more often than to celebrate heroism or destruction.

1. Why do we hear more now about the problems caused by war than about heroic fighting?

2. Why are war and conflict appealing subjects for literature?

3. What kind of emotions can war poetry excite?

Ancient heroes were portrayed with swords and shields

LEARNING POINTS

▶ To explore the distinctive features of poetry texts, linked by theme

▶ To analyse the effects of rhyme, rhythm, and stanza form

▶ To see patterns of words and imagery in poetry

▶ To use details of language and form to understand tone

▶ To interpret the meaning of poems by exploring mood

4.1 The call to arms

Poetry gives shape to powerful feelings, by applying a strong rhythm and memorable images to the idea of conflict and destruction. British poets John Scott (1731–83) and A.E. Housman (1859–1936) call up the music and the images of the recruiting drum, which in the past was used to literally drum up support for the wars which the British fought abroad, while establishing their Empire. As the military band sounded their drums, young men would be called up to go off to fight, usually in other countries.

As you read the first poem, try to hear the beat of the drum and to picture the scenes Scott describes.

A poster showing the recruiting drum

'The Drum' by John Scott (1782)

I hate that drum's discordant sound,
Parading round, and round, and round:
To thoughtless youth it pleasure yields
And lures from cities and from fields,
To sell their liberty for charms
Of tawdry lace, and glittering arms:
And when Ambition's voice commands,
To march, and fight, and fall, in foreign lands.

I hate that drum's discordant sound,
Parading round, and round, and round:
To me it talks of ravaged plains,
And burning towns, and ruined swains,
And mangled limbs, and dying groans,
And widows' tears and orphans' moans
And all that Misery's hand bestows,
To fill the catalogue of human woes.

tawdry = *cheap and nasty*

discordant = *harsh, unmusical*

swains = *young men*

bestows = *gives out*

RHYME AND SYNTAX

Repetition and pattern are clearly important elements of the poem's structure. Poetic form relies on a number of elements which give the poem its shape and its sound. This poem is clearly divided into two **stanzas**: a stanza is the correct name for a verse paragraph (sometimes just called a verse). This poem also uses one of the most common forms of shaping a pattern in sound: rhyme. When pairs of lines rhyme in this way, we call them rhyming couplets.

Notice that the stanzas also provide the sentence structure or syntax of the poem.

 Check your understanding

Look again at the poem.

1. Can you find the full stops?
2. What is the effect of these long-running sentences?
3. Is it easy to stop the flow, or to pause for thought?

A soldier in uniform

You should now learn to mark up the key features of a poem on a paper copy of the text, or on a whiteboard. Here the **rhyming couplets** have been underlined.

> I hate that drum's discordant <u>sound</u>,
> Parading round, and round, and <u>round</u>:
> To thoughtless youth it pleasure <u>yields</u>
> And lures from cities and from <u>fields</u>,
> To sell their liberty for ch<u>arms</u>
> Of tawdry lace, and glittering <u>arms</u>:
> And when Ambition's voice comm<u>ands</u>,
> To march, and fight, and fall, in foreign <u>lands</u>.

The rhymes make the poem sound insistent and predictable, as if you cannot resist what comes next. In the past, words did not always sound the same as today: pronunciation of English varies a lot, which gives poets a degree of **poetic licence**.

The shading highlights the most often repeated word in the poem. What is the effect of this?

Now mark up the next stanza in the same way.

RHYTHM

Having looked at rhyme and **syntax**, another important element in this poem is rhythm. The most common form of rhythm is the **iambic** rhythm of weak STRONG, often represented as x/. Rhythms in English poetry usually depend on **stress**, which means the words you place stress or emphasis on when speaking.

```
x  /  x   /        x  /  x   /
I hate that drum's    discordant sound,
x / x   /    x   /   x   /
Parading round, and round, and round:
```

KEY TERMS

stanza = the correct name for a paragraph of verse, sometimes called a verse.

rhyming couplets = pairs of lines that rhyme, a common pattern in English verse.

poetic licence = the freedom which poets have to break or bend the rules, particularly over patterns of rhyme but also over what is real and what is imagined.

syntax = sentence structure.

iambic = iambic pentameter is the verse line most commonly used by Shakespeare and other verse dramatists, and very common in longer English poems. It is made up of a line with five beats in it following a weak STRONG rhythm. This is also the rhythm most common in English speech patterns.

stress = where you put the emphasis when reading aloud, sometimes called the 'beat'.

🗨 Pair and share

Notice the weak stress on the first syllable and the strong stress on the last.

1. Does this help you to hear the regular sound of the drum?
2. Why does the poet call the music of the drum 'discordant'?
3. Discuss what you think the poet feels about the sound of the recruiting drum and why he feels that way.

Extend your learning

Imagery

Poems are highly visual as well as musical: they set up images as well as a soundtrack. As you have seen in previous chapters, we use the word **imagery** for language which is figurative or non-literal. A comparison, such as a **metaphor** or a simile, is used to create an image related to the object that is being described. Another form of imagery is personification: when an idea is presented as if it were a person. When an idea is personified, it often has a capital letter, so this kind of personification is easy to spot and to imagine.

1. Scott uses personification in the penultimate line of each verse: what do you think Ambition or Misery might sound or look like?

There is another form of personification which is much more subtle.

2. If you look at phrases like 'to thoughtless youth it pleasure leads' and words like 'lures', 'charms' and 'glittering arms', what do they suggest is attracting the young men to military life?

3. Is 'it' the drum? Or a woman?

4. How does this help you to picture the effect the drum has on the young men it is calling to?

 Pair and share

Choice of words and patterns

Diction is another word for a poet's choice of words: Scott chooses words for what they suggest to you as well as what they describe.

1. Why does he use words like 'tawdry' or 'glittering'?

2. What does it suggest about the rewards the men get for agreeing to 'sell their liberty'?

3. Why do they join up, and why do they get less than they expect?

Repetition is the key to the patterns in this poem, imitating the **repetitive** rhythms of the drum. The same technique can have very different effects in different places. Two examples of lists from the poem appear below. Comment on the effects of each.

a. To march, and fight, and *fall*, in foreign lands

b. And burning towns …, And mangled limbs …, And widows' tears …, And *all* that Misery's hand bestows

 Viewpoints

Interpreting the poet's purpose

Notice how sound effects like rhyme and rhythm add to the emphasis here. The word 'and' suggests that everything is connected and follows in a logical sequence. The word 'fall' goes further than just 'fall down'. In the United States, the autumn season is called 'fall' and the word is applied to death. War monuments are sometimes inscribed with the message 'For the Fallen'. Scott is suggesting that death is an inevitable consequence of joining the army. It is all part of the 'catalogue of human woes' that result from following the call of the drum. Do you agree?

Scott does not just use rhyme, a technique English poets borrowed from the French and Italians, but also an older, rougher, and Anglo-Saxon way of linking words together called **alliteration**: To march, and **f**ight, and **f**all, in **f**oreign lands. It isn't just the word 'fall' which is emphasized here, but also 'foreign'.

1. What do you think Scott might be suggesting about the wars the men were recruited to fight?

2. Do you share his bitter ideas about war?

Practice question

How does Scott's writing memorably convey to you his feelings when he hears the sound of the recruiting drum?

Look carefully at this question. It might help you to answer it if you break it up into different parts.

1. How does Scott's writing	Understanding of the writer's techniques and choice of words
2. memorably convey to you	Analysis of the effect of his techniques on the reader
3. his feelings	Your evaluation of the message of the poem
4. when he hears the sound of the recruiting drum?	Your knowledge of the scene he describes and your appreciation of the poem's sound effects

Now rearrange the different parts of the question so that you can answer it in the most suitable way.

Remember the following formula:

Knowledge > **U**nderstanding > **A**nalysis > **E**valuation

In other words, ask *what* the poem shows, then *how* it works and finally *why* it has an effect on the reader (so part 4, followed by part 1, then 2, concluding with 3).

You should aim to write about 200 words.

Share your work with a partner, as well as your teacher. How clear is your understanding? How thorough and developed is your response to language?

4.2 Comparison and contrast

When studying poetry you will often find that you are asked to compare poems on a similar theme. Although comparison is not required as part of the Cambridge Literature in English exam, nor is it necessary in coursework, your teachers may ask you to compare poems on related themes. When teachers use the word 'compare' they mean explore both similarities and differences (sometimes called contrasts, as we have seen).

The next poem by A.E. Housman has many similarities with Scott's.

A.E. Housman

'On the Idle Hill' by A.E. Housman (1896)

On the idle hill of summer,
    Sleepy with the flow of streams,
Far I hear the steady drummer
    Drumming like a noise in dreams.

Far and near and low and louder
    On the roads of earth go by,
Dear to friends and food for powder,
    Soldiers marching, all to die.

East and west on fields forgotten
    Bleach the bones of comrades slain,
Lovely lads and dead and rotten;
    None that go return again.

Far the calling bugles hollo,
    High the screaming fife replies,
Gay the files of scarlet follow
    Woman bore me, I will rise.

powder = (here) gunpowder, explosive

hollo = call out

fife = high-pitched flute

scarlet = the traditional colour of British military uniforms

This poem is written in **quatrains**, one of the most common building blocks of English poetry. A quatrain is a four-line stanza. These use alternating rhyme, in other words the last words rhyme *abab* and there is a regular rhythm, just like in Scott's poem, to link the lines together and give the poem its 'logic'.

There is, however, a crucial difference in the rhythm or beat of the poem, isn't there? Housman hears the sound of the drum differently. Instead of weak STRONG he hears a sound which is STRONG weak:

  /   x /x /   x /   x

On the idle hill of summer,

   / x /   x /   x   /

Sleepy with the flow of dreams.

We call this rhythm **trochaic**. A trochee is the opposite of an iamb and has a falling rather than a rising rhythm. Why might this suit the mood of the poem?

✎ Check your understanding

- Mark up your own copy of the poem, as you learned to do earlier.
- Mark in the rhythmic stresses.
- Mark in the rhymes.
- Mark the ways in which sentences follow stanza form.

The rhyme is very different too: there are no rhyming couplets, but instead an alternating rhyme scheme (*abab*). Notice the rhythm of the *b* lines is different: it is cut short or curtailed.

1. Why does he use this effect?
2. What else is cut short or curtailed in the poem?

Pair and share

Tone and mood

Once you have noticed the key differences to the music of the poems, the tone used by the writer, you will notice a lot of similarities in techniques and mood. Mood is the effect of the writing on the reader. It is the atmosphere created by the writer's choices, including tone, and the impact on us as we read.

Your task here is to use the same techniques to analyse this poem. Working together, find the quotations that show Housman's use of poetic techniques, and add a brief comment on their effect on the reader. Some have been done for you.

Technique	Quotation	Effect
Alliteration	sleepy with the flow of streams	
	drumming like a noise in dreams	
Repetition		Creating a sense that war and its consequences are everywhere
	Lovely lads and dead and rotten	
Personification		
Diction	screaming fife	
Use of colour	files of scarlet (note that soldiers still wore red uniforms for parade)	
Stress used for emphasis	**all** to **die**	

Do the words as well as the rhythms of the poem have a different effect on us?

Discuss the answers to the following questions.

1. Is the tone (that is, the music of the poem) very different from the first poem?
2. Which of the two poets we have looked at seems to you to be the more angry or bitter about war?
3. Which creates a rhythm most like a drum?
4. Who has the greater effect on the reader's mood?

Notice there is no right or wrong answer to these questions. Did you and your partner have different views? It is about your *personal* response. This is what we mean by 'mood'. Just make sure you support your opinion with detail, and with appreciation of the poet's 'tone', his choice of voice, and the music of the verse.

 Viewpoints

In pairs, take different positions on the poems.

1. Which do you think is the most powerful in communicating an anti-war message and why?
2. Why do you think both poets choose to use the insistent rhythm of the recruiting drum?
3. Do you find their personal, different messages as relentless as the sound of the drum?

4.3 On the front line

The next poem looks at the situation of being at war, rather than reacting to the sound of men being called to fight. The poet, Wilfred Owen, had first-hand experience of being in the trenches in France in the First World War as an officer, and was killed in 1918. He shows that real war is often about waiting.

This is a much longer poem, so take time to read it carefully twice, paying attention to *sounds* as well as sense. Sentences help you to make sense of the text, but the sounds introduce you to the emotional world of the poem.

'Exposure' by Wilfred Owen (1917)

Our brains ache, in the merciless iced east winds that knive us ...
Wearied we keep awake because the night is silent ...
Low drooping flares confuse our memory of the salient ...
Worried by silence, sentries whisper, curious, nervous,
     But nothing happens.

Watching, we hear the mad gusts tugging on the wire.
Like twitching agonies of men among its brambles.
Northward incessantly, the flickering gunnery rumbles,
Far off, like a dull rumour of some other war.
     What are we doing here?

The poignant misery of dawn begins to grow ...
We only know war lasts, rain soaks, and clouds sag stormy.
Dawn massing in the east her melancholy army
Attacks once more in ranks on shivering ranks of gray,
     But nothing happens.

Sudden successive flights of bullets streak the silence.
Less deadly than the air that shudders black with snow,
With sidelong flowing flakes that flock, pause and renew,
We watch them wandering up and down the wind's nonchalance,
     But nothing happens.

Pale flakes with lingering stealth come feeling for our faces--
We cringe in holes, back on forgotten dreams, and stare, snow-dazed,
Deep into grassier ditches. So we drowse, sun-dozed,
Littered with blossoms trickling where the blackbird fusses.
     -- Is it that we are dying?

salient = *angle in a fortified trench*

nonchalance = *indifference*

Slowly our ghosts drag home: glimpsing the sunk fires glozed   *glozed* = decorated or enhanced
With crusted dark-red jewels; crickets jingle there;
For hours the innocent mice rejoice: the house is theirs;
Shutters and doors all closed: on us the doors are closed--
     We turn back to our dying.

Since we believe not otherwise can kind fires burn;
Nor ever suns smile true on child, or field, or fruit.
For God's invincible spring our love is made afraid;
Therefore, not loath, we lie out here; therefore were born,   *loath* = reluctant
     For love of God seems dying.

To-night, this frost will fasten on this mud and us,
Shrivelling many hands and puckering foreheads crisp.   *puckering* = wrinkling
The burying-party, picks and shovels in their shaking grasp,
Pause over half-known faces. All their eyes are ice,
     But nothing happens.

 ## Pair and share

Performing the poem

Don't worry about the lines that are difficult: remember that the meaning will become clearer if you give the poem time. Instead perform the poem as a group activity.

1. First think about the title: the men are exposed in their trenches, not just to the hostility of the enemy but also to the winter wind and frost. The poet says the bullets are less deadly than the snow.

2. There are eight stanzas, so work as a class, dividing into eight groups taking a stanza each, and take up your positions in the trenches.

3. Recite the lines, as a chorus, chanting them together. In Ancient Greek drama and many other dramatic traditions, the chorus both comment on and take part in the action.

4. Here there is a lack of action. As you perform, try to communicate the emotions of the men, as they wait through the night, frozen and cold.

5. They should question what they are doing and even begin to hallucinate through exposure.

6. Will anyone at home understand what they are going through?

By performing the poem, you become more familiar with the story, or narrative, the soldiers exposed as much to the cold of winter as to enemy fire, asking what they are doing there, why nothing happens, and whether they are even dead or alive, as their comrades die around them. The language is strong and emotive: it makes an appeal to the reader's emotions. Owen himself said 'the poetry is in the pity'.

Using the terms and techniques you learned in the previous section, you are now well equipped to work your way through this poem. We will look at the structure, rhythm, diction, imagery, tone, and mood in order to explore not only what the poem says, but how it works.

Language links

Hearing stress patterns

To hear the rhythm, you need to put an emphasis on the syllable which you stress. You will have done this while performing the poem, even if you did not notice at the time. We especially put stress on those syllables with long vowel sounds. For example:

x   x   / x x / x x / x   /   x   / x

Our brains ache, in the merciless iced east winds that knive us

A more regular line is:

x   /   x /x x x / x / x /   x

Like twitching agonies of men among its branches

Do you see how each line has five stresses?

Find the stress pattern in five more lines (perhaps different groups could explore different stanzas) and comment on the effect of the variations in rhythms.

 # Check your understanding

Structure and rhythm

1. How many stanzas are there? Is there any difference between the first half of the poem and the second?

2. Can you discover a regular rhyme scheme? Compare Owen's choice of stanza form and Housman's choice. What is similar and what is different? What is Owen doing with the last line of each stanza and what is the effect on the reader?

3. How does he use repetition and what effect do you think it has on the reader?

4. It is much harder to find a regular rhythm and beat in this poem than in those of Scott and Housman. Owen is making a point here about the rhythm of the soldiers' lives; what do you think the effect on the reader is meant to be? Why is it so different from the rhythms of the two older poems? What pattern have you discovered?

5. The basic rhythm is iambic (weak STRONG) and there are five beats, or strong stresses, in each of the longer lines, making them iambic pentameters, the verse line most often used by Shakespeare and often thought to be close to the rhythms of English speech. But very few lines actually are very close to this regular pattern.

   How does the rhythm change in the line below?

   Sudden successive flights of bullets streak the silence

6. Look at the repetition of the sound 's'. What other technique is Owen using here? What is the effect on the reader of this sound effect?

7. What is the rhythmic effect of the short or curtailed lines at the end of each stanza?

Pair and share

Diction

We called the language of the poem emotive: it is made up of language which appeals to the emotions of the reader and stirs them up.

Consider the effect of words or groups of words such as:

- *merciless*
- *knive*
- *agonies*
- *dull*

- *poignant*
- *shivering*
- *shudders*
- *fingering stealth*

- *ghosts drag*
- *love is made afraid*
- *Shrivelling … puckering … shaking.*

Many of the verbs describe the situation of the men suffering from exposure, even if the description is sometimes shifted to the things they see, or imagine they are seeing.

Can you find examples?

 Language links

Imagery

In this poem, personification is again a very important technique.

1. Look for the ways in which various objects are treated as if they were alive or people.
2. Find quotations that personify the flares, the gusts of wind, and the dawn.
3. How does this show the way in which the conditions are the enemy of the soldiers as much as the men on the other side?

4. How does the imagery make the snow sound even more deadly than the bullets in stanzas four and five?

Consider the effect of the words:

> *Pale flakes with fingering stealth*
> *come feeling for our faces*

In reading papers, you are asked to use quotation and comment in order to identify writers' effects and comment on their impact on the reader. Ask yourself what the effects make you feel or imagine.

 Viewpoints

Tone

Whose experience does this poem really describe? The viewpoint changes later in the poem, which changes the way we understand it.

There is a major change in tone in the last four stanzas. Now the poem becomes less realistic and the images are no longer of the men in the trenches. Instead, we enter the imagination of the men. The exposure they are suffering from makes them dream in a 'snow-dazed' way and they imagine returning home, not as real people but as ghosts, no longer welcome.

1. How do the images, the way Owen pictures the home fires, make the idea of home both attractive and unwelcoming?
2. Answer this question by looking closely at the description in stanza six.

Some lines in poems depend on personal response: everyone will have their own idea, based on what they have already read, about what they mean. This is what we mean by the mood of the poem.

Pair and share

In pairs, debate your own ideas of what the following line means:

For God's invincible spring our love is made afraid

1. Now compare your ideas with the rest of the class and try to come to some conclusions about the meaning of this whole stanza.

2. What does it suggest about the kind of sacrifice the men are making, and what do you think the poet wanted his readers to feel about it?

3. How do the horrifying images of death in the final stanza create a final and lingering memory of life and death in the trenches?

4. Look at the use of metaphor. What is meant when the poet says 'all their eyes are ice'? (You can have more than one answer to this question.)

Compare your answers with the rest of the class, and discuss the following question:

How does this stanza achieve the "pity" which Owen said is the purpose of his poetry?

Practice question

You can gather all your observations into an essay form by using them to answer this question.

In what ways does Owen's writing create a powerful response to the sufferings of soldiers in 'Exposure'?

As you learned when answering the question on the drum poems, ask *what* the poem shows, then *how* it works, and finally *why* it has an effect on the reader, in order to give your essay structure.

Pair and share

Perform the poem once again in groups.

1. Can you make your performance more rhythmic and give your audience a sense of the poem's structure?

2. How has the close study of words, imagery, and their effect changed the way you perform the poem?

3. Can you communicate the sense of the poem's more difficult words?

4. How will you accompany your reading with movement and gesture?

5. Can your actions show developments and changes in the poem?

6. Can you give the poem tone?

7. How can you use the words to move your audience to pity (mood)?

Different parts of the class could compete for the most effective dramatic version.

4.4 Behind the lines

As war became a global event in the twentieth century, it was the civilian population behind the lines who suffered as much as the apparently abandoned soldiers on the front line. While the focus of First World War poems was often on the experience of the individual soldier, more recent conflicts have exposed whole communities to war's destructive potential. We will now read a series of poems that explore the damage done by global conflict and the effect on ordinary women and men.

The next poem provides painful images of the suffering of war and creates disturbing and controversial images. It is based on a moment near the beginning of the Second World War when Western Europe must have seemed on the point of collapse and people would do anything to survive.

'Road 1940' by Sylvia Townsend Warner (1940)

Who do I carry, she said,
This child that is no child of mine?
Through the heat of the day it did nothing but fidget and whine,
Now it scuffles under the dew and the cold star-shine,
And lies across my heart as heavy as lead,
Heavy as the dead.

Why did I do it, she said.
What have I saved for the world's use?
If it grow to hero it will die or let loose
Death, or to hireling, nature already is too profuse
Of such, who hope and are disinherited,
Plough and are not fed.

But since I've carried it, she said,
So far I might as well carry it still.
If we ever should come to kindness someone will
Pity me, perhaps as the mother of a child so ill,
Grant me even to lie down on a bed;
Give me at least bread.

Refugees transport their belongings in a handcart

hireling = *agricultural labourer*
profuse = *overgenerous*

In this poem, the poet imagines the thoughts of a woman in wartime who has picked up an abandoned child and is taking it with her to safety. To analyse this text, you might consider:

- the way the poet shows the woman's feelings about the child and her action in attempting to save the child
- how the poet shows the woman's thoughts and feelings about the future
- the impact the poem as a whole has on you.

Check your understanding

The first bullet point asks about the way the poet shows the woman's feelings about the child and her action in attempting to save the child.

This is a 'what' question that can be answered by writing about the effect her thoughts and feelings have on you as you read them. You can use a table like the one that appears below to prepare your response.

1. What has the woman done?
2. Why did she pick up a stranger's child?

Words from the poem	What it shows
no child of mine	
it did nothing but fidget and whine	
lies across my heart heavy as lead	This simile suggests that the woman feels that the child is a burden, not only on her body but also her emotions, as the heart is seen symbolically as the home of feelings.
If it grow to hero it will die or let loose/Death or to hireling, nature already is too profuse/Of such	Here too the woman is thinking about the future of the child: if is does not grow to be a death-doomed hero, it will simply be a 'hireling', little better than a slave to others. She thinks there are too many such people already.
I might as well carry it still	The woman expresses a wish to continue bearing the child, perhaps more for what it can do for her than because of what she can do for it.

 # Pair and share

The second bullet point asks how the poet shows the woman's thoughts and feelings about the future. This is a 'how' question. In filling in your responses to the quotations, you have already looked at how the poem works and the way the woman thinks about the future. Not only is the child 'heavy as the dead', reminding her of the past, but it also makes her think about a grim future of heroes and hirelings.

What does this suggest about the future world she sees emerging from war and conflict?

With your partner, discuss a response to these lines:

> *nature already is too profuse*
> *Of such, who hope and are disinherited,*
> *Plough and are not fed.*

1. What does Townsend Warner suggest about the relationship between work and ownership, or about ordinary people's chances of being fed?

2. Why do you think she suggests that a 'hero' is not the answer?

3. Do you think the baby is a boy or a girl? Does it make a difference?

Notice the syntax, or sentence structure, of the poem. It begins with questions to which the woman gives her own answers.

4. Do you agree with her? By forming your own personal response you are beginning to evaluate and judge the poem.

5. Does the poet want us to admire or pity the woman? To agree with her, or be disturbed by her action and attitudes?

6. Is she doing the right thing for the wrong reasons? What do you feel about this?

Shape your own response to these questions. This shows you how you can use a question and answer technique to create your own ideas, based around the words of the poem.

Viewpoints

The last bullet point asks about your personal response to the whole poem or the impact the poem as a whole has on you. You will need to produce an argued viewpoint of your own.

To answer this question, you need to bring your observations together. A good way of doing this is to concentrate on the impact of the final stanza and the final lines. The poet imagines finding some kindness or sympathy, and imagines that carrying the child will help her to obtain her immediate needs, whatever the uncertainty of the future.

> *Pity me, perhaps as the mother of a child so ill,*
> *Grant me even to lie down on a bed;*
> *Give me at least bread.*

What is the impact of hearing the repetition in the last three lines? Instead of questioning, the woman is now pleading, using imperatives: pity, grant, give.

She sounds like a beggar: do you find her pitiful or repulsive? Or a little of both?

What do you make of the repetition of the word 'me'? Is this moving, or proof of her self-pity? Sympathy for the woman would be based on a lie 'as the mother of a child so ill'.

The repetitions and voice of the poem give it tone. The mood is what you, as a reader, feel like after reading it.

If you feel sympathy, you are feeling pity, the emotion Owen aims for in his poem. You understand her feelings and feel sorry for them, even if you could not imagine having similar feelings yourself.

If you feel empathy, you know what it feels like to be in that woman's shoes, and to see the world from her position, even if you do not agree with it, or have never been so unfortunate yourself.

1. Which is the more powerful feeling for you as a reader?

2. Which one fits this poem best?

Pair and share

Below are examples of responses candidates could have given to a question on the impact of this poem. Read them and then discuss which answer you agree with the most.

Student A

This poem had a big impact on me from the way the persona is thinking. She should not question herself for saving a baby, it would have been morally wrong to leave it for dead. Another thing is that at the end of the poem the persona thinks only about herself and using the baby, so I feel that this woman is not suitable to take care of a baby because she only thinks about herself.

Student B

At the beginning of the poem we aren't sure of how nice the lady is and whether or not she's prepared to carry the baby all the way to safety but by the end of the poem, the lady takes on a motherly role and we really feel for her.

Student C

The poem strikes me as rather contradictory, where the woman hates, yet cares for the child. Still, this poem speaks of care, no matter how the woman complains, she still picked the child up, and cared for it, saving its life. The poem has an impact on me, relating to time. Time is the solution to her hatred of the child, as the first two stanzas explain hate, and regret, while the last two explore concealed emotions of love and care.

Student D

The overall impact that the poem had on us is shocking; the poem shows several ideas, and how they are changed by conflict. We see the direct story of a woman saving a baby; we see her reasons, which include survival; and we see the persona's outlook on life, and how it changes due to conflict. All three ideas have the potential to shock, as they are so negative compared to our 'rosy' ideas about life. After reading the poem, our outlook changes and we value the things around us more.

Extend your learning

If you want to read similarly disturbing but thought-provoking accounts of the effect of war on ordinary people in the mid-twentieth century, you could read:

- *The Siege* by Helen Dunmore
- *The Joy Luck Club* by Amy Tan.

4.5 Writing a response to a poem

Poems are meant to encourage debate and argument and like novels will stimulate discussion as they won't give away their meaning straight away.

This poem was written in the 1920s and uses many of the techniques you have already explored in this chapter.

'There Will Come Soft Rains' by Sara Teasdale (1920)

There will come soft rains and the smell of the
   ground,
And swallows circling with their shimmering sound;
And frogs in the pools, singing at night,
And wild plum trees in tremulous white,
Robins will wear their feathery fire,
Whistling their whims on a low fence-wire;

And not one will know of the war, not one
Will care at last when it is done.
Not one would mind, neither bird nor tree,
If mankind perished utterly;
And Spring herself, when she woke at dawn,
Would scarcely know that we were gone.

Practice question

Write a detailed personal response, using quotation and comment, in answer to the question which follows. You should allow yourself 45 minutes and aim to write about 300–400 words.

> *How does the poet's language help you to imagine what a post-war future could be like?*

To help you answer this question, you might consider:

- the ways in which the natural world is portrayed in the future
- how the poet shows the destruction of the human world by war
- how the whole poem affects you as a response to war.

✎ Check your understanding

Review your work and mark it together. Swap written responses and use the checklist here to help you give a mark to each other's work. Check if your partner has addressed questions 1 to 7, and then evaluate the essay by using questions 8 and 9.

1. What is the effect of the rhyming couplets and verse form?
2. What is the effect of the alliteration of 's' and 'w' sounds?
3. What is suggested by the description of the smells and sounds of nature?
4. What does the imagery suggest about nature's response to the war?
5. How does the poet use personification to show Spring's response to the war, and what does she mean by it?
6. What is implied by the third line from the end? What has happened to the human world?
7. Why does nature not care?
8. Is there an argued personal response, exploring the implied meaning of the poem?
9. How well supported is that response by quotation and comment on the language and effects used by the writer?

4.6 What do we now know about poetry?

We have explored the importance when writing about poetry of the following elements of poetic form:

- rhyme and rhythm
- syntax (sentence structure)
- repetition (word patterns)
- diction (choices of words)
- imagery (metaphors, similes, and personification)
- tone (the 'voice' and music of the poem)
- mood (its effect on the reader, and your personal response).

Modern-day war relies on heavy machinery

We will now apply these tools to a final poem and use them to shape a personal response which interprets the overall effect on the reader.

The final poem brings the subject of war even more up to date. This poem was written during the first Gulf War (after the invasion of Kuwait by Iraq in 1991 and the bombing of Iraq by the USA and Great Britain). The poet based her response on clips from news broadcasts and newspaper reports that she read at the time. The images include seabirds and sea creatures suffering because of the pollution caused by the destruction of oilfields and also the human victims of war, both soldiers and civilians.

'Lament' by Gillian Clarke (circa 1991)

For the green turtle with her pulsing burden,
in search of the breeding-ground.
For her eggs laid in their nest of sickness.

For the cormorant in his funeral silk,
the veil of iridescence upon the sand,
the shadow on the sea.

For the ocean's lap with its mortal stain.
For Ahmed at the closed border.
For the soldier in his uniform of fire.

For the gunsmith and the armourer,
the boy fusilier who joined for the company,
the farmer's sons in it for the music.

For the hook-beaked turtles,
the dugong and the dolphin,
the whale struck dumb by the missile's thunder.

For the tern, the gull and the restless wader,
the long migrations and the slow dying,
the veiled sun and the stink of anger.

For the burnt earth and the sun put out,
the scalded ocean and the blazing well.
For vengeance, and the ashes of language.

cormorant, tern, gull, wader = types of seabird

iridescence = a surface of shimmering colours

fusilier = rifleman

dugong = large aquatic mammal

✎ Check your understanding

1. This poem does not rhyme. What gives the poem its rhythm?
2. The sentences are very short (none run over into the next stanza) and not quite complete. What is the effect of this form of syntax?
3. What are the patterns of repetition that give this poem its shape?
4. The words of the poem are highly descriptive. Which elements of diction strike you as especially memorable or unusual and what is their effect?
5. What is the effect of imagery such as 'their nest of sickness', 'the cormorant in his funeral silk', the 'shadow on the sea', 'the stink of anger', and the 'ashes of language'?
6. What happens to the tone of the poem as you read it? Do the words and images become harsher?
7. What mood is conveyed to you? What does the poem make you feel about the effects of modern warfare?

A seabird covered in oil

 See the worksheet on mood and tone.

💡 Viewpoints

Which single word would you apply most strongly to the emotions portrayed in this poem? Discuss the options with a partner.

Extend your learning

To explore your understanding of this poem further, look ahead to chapter 6, which will help you to write an essay based on this text.

Looking back

1. What have you learned in this chapter about changing patterns and forms in poetry?
2. What have you learned about the ways in which the writer's choices of diction and imagery influence the tone of a poem?
3. How does the tone of a poem influence the mood of the reader?
4. What have you learned about changing responses to war and its impact?

We will explore the forms and language of poetry in more depth in chapter 9.

Developing writing skills

Preparing to write

This unit will explore and develop different ways of writing about and responding to literature, preparing you for essay writing by looking at how we can use reviews, notes, commentary, character study, **empathy**, and passage-based work.

Are you ready to write?

Writing a response to literature

5.1 Writing a review

Think ahead

How have you shown your understanding and appreciation of your reading in English lessons? How many of the following have you already written, either as part of this course, or in the last two years?

▶ Answers to comprehension questions

▶ Reviews of books you have read or plays you have seen

▶ Short play scripts or interviews using characters from texts you have read

▶ Letters or diaries in the voice of a character from a text

▶ Character sketches

▶ Discursive essays looking at a question and debating it, supported by evidence from the text.

You will see the similarity with work you are also doing in English language. You may not yet have practised all of these styles of writing, but they prepare you well for the most difficult task in the list, the last one. In a literature exam, you will answer the question set by writing a complete essay (about 2–3 sides or 500–700 words). This could be in response to a particular extract from your text, or in answer to a more discursive question. We call this criticism, not because your opinions are expected to be negative, but because your reaction should be based on evidence from the text.

LEARNING POINTS

▶ To learn to write notes on your reading

▶ To explore the language used in a text

▶ To explore characters and their actions

Writing techniques

Good responses include:

● relevance to the task set

● a planned argument

● detailed support from the text

● analytical comment on language

● an evaluative personal response, with conclusions based on evidence.

While comprehension answers allow you to explore the evidence to support an opinion about a text, and help you to feel sure you understand what is happening, they don't give you much scope to express your opinions. A personal response in literature means having views of your own about a text, but you must support them with details from what you have read or seen performed, so that your comments are fair and justified.

 Viewpoints

In everyday life, you will find plenty of reviews of plays, films, and books. They appear in newspapers, magazines, and especially on the internet, on the websites of booksellers such as Amazon, or film websites like www.imdb.com.

Although you will not be asked to write a review in a Cambridge exam or piece of coursework, reviews will help you to construct personal responses, which are a key element of the course.

Which reviews do you pay attention to, and which ones do you not? What do you think makes a review:

- readable
- authoritative
- reliable
- fair
- helpful?

You will probably conclude that reviewers need to express themselves clearly and concisely; know what they are talking about; provide evidence to show that they have done their research; avoid too much bias and consider other peoples' opinions as well as their own; and that they make useful recommendations to their readers ('if you liked x, you would like y').

 Pair and share

In chapter 2, you read three extracts from *The Importance of Being Earnest* in detail, and you interviewed the writer after the first performance. Now plan a review in which you express your opinions about the play.

All writing requires planning, and it is often a good idea to share your plan with a partner. You will notice that many bullet points in this chapter follow a 'rule of five'. It can help to look for five areas which you plan to write about. With your partner, look back at chapter 2 and find details to fit the following five points.

1. Find a starting point. This should show the overall impression the play made on you. What kind of play is it? Comment on setting and characters.

2. Develop your review through your choice of details. You have learned how problems and confrontations allow plots to develop in interesting ways. How do characters conflict with each other and get into quarrels?

3. Look at form and structure. How does the play's form as a comedy influence the ways in which the action goes on to a resolution?

4. Look at language. What makes the play funny? Give examples of the more outrageous things characters say or do. Can you look back and find some of Wilde's witty epigrams?

5. Make a recommendation. Remember you should not give the whole plot away in a review (this is sometimes called a 'spoiler'). You can hint at the direction the plot is going in. Instead describe what kind of person would enjoy this play and why.

Viewpoints

You are a reviewer for the London newspaper *The Times* in 1895 when Mr Wilde is at the height of his success. Can you recommend this play to your readers? Use the five-part plan you have just worked on in order to write a 300-word review, set out in newspaper format, with five short paragraphs that explain how the play works and why it is so popular.

Extend your learning

Search online for reviews of both theatre and film performances of *The Importance of Being Earnest*. The play is still very popular with both amateur and professional actors. Can you find a performance near you?

There are two well-known film adaptations of *The Importance of Being Earnest*, one by Anthony Asquith (1952) and another by Oliver Parker (2002). Watch either or both of these adaptations.

Write a review giving examples of:

1. the director's choices of setting and actors
2. what worked especially well
3. what did not work
4. how successfully the film caught the spirit of the play
5. whether you would recommend the film to your classmates.

The Times newspaper

The cast from the 1952 film adaptation of *The Importance of Being Earnest*

5.2 Writing notes and commentary to explore language

The next text you will write about is a prose text, from much earlier in the Victorian period. *Jane Eyre* is a **bildungsroman**, a novel which shows the development and education of the main character (or **protagonist**). A bildungsroman often has a first-person narrator so that the novel sounds like an autobiography in which a character looks back and reflects on their childhood, their relationships and their learning experiences as they journey through life. The narrating voice has a close relationship with the reader. In *Jane Eyre*, the narrator even addresses the reader directly. We are presented with a fictionalized version of the past, not necessarily as it happened at the time, but as the narrator now sees it. The language will therefore be heightened in order to communicate the protagonist's emotional state to the reader. Victorian readers loved *Jane Eyre*: it presents the narrator as an empowered woman who succeeds in improving her social position through her education, her moral integrity, her capacity for love and a little luck. She triumphs over darker emotions and circumstances which threaten to overwhelm her. Jane has some similarities to her author, Charlotte Brontë: both had to teach as their families did not have enough money to sustain a high social position. Charlotte and her sisters famously had to pretend to be men in order to get their first novels published.

KEY TERMS

bildungsroman = novel about learning and growing up.

protagonist = the main character.

In this scene, Jane is looking back to how, as a very young girl with a vivid imagination, she was given an unfair punishment by being locked in the Red Room. This room has been left untouched since her uncle, Mr Reed, died in it. As Jane explains, she was adopted as an orphan and Mr Reed made his wife promise to bring up Jane as if she was one of their own children. Jane (rightly) does not feel she is treated equally or fairly. Bessie and Abbot are two servants: Bessie is kind to her, but Abbot is not. The **revelation** of the supernatural is a moment when the novel appears to be in the Gothic tradition, while the **flashback** to the deathbed agreement between the Reeds is one of the moments when the novel is much more realistic, and grounded in the psychological accuracy of the bildungsroman tradition. The early chapters of a novel establish its genre, and your notes will need to reflect the writing and how its effect on the reader prepares them for how the novel will develop within the tradition the writer has chosen.

KEY TERMS

revelation = when readers discover something, either good or bad, which they did not expect.

flashback = when a narrative takes the reader back in time to explain something which has already happened.

Jane Eyre by Charlotte Brontë (1847)

Daylight began to forsake the red-room; it was past four o'clock, and the beclouded afternoon was tending to drear twilight. I heard the rain still beating continuously on the staircase window, and the wind howling in the grove behind the hall; I grew by degrees cold as a stone, and then my courage sank. My habitual mood of humiliation, self-doubt, forlorn depression, fell damp on the embers of my decaying ire.

forsake = *abandon*

fell damp on the embers of my decaying ire = *puts water on the flames of her decreasing anger*

All said I was wicked, and perhaps I might be so: what thought had I been but just conceiving of starving myself to death? That certainly was a crime: and was I fit to die? Or was the vault under the chancel of Gateshead Church an inviting bourne? In such vault I had been told did Mr Reed lie buried; and led by this thought to recall his idea, I dwelt on it with gathering dread. I could not remember him, but I knew that he was my own uncle – my mother's brother – that he had taken me when a parentless infant to his house; and that in his last moments he had required a promise of Mrs Reed that she would rear and maintain me as one of her own children. Mrs Reed probably considered she had kept this promise; and so she had, I dare say, as well as her nature would permit her: but how could she really like an interloper, not of her race, and unconnected with her, after her husband's death, by any tie? It must have been most irksome to find herself bound by a hard-wrung pledge to stand in the stead of a parent to a strange child she could not love, and to see an uncongenial alien permanently intruded on her own family group.

A singular notion dawned upon me. I doubted not – never doubted – that if Mr Reed had been alive he would have treated me kindly; and now, as I sat looking at the white bed and overshadowed walls – occasionally also turning a fascinated eye towards the dimly gleaming mirror – I began to recall what I had heard of dead men, troubled in their graves by the violation of their last wishes, revisiting the earth to punish the perjured and avenge the oppressed; and I thought Mr Reed's spirit, harassed by the wrongs of his sister's child, might quit its abode – whether in the church vault or in the unknown world of the departed – and rise before me in this chamber. I wiped my tears and hushed my sobs, fearful lest any sign of violent grief might waken a preternatural voice to comfort me, or elicit from the gloom some haloed face, bending over me with strange pity. This idea, consolatory in theory, I felt would be terrible if realized: with all my might I endeavoured to stifle it – I endeavoured to be firm. Shaking my hair from my eyes, I lifted my head and tried to look boldly round the dark room; at this moment a light gleamed on the wall. Was it, I asked myself, a ray from the moon penetrating some aperture in the blind? No; moonlight was still, and this stirred; while I gazed, it glided up to the ceiling and quivered over my head. I can now conjecture readily that this streak of light was, in all likelihood, a gleam from a lantern carried by some one across the lawn; but then, prepared as my mind was for horror, shaken as my nerves were by agitation, I thought the swift-darting beam was a herald of some coming vision from another world. My heart beat thick, my head grew hot; a sound filled my ears, which I deemed the rushing of wings; something seemed near me; I was oppressed, suffocated: endurance broke down; I rushed to the door and shook the lock in desperate effort. Steps came running along the outer passage; the key turned, Bessie and Abbot entered.

an inviting bourne = *a good place to end up (after death)*

interloper = *intruder*

violation of their last wishes = *breaking of final promises to them*

the perjured = *those who made false promises*

preternatural = *supernatural or ghostly*

haloed = *like an angel*

'Miss Eyre, are you ill?' said Bessie.

'What a dreadful noise! It went quite through me!' exclaimed Abbot.

'Take me out! Let me go into the nursery!' was my cry.

'What for? Are you hurt? Have you seen something?' again demanded Bessie.

'Oh! I saw a light, and I thought a ghost would come.' I had now got hold of Bessie's hand, and she did not snatch it from me.

'She has screamed out on purpose,' declared Abbot, in some disgust. 'And what a scream! If she had been in great pain one would have excused it, but she only wanted to bring us all here; I know her naughty tricks.'

A young Jane Eyre

✎ Check your understanding

The purpose of this section is to help you to make more effective notes while you are getting to know a new text, so that you can collect the details which will help you to write an essay.

Remembering the 'rule of five', you will begin by finding five things which the reader finds out about in this scene. On your own copy, highlight and mark up the parts of the text which tell you about:

1. the gathering gloom in the Red Room and its effect on Jane's mood

2. Jane's memories of Mr Reed and feelings about Mrs Reed

3. how she uses her imagination to think about Mr Reed's ghost

4. the ghost's 'appearance' to Jane

5. the very different reactions of Bessie and Abbot.

Now divide up your exercise book or notes into five sections with a column for each of the bullets above. Using the **PEA technique**, look for evidence from the writing which shows that the impression the story makes is that Jane has a vivid imagination and powerful emotions.

Base your response around a selection of three short quotations for each bullet. Some of the work has been done for you.

KEY TERM

PEA technique = using points which respond to the question, evidence from the text and analysis of their effect on the reader.

	Gathering gloom	Memories	Imagining the ghost	The ghost's 'appearance'	Reactions
Point		Jane actually knows little about Mr Reed		The young Jane is convinced that the light comes from the world of the dead	
Evidence			'revisiting the earth to punish the perjured and avenge the oppressed'		
Analysis	Suggests the gloom of the evening has affected Jane's feelings				Shows that Bessie is worried about Jane
Point					However, Abbot is convinced that Jane is attention-seeking
Evidence	'fell damp on the embers of my decaying ire'	'how could she really like an interloper'	'and rise before me in this chamber'		
Analysis				The language suggests all of the young Jane's senses were stirred up at once	
Point	Jane questions whether she will be punished after death			The older Jane, looking back, realizes that it was not really a ghost	
Evidence		'bound by a hard-wrung pledge'			'"I know her naughty tricks"'
Analysis			This suggests that Jane would really rather not see any kind of ghost		

Pair and share

Bessie and Abbot take different views of Jane. One of them feels sorry for her and thinks she has been made ill by her fears and unfair treatment. Abbot thinks she just has an overactive imagination and pretends to see things in order to get attention from others. There is evidence on both sides: in pairs, one of you can take Bessie's view and the other Abbot's. Find the evidence on your side and then debate together whether we should sympathize with Jane or decide she is trying to manipulate our feelings.

Later events in the novel also make us wonder if the supernatural is at work, or there is a realistic solution. How do the **Gothic** elements in this passage make the reader aware of Jane's real distress? How does the appearance of the 'ghost' highlight her feelings of oppression and unfairness for you? Discuss with your partner the effect of the supernatural element on the reader's sympathy.

Now write some notes on how far this episode develops the reader's sympathies with Jane, and our understanding of why her childhood was unhappy.

Viewpoints

Looking back over your notes, you should now be able to write a short commentary to address the following five questions.

1. What important information does the reader gain from this episode?
2. How does the writing present Jane's feelings of guilt and fear?
3. How does the writing suggest that she feels an outsider in her own family?
4. How does Brontë bring out differences between the older and younger Jane?
5. How does Brontë use language to bring out Jane's vivid imagination and powerful feelings?

Support your comments with quotations and comments on the writing. Remember that the opening of a novel wants the reader to ask questions: there is no need to give all the answers!

KEY TERM

Gothic = literature which uses the supernatural to explore human fears.

Extend your learning

Find out more about the **Gothic** genre. Explore websites such as www.litgothic.com or www. victorianweb.org. Are there modern stories and films which also use elements of the Gothic genre? Examples of these are:

1. semi-ruinous locations
2. midnight settings
3. challenging the norms of society
4. dark secrets from the past
5. hints of transgressive sexuality
6. elements of the supernatural.

Why is the Gothic still such a popular and interesting genre?

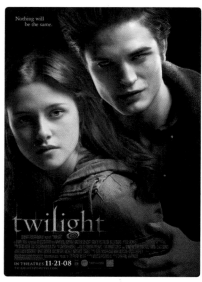

Twilight could be seen as modern Gothic literature

5.3 Exploring character through empathy: Romeo and Juliet

The plays of William Shakespeare are not just popular in school classrooms; they remain popular in theatres all over the world. As we saw in chapter 2, it is important not to let the difficulties of his language get in the way of your appreciation of character and action. One way of doing this is to use your own language to express the feelings of characters.

We can respond to characters by recreating their voices through empathic writing. This is a good way for you to find your way into text imaginatively; actors need to do this when creating a character.

Think ahead

▶ To write empathically, you need a good idea of exactly what is happening at that moment in a text.

▶ You must create a voice as similar as possible to that of the character at that moment in the play.

▶ When first reading Shakespeare's plays, the language of the past can often be a barrier, as can the verse. However, by putting the emotions of characters into your own words and language, you can get inside the meaning of the text, without letting language get in the way.

▶ You can also show that you understand both the literal meaning of Shakespeare's words, and the emotional impact of his metaphors.

This scene from Act One Scene Two presents Juliet Capulet to the audience for the first time. Her story, like Jane Eyre's, shows how little freedom of choice young women had in earlier times. Only 14 years old and an only child, she is already expected to be married. The marriage will be an arranged match made for dynastic and family reasons, not a love match. Juliet's mother (Lady Capulet) was married at a similar age for similar reasons, so she is not sympathetic to her. Juliet has largely been brought up by the talkative and slightly embarrassing Nurse, who will have breastfed her. The Nurse is preoccupied with the physical aspects of marriage and childbirth (because they are all she knows) and has just made a joke about this, in very dubious taste.

The audience actually find out very little about Juliet's character in this scene because she says so little. The conventions of the time mean that she cannot express disobedience towards her parents and we do not know what she really feels about this proposed marriage – although at the party she will flirt with Romeo, an uninvited guest from the rival Montague family, and not with Paris, her intended husband. Different directors can make different decisions about how reluctant Juliet is to be married. You

Juliet with Lady Capulet and the Nurse, from Franco Zeffirelli's 1968 film adaptation of *Romeo and Juliet*

might compare the different portrayals of Juliet's first scene in the films by Franco Zeffirelli (in a traditional historical setting) and Baz Luhrmann (updated to a modern American setting).

In an empathy question, you will write the character's thoughts at that moment in the play, using the knowledge which you have of them from the text, and using a voice appropriate to the character – but in modern English. Juliet will have been brought up to obey, but what might make her rebel against her parents' plans? What excites her about the party they are planning? What is she afraid of? Remember that Juliet will have had a very sheltered upbringing up to this point, and very little social life. Being presented in public gives a signal that she is ready for marriage, but it is also a chance to see more of the world.

Romeo and Juliet by **Shakespeare (circa 1597)**

NURSE
> Thou wast the prettiest babe that e'er I nurs'd.
> And I might live to see thee married once,
> I have my wish.

LADY CAPULET
> Marry, that 'marry' is the very theme
> I came to talk of. Tell me, daughter Juliet,
> How stands your disposition to be married?

JULIET
> It is an honour that I dream not of.

NURSE
> An honour! were not I thine only nurse,
> I would say thou hadst suck'd wisdom from thy teat.

LADY CAPULET
> Well, think of marriage now; younger than you,
> Here in Verona, ladies of esteem,
> Are made already mothers. By my count,
> I was your mother much upon these years
> That you are now a maid. Thus then in brief:
> The valiant Paris seeks you for his love.

NURSE
> A man, young lady! lady, such a man
> As all the world – Why, he's a man of wax.

LADY CAPULET
> Verona's summer hath not such a flower.

NURSE
> Nay, he's a flower, in faith, a very flower.

how stands your disposition to be married? = *how do you feel about getting married?*

were not I thine only nurse … thou hadst suck'd wisdom from thy teat = *I would have said you sucked intelligence from the breast when you were a baby – except that I was your only nurse (and I am not very clever)*

I was your mother much upon these years = *I had already become your mother before I was your age*

LADY CAPULET
What say you, can you love the gentleman?
This night you shall behold him at our feast;
Read o'er the volume of young Paris' face,
And find delight writ there with beauty's pen;
Examine every married lineament,
And see how one another lends content;
And what obscur'd in this fair volume lies
Find written in the margent of his eyes.
This precious book of love, this unbound lover,
To beautify him, only lacks a cover.
The fish lives in the sea, and 'tis much pride
For fair without the fair within to hide;
That book in many's eyes doth share the glory
That in gold clasps locks in the golden story:
So shall you share all that he doth possess,
By having him, making yourself no less.

NURSE
No less! nay, bigger women grow by men.

LADY CAPULET
Speak briefly, can you like of Paris' love?

JULIET
I'll look to like, if looking liking move;
But no more deep will I endart mine eye
Than your consent gives strength to make it fly.

Read o'er the volume of young Paris' face = look at him like a book (extended metaphor), and learn about love

margent = margin

the fish lives in the sea ... = the sea is a place for fish to hide, but the 'fair' (beautiful) should not submerge themselves

that book ... the golden story = the best ending is for you to be locked in Paris's beautiful book of love

endart mine eye = I won't look more deeply without permission (metaphor involves the arrows of love)

Pair and share

The glossary terms provided are to help you understand the literal meaning of the imagery used, as well as to help you with difficult words. Read the scene twice with a partner, one of you doubling as a Nurse and Juliet. Notice just how little Juliet says. But remember that the audience will be able to see her reactions in a staged performance. Which lines do you think she will react to most? Why do you think she says nothing when Paris's name is mentioned (unlike the Nurse). Notice that Lady Capulet's lines turn into rhyming couplets. What is the effect of this very artificial way of speaking? What does Juliet mean by her final lines and how does she say them?

Viewpoints

Why do you think Juliet and her mother speak in couplets and metaphors? What does this tell us about their relationship and their attitudes towards love? Discuss with your partner.

Check your understanding

To create Juliet's voice, you need to identify key aspects of her character. In the extract, what is said which shows that:

a. the Nurse loves her more than her mother

b. her mother expects her to follow conventions

c. her mother was married when she was younger than Juliet is now

d. both Lady Capulet and the Nurse think highly of Paris – although Juliet says nothing

e. that Lady Capulet appears to care more about what will be good for Paris than for Juliet

f. that she hints that Paris is rich and will make Juliet rich too

g. that the Nurse thinks marriage is all about having children

h. that Juliet is not very keen to rush things on

i. that women in Shakespeare's world get very little say about what happens to them except through the process of courtship and marriage.

What does the scene encourage you to think about Juliet's attitude to her mother and her Nurse?

To answer the last question, you need to appreciate that Shakespeare's society, just like our own, was very preoccupied with status. Actors use this term in order to establish who should stand where on the stage, and how they should move, act, and react. Clearly Juliet is of high status, but defers completely to her mother, whereas the Nurse feels she can interrupt because of her close relationship with Juliet.

Pair and share

In groups of three, you could now act out this scene, demonstrating the slightly embarrassing nature of the relationships here. Lady Capulet is embarrassed to have a teenage daughter as she is not even 30 herself. The Nurse is embarrassing because she keeps talking about bodily functions: Lady Capulet left all the physical aspects of motherhood to her. Juliet has an independent spirit, but does not feel she is allowed to express herself.

1. Who would stand upstage (the most powerful position)?

2. Who breaks the rules of convention and moves around most?

3. Who is sitting and who is standing?

4. Try changing positions several times in the scene, to show how both Lady Capulet and the Nurse are making claims over Juliet, but that she may feel embarrassed by both of them.

Romeo and Juliet is a tragedy governed by fate, but the Nurse is clearly a comic character. How much should this scene be played for comedy and how much should be serious? Try acting this scene for different effects, playing with tone and mood.

Remember it is only Scene Two, so it is good dramatic practice to leave the audience confused and intrigued. They will want to find out the answers as the play goes on!

Pair and share

Your written response will work if it sounds like Juliet. Actors call this process thought tracking. Your writing should sound as if it really is Juliet talking to us.

If you find this difficult, you could begin by getting help from your friends. Take up the role of Juliet and sit in the hot seat. Your friends can ask you questions, but you need to answer in character. If you think a question is cheeky, you don't need to give a straight answer.

Try to answer the questions as far as possible from evidence in the play, although you can invent some back story if it sounds plausible. Shakespeare tells us nothing, for example, about Juliet's early childhood apart from that rather embarrassing anecdote told by the Nurse.

 ## Pair and share

Later in the play, we will find out a lot more about what Juliet really thinks through a technique called soliloquy, in which a character speaks out their true thoughts. You are now putting those thoughts into your own words.

 ## Viewpoints

In your re-creative response you don't need to answer all the questions: it is better to leave some aspects of Juliet's character ambiguous and uncertain, because she isn't so sure herself.

Now write your response to the question below, remembering the rule of five.

> *You are Juliet at the end of Act One Scene Two. Lady Capulet has just explained to you that a party will be held so that you can meet the Count Paris. Your parents intend you to marry him. Write your thoughts.*

You should aim to write about 500 words.

Plan your writing using five paragraphs. Think about five different aspects of the scene:

1. Juliet's feelings about having this conversation with her mother
2. Juliet's feelings about the Nurse's interruptions
3. What Juliet makes of Paris
4. What Juliet feels about the 'feast' or party
5. The advantages and disadvantages of marriage for a girl of her age and her social position.

Extend your learning

You will need to remember the importance of cultural background. In Shakespeare's society, a woman had considerable control over men only while they were trying to get her to agree to marry them. After marriage, women had to obey and be loyal to their husbands. Well born young women had few chances to go outside the family home unless they had a chaperone, usually an older woman. It was also quite normal for their education to be left to servants, such as wet nurses, who breastfed the children so that the mother would not have to. Marriage as a teenager was quite common, and often to a man much older than the bride. This seems to have happened to Lady Capulet, but she hints that this had some advantages for her.

Look up marriage in Shakespeare's time on the internet. What have you discovered about Shakespeare's own marriage?

5.4 Exploring character through viewpoint

As we have seen, there is plenty you can write about the opening of a text, even before you know how it will end. You can look at the writer's descriptive language and techniques, and explore characterization. Here is a passage from early on in another famous novel, in a very different style, written in the middle of the twentieth century.

Big Brother from the 1956 film adaptation of *Nineteen Eighty-Four*

Winston Smith, in George Orwell's *Nineteen Eighty-Four,* is a character in search of his past, his personal freedom and identity. In this respect, he is quite similar to Jane and Juliet: he lives in a world that denies him individuality and makes his own history obscure. In his case, this is because of politics rather than gender. *Nineteen Eighty-Four* belongs to a genre called dystopian fiction, about an alternative world much worse than the real world (Orwell's novel was written in 1948), in this case a totalitarian future run by a police state under the leadership of a cult figure called Big Brother. The state of Oceania controls the lives of its people by spying on them, denying them freedom, rewriting history and encouraging citizens, even children, to denounce one another for 'thoughtcrimes'.

Nineteen Eighty-Four by George Orwell (1948)

The pain of the coughing fit had not quite driven out of Winston's mind the impression made by his dream, and the rhythmic movements of the exercise restored it somewhat. As he mechanically shot his arms back and forth, wearing on his face the look of grim enjoyment which was considered proper during the Physical Jerks, he was struggling to think his way backward into the dim period of his early childhood. It was extraordinarily difficult. Beyond the late 'fifties everything faded. When there were no external records that you could refer to, even the outline of your own life lost its sharpness. You remembered huge events which had quite probably not happened, you remembered the detail of incidents without being able to recapture their atmosphere, and there were long blank periods to which you could assign nothing. Everything had been different then. Even the names of countries, and their shapes on the map, had been different. Airstrip One, for instance, had not been so called in those days: it had been called England or Britain, though London, he felt fairly certain, had always been called London.

Winston could not definitely remember a time when his country had not been at war, but it was evident that there had been a fairly long interval of peace during his childhood, because one of his early memories was of an air raid which appeared to take everyone by surprise. Perhaps it was the time when the atomic bomb had fallen on Colchester. He did not remember the raid itself, but he did remember his father's hand clutching his own as they hurried down, down, down into some place deep in the earth, round and round a spiral staircase which rang under his feet and which finally so wearied his legs that he began whimpering and they had to stop and rest. His mother, in her slow dreamy way, was following a long way behind them. She was carrying his baby sister – or perhaps it was only a bundle of blankets that she was carrying: he was not certain whether his sister had been born then. Finally they had emerged into a noisy, crowded place which he had realized to be a Tube station.

There were people sitting all over the stone-flagged floor, and other people, packed tightly together, were sitting on metal bunks, one above the other. Winston and his mother and father found themselves a place on the floor, and near them an old man and an old woman were sitting side by side on a bunk. The old man had on a decent dark suit and a black cloth cap pushed back from very white hair: his face was scarlet and his eyes were blue and full of tears. He reeked of gin. It seemed to breathe out of his skin in place of sweat, and one could have fancied that the tears welling from his eyes were pure gin. But though slightly drunk he was also suffering under some grief that was genuine and unbearable. In his childish way Winston grasped that some terrible thing, something that was beyond forgiveness and could never be remedied, had just happened. It also seemed to him that he knew what it was. Someone whom the old man loved, a little granddaughter perhaps, had been killed. Every five minutes the old man kept repeating:

'We didn't ought to 'ave trusted 'em, I said so, Ma, didn't I? That's what come of trusting 'em. I said so all along. We didn't ought to 'ave trusted the buggers.'

But which buggers they didn't ought to have trusted Winston could not now remember.

Physical Jerks = *compulsory exercises communicated on the telescreen*

Colchester = *large town in the south east of England*

Tube = *the London underground*

gin = *alcoholic spirit*

we didn't ought to 'ave trusted the buggers = *(slang) we should have not have trusted people who were out to get us*

Check your understanding

1. Although this novel is told as a third-person narrative, we clearly see things from Winston's viewpoint. What evidence can you find in the first sentence which shows that?
2. Which phrases show that Winston is not really enjoying the 'Physical Jerks'?
3. What is the main reason why it is hard for him to remember his childhood?
4. Why do you think England is now called 'Airstrip One'?
5. Why is it so hard for him to imagine a period of peace?
6. What has happened in the past which has destroyed a lot of what used to be 'England'?
7. What was it that made going down into the tube station memorable?
8. What have we learned about the character of Winston's mother?
9. Why do you think so many people are packed in the tube station?
10. What are the different things he remembers about the old man?
11. Why do you think the old man feels he was betrayed?
12. Why is it revealing that Winston no longer remembers who betrayed them?

 ## Pair and share

Put Winston Smith on trial for 'thoughtcrimes'. Thoughtcrimes are defined by Big Brother, the leader of the only party in control of Oceania. They are any negative thoughts about the country, the party or other people, or indeed any form of thinking for yourself instead of thinking what the party wants you to think.

You each need to gather quotations as evidence.

1. Which phrases show Winston does not enjoy the things the party requires him to do?
2. Which phrases show he is trying to recover memories of the past?
3. Which phrases show he is thinking about his family?
4. Which phrases show he distrusts the way the party handles history?
5. Where can you find evidence that he sympathizes with defeatist or unpatriotic thinking?

To extend your ideas about him in role play, you and a partner can imagine what Winston might say if he were placed under arrest. Has he actually done or said anything which is wrong yet? Now cross-examine him in the witness box as Prosecutor and try to find out why he had these thoughts. How will the Defence argue that he is still loyal to Big Brother?

💡 Viewpoints

You can see that the narrator adopts what we can call a third-person limited perspective. We see and feel things the way Winston sees them. What are the limits of this kind of narrative? What are its benefits?

Where does Winston himself admit the limitations of his own viewpoint?

Discuss why this kind of viewpoint is particularly suited to the **dystopian novel**. How do we discover the reality of the oppressive regime Winston lives under? What is the effect on the reader's sympathies?

KEY TERM

dystopian novel = novel warning about an unhappy alternative world.

Write a character sketch of Winston using the passage as evidence. What kind of person is he? Find quotations to show he is:

- dissatisfied
- imaginative
- curious
- observant
- emotionally needy
- sympathetic to others
- able to remember details
- keen to establish the truth.

What have we discovered about the difficulties of his search for the truth by reading this text?

Viewpoint has a big influence on the way we judge characters. Which characters in texts you are studying do we discover from the inside (by understanding their thoughts and feelings) and which ones do we only see from the outside? What is the effect on our sympathies?

Collect the evidence from this passage that Winston is not only passionate about the truth, but also cares about other people and their stories.

Irony is present when we know or suspect more than a character does. Where can you find evidence that Winston does not fully understand what has happened to him, and the dangers of thinking in the way he does?

How does viewpoint influence how you judge characters in your set texts? What do characters know and not know about themselves?

✎ Check your understanding

Key terms

Revise the meaning of the following terms. You can use the glossary on the website or refer back to earlier chapters.

- status
- contrast
- flashback
- dialogue
- viewpoint
- irony
- character sketch.

Extend your learning

Complete the following task:

Explore how we discover the effect of Oceania's recent history through the way Winston remembers things in this passage.

Write about 500 words including quotations. You should illustrate your sketch with lots of examples of how Winston sees things and what they mean to the reader. Explain how the writer's language shows us what Oceania and Winston are like.

Keep tracking notes on characters in your set texts as you are introduced to them. Consider:

- how they see themselves
- how others see them
- the influence of the narrative point of view
- the influence of genre, the type of drama or narrative you are reading
- collect quotations and comment on what the language shows.

Looking back

You should now appreciate that the key to good writing about literature relies on sticking to the following principles.

- Make sure you plan your writing effectively so that you have something relevant and well supported to say.

- Find quotations and make reference to the language used by characters.

- Use the PEA (point, evidence, analysis) technique to ensure that you are making analytical points about the writer's use of language, especially in descriptive passages.

- Engage with characters and their viewpoints but be alert to irony: the character's viewpoint is not the same as the author's.

- Appreciate the language used by characters and try imitating it.

- Explore the voice of the narrator through description and how dialogue is reported.

- Keep a good set of notes, tracking important introductions and developments of both character and setting, so that you can compare and contrast ideas when you write critical essays.

In chapter 6, we will apply these ideas to writing a critical essay based on a single poem. You should then be able to use the same writing techniques to write effective reviews, notes, commentaries and essays when writing about your set texts in class.

In online chapter 10, you will go on to develop your writing skills further, but first we will explore the structure of the 'critical essay', the format your teachers will want you to use for coursework and in all your writing as you develop a deeper understanding of your texts.

Writing an essay

6.1 Writing a critical essay

We will return to the last poem that we looked at in chapter 4, reproduced below. This time we will focus on producing a continuous piece of writing and we will use an exam-style question. As we have seen, you will first need to read the question carefully and apply it to the text. The question is:

In 'Lament' how do Gillian Clarke's language and word choice evoke a sense of bitterness?

LEARNING POINTS

▶ To build on the skills developed in the previous chapter to write a complete essay

▶ To write about a single poem in depth and detail

▶ To use quotation to show close analysis of language

▶ To use research to develop an evaluative approach

▶ To compare different student responses and look at the success criteria

Think ahead

Remind yourself of what you have already learned about this poem and how it was written, and have a look at Gillian Clarke's very helpful website www.gillianclarke.co.uk. What can you find out about the first Gulf War and US actions after the invasion of Kuwait?

'Lament' by Gillian Clarke (circa 1991)

For the green turtle with her pulsing burden,
in search of the breeding-ground.
For her eggs laid in their nest of sickness.

For the cormorant in his funeral silk,
the veil of iridescence upon the sand,
the shadow on the sea.

For the ocean's lap with its mortal stain.
For Ahmed at the closed border.
For the soldier in his uniform of fire.

For the gunsmith and the armourer,
the boy fusilier who joined for the company,
the farmer's sons in it for the music.

For the hook-beaked turtles,
the dugong and the dolphin,
the whale struck dumb by the missile's thunder.

For the tern, the gull and the restless wader,
the long migrations and the slow dying,
the veiled sun and the stink of anger.

For the burnt earth and the sun put out,
the scalded ocean and the blazing well.
For vengeance, and the ashes of language.

✎ Check your understanding

Remember that your first priority when writing is to produce a relevant response which addresses the key term in the question.

1. What do you understand by the term 'bitterness'?
2. Why is it different from 'sadness' or 'regret'?
3. How could you associate that term with the title of the poem?
4. What kind of sound conveys bitterness?
5. What kind of images would a poem expressing bitterness focus on?
6. How would emotions of bitterness develop? Would they change? Or simply become stronger over time?

Now begin to draw up a plan. How could you show that the poem does the following?

- It begins by lamenting and showing distress at damage the poet can do nothing about.
- It continues with increasingly powerful feelings about the senselessness and damage of war.
- It ends with an expression of anger and despair.

Divide the poem into four sections to show how it develops; this will help your paragraph planning.

Then think of a strong opening statement. This needs to give an **overview** of the poem, mention the key term of the question, and explain how both your argument and the poem will develop. Remember to mention the writer's name, and the effect of the poem on the reader.

Compare your opening sentences with those of others in the class.

a. Which one gives the strongest sense of an overview of the poem?
b. Which one gives a powerful sense of the writer's purpose?
c. Which one most clearly answers the question?
d. Does anyone's opening do all of these?

💬 Pair and share

What do you and your partner think of the three opening paragraphs which follow? Compare them, look at the comments, and compare these statements with your own.

Student A

'Lament' is a poem written by Gillian Clarke in which she explores and describes the ways in which humans have destroyed, polluted, and killed our planet and its inhabitants.

Comments

This answer can only get better. At the moment, the question is not addressed very directly, nor is there very clear knowledge of the poem and its context. However, the triplet 'destroyed, polluted, and killed' our planet and its inhabitants does show some understanding of the writer's purpose and the poem's development and that it will go on to link the natural world, animals, and humans.

Student B

Gillian Clarke vividly conveys a feeling of bitterness in the poem 'Lament' through her portrayal of the theme of the lack of respect humans have for nature, and the amount of respect and responsibility they should have when it comes to nature. She also conveys a feeling of bitterness through her use of enjambment, metaphors and diction.

Comments

This certainly addresses the terms of the question and begins to define a response when talking about 'responsibility'. This comment shows some clarity of understanding. When using technical terms, it is better to introduce them as part of your analysis, rather than to simply list them. If you mention a literary device, make sure you comment on how it is being used.

Student C

Gillian Clarke shows increasing bitterness and anger in her 'Lament' for all the damage done in consequence of war in the Gulf. A series of powerful images shows that man and the natural world are united in suffering, and the future for the world portrayed in the poem is bleak. The poem's harsh sounds become a crescendo of bleak feelings about the future, culminating in a very dark final couplet.

Comments

This answer shows knowledge of who wrote the poem and why, of the structure of the whole poem, and of its visual and sensory effects. It addresses the language of the question and suggests that the most bitter part of the poem is the way it ends. The candidate has set up a strong opening statement with an argument to prove in the rest of the essay.

You can see how a good introductory paragraph will help you to position what you want to say in the rest of your essay.

💡 Viewpoints

Consider the way Clarke constructs her own viewpoint and portrays her emotions in this poem. It is literally a 'bird's eye view': she is looking down on the world of the poem and lamenting what she sees.

1. What makes the poem list-like?
2. Why might the poet be at a distance from what she describes?
3. Does this limit her ability to intervene or change anything?
4. What effect does this have on the reader?
5. How would this fit the idea of seeing everything from the outside, unable to change or alter things? Why is this appropriate to the idea of a 'lament' or **elegy**?

A 'bird's eye view' allows us to look down on the world

 See Worksheet 1 for further help with this poem.

Writing about language

As we have seen, poems work through a combination of sensory effects, using sound patterns and images (or pictures in words). Let's begin with the sounds. Which sound effects would best convey bitterness: soft or harsh?

Using the skills you developed in chapter 4, identify the sound patterns which link the groups of words in the table that follows. Then comment on the effect of combining these particular words through their sounds. What does this make the reader feel? Remember that commenting on sound effects is worthwhile if you can link the effect to its meaning.

Sound pattern	Identified as	Effect on reader of words and sounds
For … for … for … funeral		
Burden … breeding		
Sand … shadow … sea		
Mortal … closed … soldier		
Fusilier … farmer … for the music		
Dugong … dolphin … dumb		
Tern … wader … long … slow		
Sun … stink … sun … scalded		
Burnt … blazing		
Scalded … ashes … language		

You can see that sound effects such as alliteration and assonance create a certain tone, which conveys emotion to the reader and thus affects our mood. Although the observations in the poem appear to be made from a distance, the poet's feelings are very strongly engaged, and it is probably right to talk about 'bitterness' when emotions are stirred up about a situation you are powerless to change.

Why is the title 'Lament' especially appropriate? What can you now say about the 'funeral music' of the poem, and the bitter feelings it expresses?

 Pair and share

As we have seen, poems are made up of images as well as sounds. They are like a slideshow, accompanied by music. Now you and your partner have a better sense of the poem's harsh music, try to link this to the very specific collection of pictures we are presented with. There is at least one strong visual image in each stanza, sometimes two.

Divide the first two stanzas between yourself and your partner, and come up with:

- a short quotation to illustrate the image

- a comment on what is unusual, disturbing, or sinister about the details.

You should, for instance, bring out the 'nest of sickness', the 'funeral silk', and the 'whale struck dumb'. What is being suggested about the damage done by the war? What kind of images are created and why would they accompany sad funeral music?

Now look together at examples of students writing about images in this poem, followed by comments on each.

Student A

Clarke conveys a feeling of bitterness through her use of metaphors and diction. The metaphor that I particularly like says that we should lament for the 'cormorant in his funeral silk' which is a metaphor which talks of how oil spills affect the cormorant in particular. The oil on the cormorant's feathers looks rather silky and it is referred to as 'funeral silk' because the oil is the cause of its death.

Comments

This shows understanding of the writer's purpose and choices, and gives some personal response. However, the candidate tends to explain rather than explore. The metaphor is identified, and its shock element is implicit, but there is no explicit comment on the effect on the reader.

Student B

After an oil spill the seabirds are coated in a thick layer of oil which entraps them and slowly leads them to their death. Even the sand is covered in oil, showing how our actions have widespread, negative consequences. The author remarks on the oil spill and refers to it as 'wearing a funeral silk'. This is powerful as it gives you the image of a poor gull trapped in black oil, unable to move, slowly dying as if it were a human, wearing a tux in a coffin.

Comments

This is a specific, detailed, and developed set of comments. There is explanation but also a link between the destruction and human actions. The image of the gull 'wearing a tux in a coffin' is especially memorable and suggests how deliberately incongruous and disturbing the metaphor is.

Following student B's example, find some striking and individual things to say (in two or three sentences) about the effect of the images in your chosen stanzas on the reader.

Look at what our two students go on to say:

Now compare your sentences with those of your partner. Are you bringing out the meaning of each image, and how we interpret not just its meaning but also its deeper implication?

Student A

This could liken to the shadow of death and informs me as the reader on just how much the oil affects the life at sea. It also obviously refers to the fact that the oil literally looks like a shadow on the sea's surface. These metaphors and use of diction convey a feeling of bitterness because it tells me as the reader just how badly some creatures are affected because of humans.

Student B

By saying 'shadow on the sea' it shows us how our mistakes are bigger than even the ocean, that we are overshadowing something so vast and beautiful. By placing a full stop after that line the author is emphasizing her message and forcing us to stop and take it all in.

Comments

Once again, student B has more to say about the effects of the choice of image, even though student A provides explanation and identifies the features of language. There is a stronger sense of the tone of the poem, the writer at work, and the impact on the careful reader in student B's answer.

As you and your partner work through the stanzas, you should be developing a sense of the mood of the poem and the ways in which it gets darker.

What does the poem go on to suggest about the following?

1. The effect of war on human beings
2. Why the soldiers joined up
3. The impact of missile warfare on rare and endangered species
4. How nature seems to be set upside down by the destruction of bombing

The work you have done together should have given you plenty of examples of the poet's growing despair at the 'slow dying' she sees through all these images.

# Viewpoints

Essays need arguments. You need something powerful and original to say. One of the problems when writing without a plan is that you discover something interesting to say much too late in your essay. A lot of weaker essays begin by saying things which are obvious. However, if you have an overview of the direction of the text as a whole, and a strong sense of where you are heading, then your essay will be much more effective.

As the final part of your preparation for writing the essay we set at the beginning of the chapter, you will need to decide on what to say about the final stanza. Then you will know where your essay is heading.

Poems, extracts from plays or prose, and also good essays don't just stop. As we have already seen, writers make very specific choices about where they begin and how they end their texts. When extracts are selected for comment and analysis in exams, the right place to end the extract has been carefully thought about. You can write your essay much more effectively if you know how you want it to end, and it is much easier to write your conclusion if you have a clear understanding of the writer's last word on the subject.

Let's explore the final stanza again:

> *For the burnt earth and the sun put out,*
> *the scalded ocean and the blazing well.*
> *For vengeance, and the ashes of language.*

There are several powerful images here, so these three lines pack in more details than any of the previous stanzas. They also express a much stronger sense of destruction. Destruction here is not just local but global: 'the sun put out'. Notice how destruction extends to each of the four elements: earth, air, water, and fire. It is almost an image of the end of the world. Some religious texts call this 'apocalypse' or 'Armageddon'. However, the reference to the 'blazing well' makes it clear that the destruction is man-made and is associated with fighting over oil and destroying the oil fields.

The final line is a separate sentence.

1. Why does the writer mention 'vengeance'?
2. What does this suggest about the consequences of war and destruction?
3. Why do you think the writer makes 'the ashes of language' the last thing she says?
4. Why might it be especially poignant to talk about the destruction of words in a poem, and especially a poem set in the Persian Gulf, one of the places where civilization and written language originated?

Having some answers to these questions should allow you to build your writing towards a powerful conclusion.

You will want to conclude in the following way.

- Return to the key term in the question (in this case 'bitterness').
- Suggest how the text has developed (showing increasing bitterness and desperation).
- Comment on the writer's purpose and choices (to demonstrate through analysis how the destruction of war affects everyone and everything, and will have lasting consequences which will bring destruction, not peace).
- Comment on the effect on the reader (the tone of the poem influences the reader's mood and understanding of the subject).
- Don't be afraid to voice your personal views (the end of an essay is the best place to use the pronoun 'I'): good answers conclude with an evaluation.

Now you have an excellent set of notes, and have highlighted and found things to say about a range of quotations. You are ready to write the essay:

> *In 'Lament' how do Gillian Clarke's language and word choice evoke a sense of bitterness?*

You should write about 700 words. Stick to a five-paragraph plan and make sure you leave plenty of time for a full conclusion.

When you have finished, look again at your essay and consider the following questions:

Have you:

- kept your answer relevant throughout?
- shown clear critical understanding (why the text was written)?
- explored deeper implications (gone beyond surface meaning)?

- responded sensitively and in detail to the writer's effects (used analysis)?
- integrated well-selected references to the text (used short quotations within your sentences)?
- constructed a developed argument working towards a personal response (an original argument, moving stage by stage towards your conclusion)?

Extend your learning

To write a more extensive, argued essay about warfare and its impact, use the techniques of analysis and comment you have learned in this chapter to write a longer essay covering two of the poems in chapter 4. A 1,000-word essay on two poems would be highly suitable for coursework submission.

A suitable title would be:

How do different poets powerfully convey to you the destruction and damage done by war through their choices of language and form?

Remember the following points.

- Refer to just two poems in detail.
- Identify the emotions and tone of the poems.
- Support your answer throughout with close reading of the language and the effect of the writers' choices of detail.
- Make a personal evaluation of the impact of each poem on you.

Looking back

We have seen that effective essay writing in this subject requires:

- analysis of the key terms of the question
- an overview of the structure of the text
- a plan
- selection of relevant details based on the writer's choice of words
- a conclusion which allows you to evaluate the effect of the whole text.

So far, we have only applied these skills to writing about a poem. What problems would you encounter when using them to write about an extract from a play or prose text which you have studied, or when answering a discursive question about a character or theme from a whole text?

Essentially, your only problem will be one of selection. Once you have studied a whole text in close detail, there will be far too much that you *could* say in answer to a question, so your plan will need to involve choosing the right details from the passage to make your points, or choosing three, or at most four, incidents from the

whole text which you can refer to in detail in order to construct your argument, whether it is about a character, a theme of the text, or a technique which the writer uses. It is better to say a lot about a little, rather than too little about a lot.

So far, we have explored a number of extracts and poems in order to develop an understanding of literary criticism and personal response. It is now time to move on to a detailed study of the texts your teachers have chosen, which are set for examination or for coursework.

As you work through your set texts, you will write a variety of essays, initially on extracts and sections of the texts, and eventually on the whole text. This unit should have helped you to understand critical writing better, to plan your essays more effectively, and to have confidence in making comments about quotations.

In the next unit, you will develop a deeper appreciation of the structure and language of texts in each genre, moving towards the point when you will feel confident in writing your own evaluation of your chosen texts.

Set texts—an introduction to close reading

How to read set texts

The next three chapters are designed to help you with your detailed study of set texts. As those texts change frequently from year to year, we will focus on genre and ways of appreciating the form and structure of literary texts. In this unit you will find a range of extracts, along with exercises, activities, and practice essay titles.

The aim is to develop and expand the skills you acquired in units 2 and 3. You will find a strong concentration on the structure of texts, encouraging you to ask questions about how writers put their texts together while you are reading your own set texts.

In the questions and activities you will find a greater emphasis on close reading of the language of the texts and on extended written responses. You need to be familiar with the terms introduced in unit 2 and with the style of critical writing introduced in unit 3.

Through close reading of passages, we shall explore the generic features of different forms of writing, and the different ways in which you can construct written arguments about them, and express an informed personal response in classwork and assessment. Online units 5 and 6 will extend these skills further and apply them to the preparation of a coursework folder and revision.

LEARNING POINTS

▶ To extend knowledge and understanding of drama, prose, and poetry texts

▶ To explore the distinctive elements of structure and form in each of the three genres and suggest ways of applying them to set texts

▶ To appreciate ways in which set texts are shaped by traditions and conventions within each genre

▶ To develop close analysis of the writers' use of language and effects

▶ To begin to explore the type of questions that could appear on an exam paper, and the detail required for exam and coursework responses

Studying drama

Structure of drama

Drama texts are perhaps the most approachable of all texts in a classroom
situation. They need to be read out aloud, just like poems. Their structure is
much more obvious than that of prose texts: plays need an effective beginning
(or opening scene) and ending (or climax), and often need to be divided into
two halves to allow for an interval. The action, therefore, often develops to
an exciting point about halfway through the play, before needing to pick up
dramatic momentum once again.

LEARNING POINTS

▶ To understand the distinct
features of drama texts,
using practical theatre
techniques

▶ To appreciate how plays
are structured

▶ To explore audience
response in relation
to dramatic form and
structure

▶ To evaluate the impact of
texts in performance and
their overall effect on an
audience

Many plays are written to be performed in theatres like this

Plays need to make sense to an audience hearing the text for the first time, so
they are not usually as dense as poems. They rarely take longer than a single
evening to perform (although there are epic dramas too!) so they are easy
to read out in full in class, unlike the prose texts which require homework
reading.

Plays always make more sense when performed, so there is plenty of scope
when you are preparing a drama set text to engage with the text through
movement and through visual elements: this can appeal to those who struggle
with lots of words. For these reasons it is a good idea to begin exploring
drama set texts early in the course.

Drama is also the most enjoyable way of exploring character, through performance and through writing, as we have seen in chapter 2. Performing drama allows you to submerge your own ideas in the thoughts and feelings of that character, creating the kind of empathy crucial for literary understanding.

However, studying texts in a literature classroom is a different process from studying them in a drama classroom: the concentration needs to be on the language of the text and on the dramatist's craft. Instead of seeing the drama text from the viewpoint of the performer, as in drama or theatre studies, literature asks you to approach texts from the viewpoint of the audience. You need to explore the structure and writing of the text as designed for an emotive effect.

Audiences go to the theatre to experience a work emotionally, in a very powerful way. The ancient Greek philosopher Aristotle called the effect of tragedy catharsis, in other words a powerful emotional response created by the chemistry of empathy, which could stir up, but perhaps also help to understand, such feelings as pity and fear. The ancient Greeks enjoyed comedy too: both tragedy and comedy take audiences out of themselves and take them into different worlds and ways of seeing them, however, they can also make us reflect critically or satirically on our own world. Above all, theatre is a communal and live experience; the interaction of performers and audience, and the greater risks involved, have meant that theatre retains its popularity even in the age of film.

Ideally you will have a chance to see your set texts performed live, or to perform them yourselves. If not, there are many good film versions of most of the texts set for study in Cambridge Literature in English. However, remember that a film is only an interpretation based on the personal response of the director. One reason why there are many versions of good drama texts and why they keep on being performed is that you can interpret them in different ways. Recent excellent reinterpretations of Shakespeare's texts have moved the action to American high schools, Bollywood, and the culture of street gangs.

This chapter is structured around the shape of a play, and the building blocks of drama. These are:

- situation
- characters
- conflict
- soliloquy or monologue
- resolution.

These building blocks allow you to follow the plot lines of the plays you are studying and the presentation of the characters in them.

Many of Shakespeare's plays have been made into films; sometimes there are many different versions of the same play

'Why do you act? You act for an audience. In the theatre, you're in their presence. Film stars don't know what it is to have an audience.' Interview with Sir Ian McKellen in *The Daily Telegraph* (November 2012)

7.1 Introducing situation

Dramatists must not only establish characters, but also situation at the beginning of a play. The first scene establishes the form and genre of the play, and creates **mood** for the audience.

Shakespeare's *Macbeth* has one of the most famous opening scenes in all drama. As in many of Shakespeare's plays, he does not begin with the principal character, but with other characters who are talking about him. He also needs to establish for the audience that this play is not a comedy, like those in chapter 2, but a tragedy. In tragedy, a character may have various choices, but the audience needs to feel that some of these are a matter of fate.

The three witches in *Macbeth*.

> **KEY TERM**
>
> **mood** = the effect of language, tone and structure on the mood of the reader or audience. Connect this to your personal response assessment objective.

Think ahead

What do audiences need to know in the first scene of a play?

1. Who the characters are
2. Where they are
3. What kind of play it will it be
4. The play's themes and ideas

Which do you rank as most important?

Compare the opening of this play to the play you are studying. How does each introduce characters, situations, genre and ideas?

In a play, audiences are given this information through action and dialogue. In Shakespeare's day, audiences did not even have a programme to tell them who was who. Not only that, but the scene needs to make an impact on them, through setting, characters and what is said.

What does Shakespeare achieve by starting this play with the weird sisters or witches?

The play is set in early medieval Scotland, and the scene is a bare (or 'blasted') heath. A battle is taking place: Macbeth and Banquo are fighting for King Duncan against an army of rebels and Norwegian invaders.

Macbeth **by William Shakespeare (1606)**

ACT I SCENE I

Thunder and lightning. Enter three Witches

First Witch   When shall we three meet again?
In thunder, lightning, or in rain?

Second Witch   When the hurly-burly's done,
When the battle's lost and won.

Third Witch   That will be ere the set of sun.

hurly-burly = fighting

First Witch	Where the place?
Second Witch	Upon the heath.
Third Witch	There to meet with Macbeth.
First Witch	I come, Graymalkin.
Second Witch	Paddock calls.
Third Witch	Anon.
ALL	Fair is foul, and foul is fair, Hover through the fog and filthy air.

Exeunt

> ***Graymalkin, Paddock*** = *the names of the witches' familiars or demons, in the form of cats or toads*
>
> ***Anon*** = *right away*
>
> ***Hover through the fog and filthy air*** = *suggests the witches can fly*

✎ Check your understanding

1. How do Shakespeare's stage directions immediately tell you that the situation is supernatural?
2. Why do they only talk about bad weather, not good?
3. Why do you think he chose to have three witches?
4. What is the effect of having them chant rhyming verse and not speak in prose or blank verse?
5. What do you know is happening offstage while they are chanting?
6. How does the audience get the impression that the witches can see into the future?
7. How can a battle be lost and won at the same time?
8. What is the effect of the witches mentioning Macbeth by name?
9. Which phrases give the impression that nothing is quite what it seems?
10. How does the last line emphasize the nastiness of the setting and situation?

Writing techniques

When writing about a play, always see it from the point of view of the audience, but as you are writing an informed personal response, you write from the point of view of someone who knows how things will end, and who understands **dramatic irony** – those situations where the audience know more than the characters.

The witches share their sense of dramatic irony with us. Like us, they know the result of the battle, and they know that winning the battle may not prove the best thing for Macbeth, as it encourages his ambition. They know he won't stay a hero ('fair') for long, but will become a villain ('foul'). By naming him, alongside their familiars, Graymalkin and Paddock, they are suggesting they have some control over him. The gloomy atmosphere suggests all will end badly.

In a tragedy, as we have already seen, there is a strong sense of structure and of patterns of fate which can't be avoided. The witches call themselves the 'weird sisters', based on the Old English word for 'fate'.

You need that same sense of fate when you write about a play: the script has already been written, and you need a sense of how the dramatist is manipulating the situation and the characters for an effect on the audience.

> **KEY TERM**
>
> **dramatic irony** = in drama, when the audience know something a character does not.

Extend your learning

Read the next scene of the play, and explore what it tells you about:

- The politics of Scotland
- Macbeth's character
- What other people think of him
- Betrayal and bloodshed
- Winners and losers

How does this scene develop themes and ideas already established in the first scene? What does it suggest about the relationship between the supernatural and realistic scenes?

The following short extract finally introduces Macbeth himself, a full scene after he was first named.

Now Macbeth and Banquo meet the witches. They greet Macbeth as Thane of Cawdor, which the audience already knows is a title the King will give him as a reward for defeating their enemies. They also tell Macbeth he will be King 'hereafter' which means in the future. The audience who know the story will realize this is planting the seed of Macbeth's own betrayal of the King.

Macbeth **by William Shakespeare (1606)**

Drum within

Third Witch	A drum, a drum, Macbeth doth come.
ALL	The weyard sisters, hand in hand, Posters of the sea and land, Thus do go about, about, Thrice to thine and thrice to mine And thrice again, to make up nine. Peace, the charm's wound up.

Enter Macbeth and Banquo

MACBETH	So foul and fair a day I have not seen.
BANQUO	How far is't called to Forres? What are these, So withered and so wild in their attire, That look not like th' inhabitants o' th' earth And yet are on't? Live you, or are you aught That man may question? You seem to understand me By each at once her choppy finger laying Upon her skinny lips. You should be women, And yet your beards forbid me to interpret That you are so.
MACBETH	Speak if you can. What are you?
First Witch	All hail, Macbeth, hail to thee, Thane of Glamis.
Second Witch	All hail, Macbeth, hail to thee, Thane of Cawdor.
Third Witch	All hail, Macbeth, thou shalt be king hereafter.

weyard = *weird*

posters of the sea and land = *again this suggests that the witches can fly, travelling 'post', that is, quickly*

the charm's wound up = *they have completed a spell*

Forres = *a place in the north of Scotland*

aught that man may question = *Macbeth is asking if the women are real or spirits*

thane of Glamis = *this is Macbeth's old title; he does not know the King has made him Thane of Cawdor*

7.2 Developing complex characters

Think ahead

We will move on to explore further the development of distinctive and complex characters through duologue. In chapter 2, we saw that duologue and double acts help to reveal what is distinct about characters. They encourage audience reaction, especially in comedy. However, they also prompt us to think about why characters are different and distinctive. We have started to look at differences between comedies and tragedies. Willy Russell's *Educating Rita* is certainly a very funny play too, but it has a more serious side, and in this chapter we will explore the ways in which drama can be comic and tragic at the same time. How does the play you are studying do the following?

1. Develop the audience's understanding of the main characters
2. Show relationships between the main characters
3. Introduce key themes
4. Balance comedy and seriousness
5. Keep the audience interested in what might happen next

Rita is a hairdresser who has started an Open University degree course and her tutor, Frank, is a heavy-drinking and disillusioned lecturer at the local university. Rita speaks non-standard English, with a heavy northern English accent. Rita has rushed out of work to tell Frank about her first experience of a Shakespeare play. As well as confronting the audience with the contrast between Rita's enthusiasm and Frank's cynicism, the playwright (like Shaw in *Pygmalion*) also interests us in whether their double act will develop into something more. Could this turn into a deeper relationship?

Julie Walters and Michael Caine in *Educating Rita*

Educating Rita by Willy Russell (1985)

Rita   [_she produces a copy of 'Macbeth'_] Look, I went out an' bought the book. Isn't it great? What I couldn't get over is how excitin' it was.

[_Frank puts his feet up on the desk_]

Rita   Wasn't his wife a cow, eh? An' that fantastic bit where he meets Macduff an' he thinks he's all invincible. I was on the edge of me seat at that bit. I wanted to shout out an' tell Macbeth, warn him.

Frank   You didn't did you?

Rita   Nah. Y' can't do that in a theatre, can y'? It was dead good. It was like a thriller.

Frank   Yes. You'll have to go and see more.

Rita   I'm goin' to. Macbeth's a tragedy, isn't it?

Frank nods

Rita   Right.

Rita   (_smiles at Frank and he smiles back at her_) Well I just – I just had to tell someone who'd understand.

Frank   I'm honoured that you chose me.

Rita   (_moving towards the door_) Well, I better get back. I've left a customer with a perm lotion. If I don't get a move on there'll be another tragedy.

Frank   No. There won't be a tragedy.

Rita   There will, y'know. I know this woman; she's dead fussy. If her perm doesn't come out right there'll be blood an' guts everywhere.

Frank   Which might be quite tragic –

He throws her an apple from his desk which she catches

But it won't be a tragedy.

Rita   What?

Frank   Well – erm – look; the tragedy of the drama has nothing to do with the sort of tragic event you're talking about. Macbeth is flawed by his ambition – yes?

Rita   (_going and sitting in the chair by the desk_) Yeh. Go on.

(_She starts to eat the apple_)

Frank   Erm – it's that flaw which forces him to take inevitable steps towards his own doom. You see?

Rita offers him the can of soft drink. He takes it and looks at it

Frank   (_putting the can down on the desk_) No thanks. Whereas, Rita, a woman's hair being reduced to an inch of stubble, or – or the sort of thing you read in the paper that's reported as being tragic, 'Man Killed by Falling Tree', is not a tragedy.

Rita   It is for the poor sod under the tree.

Frank   Yes, it's tragic, absolutely tragic. But it's not a tragedy in the way that Macbeth is a tragedy. Tragedy in dramatic terms is inevitable, pre-ordained. Look, now, even without ever having heard the story of Macbeth you wanted to shout out, to warn him and prevent him going on, didn't you? But you wouldn't have been able to stop him would you?

Rita   No.

Frank   Why?

Rita   They would have thrown me out the theatre.

Frank   But what I mean is that your warning would have been ignored. He's warned in the play. But he can't go back. He still treads the path to doom. But the poor old fellow under the tree hasn't arrived there by following any inevitable steps has he?

Rita   No.

Frank   There's no particular flaw in his character that has dictated his end. If he'd been warned of the consequences of standing beneath that particular tree he wouldn't have done it, would he? Understand?

Rita   So – so Macbeth brings it on himself?

| Frank | Yes. You see he goes blindly on and on and with every step he's spinning one more piece of thread which will eventually make up the network of his own tragedy. Do you see? | Frank | It's quite easy, Rita. |
| Rita | I think so. I'm not used to thinking like this. | Rita | It is for you. I just thought it was a dead excitin' story. But the way you tell it you make me see all sorts of things in it. (*After a pause*) It's fun, tragedy, isn't it? |

✎ Check your understanding

You should be able to see that this is a key scene in Rita's education about the criticism of literature. As Frank explains, words in literary criticism often have a more precise meaning than in everyday life. What does he tell you about the concept of tragedy? How is it linked to fate, or the concept of the inevitable, and who is most aware of this in the theatre?

Answer the following questions to track the development of the scene.

1. What does Rita find enjoyable about the experience of theatre?

2. Which comment shows that she is beginning to understand the concept of dramatic irony, even if she doesn't yet know the term?

3. What shows her understanding of conventions in the theatre?

4. What does Frank's choice of the word 'honoured' show?

5. Why, according to Frank, is a tragic event not a tragedy?

6. Why is Macbeth's fate inevitable, according to Frank?

7. How is this linked to the audience's reactions to the drama?

8. How does the tragic **hero** treat the warnings of his doom?

9. Can you link this to the way a tragedy is constructed?

10. Why would an audience laugh at Rita's phrase 'It's fun, tragedy'?

KEY TERM

hero or heroine = the main character, whether we approve of them or not.

Pair and share

Discuss the characterization of Frank and Rita before producing a dramatic paired reading of their duologue.

1. What are the contrasts which make Rita and Frank so interesting as characters?

2. What is lively and surprising about her attitudes and stories?

3. What qualities does she have which make her different from Frank's other students?

4. As Frank is an alcoholic, there are certain tragic elements in his own character (notice he refuses Rita's soft drink). What are they?

5. Like Shaw, Willy Russell uses stage directions to show the dynamic between the characters.

Can you see ways in which they are getting closer?

Present the scene to your class dramatically, with actions and movement as well as words.

Pay particular attention to each stage direction and explore what is implied, as well as explicit. Why does Frank offer Rita an apple? What might this gesture imply? (Look up the story of Adam and Eve and the Tree of Knowledge.)

Afterwards, each character should answer questions from the rest of the class in the hot seat. In drama, once a character is in the 'hot seat' they must tell the truth as their character sees it, and explain to the audience what they are feeling at that particular moment.

Viewpoints

We have seen that literature texts raise debates and ask us questions which are not completely resolved. In the theatre this creates suspense or tension. This will keep the audience interested: in a performance, this scene takes place about 15 minutes before the interval. Discuss and debate the questions below.

1. Will Rita's education be an entirely good thing?

2. She wants to learn the technical terms so that she can speak about literature in the same way as Frank's other students. However, if she achieves this, what will be lost?

3. Can you compare her to Eliza in *Pygmalion* (in chapter 2)?

4. By changing her vocabulary, and her way of thinking, Rita is also likely to change her language and her social status. Why might that cause problems?

5. Alcoholism is not a choice. What seems to be Frank's attitude to his own fate?

6. Why does this create a sharp contrast between his character and that of Rita?

7. How does this scene, therefore, sow the seeds of further developments and deeper contrasts between the characters?

Extend your learning

Have another look at Frank's explanation of the difference between the tragic and tragedy. Is the drama text you are studying a tragedy or a comedy? Or does it mix elements of the two? We have seen that there are serious elements to comedy, and there are also possible laughs in tragedies. Both forms use plenty of irony. When writing about plays, we use the term 'dramatic irony' (when the audience knows something that a character does not).

1. Can you link this term to the moment when Rita wanted to warn Macbeth about Macduff (the man who is fated to kill him)?

2. How might an audience react to a character's fate?

3. What are the theatre conventions which stop an audience warning the character of his fate?

4. Why, according to Frank, do tragic characters fail to listen to any warnings in the play?

5. Can you link this idea to the way the writer has deliberately crafted the play?

6. What do these flaws in tragic characters suggest to you about human nature?

 See Worksheet 2 for further help in looking at what makes a tragedy.

7.3 Playing: plays within plays

Willy Russell's play shows how the engagement of the audience is crucial in both tragedy and comedy. Their laughter and their sense of irony create the drama. Rita's lively and fresh reaction – 'It's fun, tragedy, isn't it?' – is just what a writer would want, and it certainly provokes even more interest in her from Frank. You will also have noticed that she reacts to Shakespeare's play as a theatrical experience. She does not worry too much about the language or the history, but enjoys the way in which the audience's emotions are engaged. What is 'tragic' in real life could be 'fun' in the theatre.

Audiences today are very aware of the tragedy that awaits characters in R.C. Sherriff's *Journey's End*. The title itself is taken from Shakespeare's comedy *Twelfth Night*, which we will look at later, but audiences at the first performance in 1928 would have been conscious that the end of this journey will be tragic, and that it remembers a lost generation killed on the Western Front in a war that ended just 10 years before. Nevertheless, there are comic scenes in this play, which also presents the different ways in which soldiers on the front line coped with the stress of conflict. Jokes, dialogue and the interplay between characters provide the audience with comic relief from the more tragic central figure, Stanhope, and his troubled relationship with the new arrival, Raleigh.

Think ahead

Theatre provides audiences with realistic situations, but presented in an exaggerated way. Dialogue and relationships between characters reflect this, and will often make an audience laugh out loud.

1. Which parts of your studied play are funny or change the mood?
2. How do characters 'play to the audience' in your drama text?
3. Is the action realistic or exaggerated (stylized)?
4. We call references to other plays, like the title of *Journey's End*, intertextuality. How does your play relate to other tragedies or comedies?
5. How do characters in your text reveal their character through the way they use language?

Raleigh has just arrived to join a platoon on the front line of the Western Front of the Great War. The soldiers are in trenches, waiting for either side to make a major attack on their enemy. Raleigh's platoon is commanded by Captain Stanhope, his schoolboy hero and engaged to his sister, but Stanhope has not given him a friendly welcome. In this scene, early the next morning, Raleigh listens to Trotter and Osborne, two older officers, who have been teasing the soldier Mason about his terrible cooking.

A scene from *Journey's End*.

Journey's End by R.C. Sherriff (1928)

TROTTER	I say, d'you realise he's washed his dish-cloth?
OSBORNE	I know. I told him about it.
TROTTER	Did you really? You've got some pluck. 'Ow did you go about it?
OSBORNE	I wrote and asked my wife for a packet of Lux. Then I gave it to Mason and suggested he tried it on something.

pluck = *courage*

a packet of Lux = *packet of soap*

TROTTER	Good man. No, he's not a bad cook. Might be a lot worse. When I was in the ranks we 'ad a prize cook – used to be a plumber before the war. Ought to 'ave seen the stew 'e made. Thin! Thin wasn't the word. Put a bucketful of 'is stew in a bath and pull the plug, and the whole lot would go down in a couple of gurgles.

MASON brings TROTTER'S porridge.

MASON	I've took the lumps out.
TROOTER	Good. Keep 'em and use 'em for dumplings next time we 'ave boiled beef.
MASON	Very good, sir. *He goes out.*
TROTTER	Yes. That plumber was a prize cook, 'e was. Lucky for us one day 'e set 'imself on fire making the tea. 'E went 'ome pretty well fried. Did Mason get that pepper?
OSBORNE	Yes.
TROTTER	Good. Must 'ave pepper.
OSBORNE	I thought you were on duty now.
TROTTER	I'm supposed to be. Stanhope sent me down to get my breakfast. He's looking after things till I finish.
OSBORNE	He's got a long job then.
TROTTER	Oh, no. I'm a quick eater. Hi! Mason! Bacon!
MASON	(*outside*) Coming, sir!
OSBORNE	It's a wonderful morning.
TROTTER	Isn't it lovely? Makes you feel sort of young and 'opeful. I was up in that old trench under the brick wall just now, and damned if a bloomin' little bird didn't start singing! Didn't 'arf sound funny. Sign of spring, I s'pose. *MASON arrives with TROTTER's bacon.* That looks all right.
MASON	If you look down straight on it from above, sir, you can see the bit o'lean quite clear.
TROTTER	Good Lord, yes! That's it, isn't it?
MASON	No, sir; that's a bit o' rust off the pan.
TROTTER	Ah! *That's* it, then!
MASON	You've got it, sir. *He goes out.*
TROTTER	Cut us a chunk of bread, Uncle. *OSBORNE cuts him off a chunk.*
OSBORNE	How are things going up there?

when I was in the ranks = *before Trotter was promoted to officer (unusual as most officers were appointed direct from officer training, and sometimes, like Raleigh, straight from school)*

the bit o'lean = *part of the bacon which is not just fat*

TROTTER	I don't like the look of things a bit.
OSBORNE	You mean – the quiet?
TROTTER	Yes. Standing up there in the dark last night there didn't seem a thing in the world alive – except the rats squeaking and my stomach grumbling about the cutlet.
OSBORNE	It's quiet even now.
TROTTER	Too damn quiet. You can bet your boots the Boche is up to something. The big attack soon, I reckon. I don't like it, Uncle. Pass the jam.

the cutlet = a piece of meat
the Boche = Germans

✎ Check your understanding

Dialogue is crucial for the development and revelation of character. Even though this scene appears at first to be comic relief, it reveals a lot about Trotter and Osborne. It also becomes much more serious at the end.

Exam passage-based questions are a similar length to this. You need to think about what has just happened dramatically, and how the scene prepares the audience for what happens next. Most importantly, you need to look in detail at the effect of individual lines on the audience. It helps to divide the scene into sections.

Part A: Trotter and Osborne

1. What is revealed about Osborne through the way he gets Mason to wash the dish-cloth?
2. What is revealed about Trotter's past?
3. What else shows audiences that he was not originally 'officer class'?
4. Which jokes of Trotter's would the audience laugh at?
5. Is there an unpleasant side to his humour?
6. How do you think Osborne and Raleigh react to his jokes?
7. Which line suggests that Osborne is making fun of Trotter?
8. Why do you think Trotter calls Osborne 'Uncle'?

Part B: Trotter and Mason

1. Why do you think food is important to Trotter?
2. How else does Trotter try to keep cheerful?
3. How does Mason show the audience that he has a sense of humour too?
4. Raleigh is there too: why might he be an audience for all this joking and playing?

Part C: Looking ahead

1. At what point does the mood change?
2. How might actors signal this in the speed of the dialogue?
3. Where does the writer use descriptions and sound in order to get the audience to pay attention to the quiet atmosphere?
4. Which words suggest that Trotter is no longer joking?
5. What does this reveal about what the jokes are actually covering up?
6. How does this scene prepare the audience for later developments?
7. How does this make you think differently about Trotter's character?
8. Look back at his speech about the singing bird. Do you think differently about it now?

Pair and share

Act out the two dialogues between Osborne and Trotter, at the beginning and end of the scene. Add as much humour as you can to the first dialogue, and as much seriousness as possible to the second. Which actions can you match to the words?

Consider how the tone of language can influence the mood of the audience. How can you reveal the serious side behind the banter and playing?

Osborne and Trotter are clearly very different characters. How does their language show this? How can you see this in their treatment of, and by, Mason?

Contrasting characters, whose attitudes conflict, make for effective drama. Where do you see this in your studied play?

Viewpoints

One character in this extract says very little and another says nothing at all. Mason keeps his opinions to himself, but we can see that he has a sense of humour. He also represents the viewpoint of the ordinary soldier rather than the officers. What does he think of the officers?

Raleigh says nothing at all. If you are studying the play, you will know that he has had his first night on duty, and that he is probably also thinking about how Stanhope treated him in Act 1. Always pay attention to all the characters on stage. The audience will be aware of them and of their facial expressions and body language.

Actors use the hot-seating technique to develop characters, and their thoughts and expression.

Choose the part of **either** Mason or Raleigh and prepare for the hot seat. Your fellow students will ask you questions about this scene.

Afterwards write up your thoughts. Think about what has just happened to the character, their feelings at this moment and their thoughts about what might happen next.

Extend your understanding

1. How do characters in your set drama text grow or develop?

2. Can you plot their 'journey' on a timeline?

3. Where will they inevitably come into conflict or challenge others?

4. Does your play depict these conflicts as comedy or tragedy?

5. How successfully does the writer you are studying combine laughter and seriousness?

6. Who does the audience sympathize with?

7. How do they react to conflict and tension between characters?

8. Is the direction of the play inevitable?

7.4 Conflict

We have explored how dramatists present the audience with contrasting characters who will need to engage and often clash with each other if they, and the plot, are going to develop. Alan Bennett's brilliant school-based drama *The History Boys* is based around the clash between two teachers who are preparing the boys for their university entrance exams. They will need to answer a special entrance paper to study history at Oxford. Hector is a traditionalist literature teacher who has encouraged them to memorize poems and filled them with cultural knowledge. The much younger Irwin, in his first teaching job, is here encouraging them to question the assumptions behind what they have learned, and to construct original arguments. The other characters are all schoolboys. They have written essays for Irwin on the First World War, which he has just marked.

The History Boys by Alan Bennett (2004)

Irwin   So. Our overall conclusion is that the origins of the Second War lie in the unsatisfactory outcome of the First.

Timms   (*doubtfully*) Yes. (*with more certainty*) Yes.

Others nod.

Irwin   First class. Bristol welcomes you with open arms. Manchester longs to have you. You can walk into Leeds. But I am a fellow of Magdalen College, Oxford, and I have just read seventy papers all saying the same thing and I am asleep …

Bristol … Manchester … Leeds = all very good universities but not as famous as Oxford and its Colleges

Scripps   But it's all true.

Irwin   What has that got to do with it? What has that got to do with anything?

Let's go back to 1914 and I'll put you a different case.

Try this for size.

Germany does not want war and if there is an arms race it is Britain who is leading it. Though there's no reason why we would want war. Nothing in it for us. Better stand back and let Germany and Russia fight it out while we take the imperial pickings.

These are the facts.

Why do we not care to acknowledge them? The cattle, the body count. We still don't like to admit the war was even partly our fault because so many of our people died. A photograph on every mantelpiece. All this mourning has veiled the truth. It's not so much lest we forget as lest we remember. Because you should realize that so far as the Cenotaph and the Last Post and all that stuff is concerned, there's no better way of forgetting something than by commemorating it.

And Dakin.

the cattle = Irwin is referring to Wilfred Owen's 'Anthem for Doomed Youth', 'What passing bell for those who die as cattle'

Cenotaph and Last Post = the way in which the British commemorate their war dead

Dakin   Sir?

Irwin	You were the one who was morally superior about Haig.
Dakin	Passchendaele. The Somme. He was a butcher, sir.
Irwin	Yes, but at least he delivered the goods. No, no, the real enemy to Haig's subsequent reputation was the Unknown Soldier. If Haig had had any sense he'd have had him disinterred and shot all over again for giving comfort to the enemy.
Lockwood	So what about the poets, then?
Irwin	What about them? If you read what they actually say as distinct from what they write, most of them seem to have enjoyed the war. Siegfried Sassoon was a good officer. Saint Wilfred Owen couldn't wait to get back to his company. Both of them surprisingly bloodthirsty.
	Poetry is good up to a point. Adds flavour. But if you want to relate the politics to the war, forget Wilfred Owen and try Kipling.
Akthar	Thanks a lot.
Irwin	'If any question why we died
	Tell them because our fathers lied.'
	In other words …
Timms	Oh no, sir. With respect, can I stop you? No, with a poem or any work of art we can never say 'in other words'. If it is a work of art there are no other words.
Lockwood	Yes, sir. That's why it is a work of art in the first place.
	You can't look at a Rembrandt and say 'in other words', can you, sir?

Irwin is puzzled where all this comes from but is distracted by Rudge.

Rudge	So what's the verdict, sir? What do I write down?
Irwin	You can write down, Rudge, that 'I must not write down every word that teacher says.'
	You can also write down that the First World War was a mistake. It was not a tragedy.
	And as for the truth, Scripps, which you were worrying about: truth is no more at issue in an examination than thirst at a wine-tasting or fashion at a striptease.
Dakin	Do you really believe that, sir, or are you just trying to make us think?
Scripps	You can't explain away the poetry, sir.
Lockwood	No, sir. Art wins in the end.

The bell goes.

Haig = *First World War general: British commander on the Western Front*

Somme … Passchendaele = *major battles on the Western Front*

Sassoon … Kipling = *other poets who wrote about the war as well as Wilfred Owen (see chapter 4)*

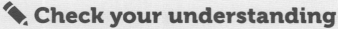

Check your understanding

1. Why does Irwin want the boys to produce arguments which are different?

2. Why doesn't he seem to care about the truth?

3. He is also challenging ideas of tragedy and inevitability. How is he suggesting the First World War came about?

4. What does he suggest 'remembrance' encourages people to forget?

5. What does he mean by saying that General Haig 'delivered the goods'?

6. Why does he suggest that we shouldn't trust First World War poets like Wilfred Owen (see chapter 4)?

7. What do you think he likes about the lines by Rudyard Kipling?

8. How do Timms and Lockwood change the terms of the argument?

9. Look at the stage direction which follows and the introductory notes. Where do the boys' ideas about art come from?

10. How does Irwin turn his ideas into epigrams (see chapter 2)?

11. How does Scripps turn this into an argument about art versus history?

12. Who do you think has won this argument?

Viewpoints

Sarcasm and provocation are important parts of Irwin's teaching style. The way he says things is controversial as well as his views.

1. Use the PEA technique to find examples of the harsh way Irwin puts things and explain why his choice of words is so provocative.

2. Look more closely at his language. Give examples of the ways in which he uses short sentences. Find examples of how his short sentences make him sound especially sure of himself or full of authority.

3. How successful are the boys at challenging or undermining that voice of authority? How do they use their own knowledge to do so?

4. Is it true that there are no words which can replace the statement made by a work of art? Why would that provide problems for literary criticism?

Pair and share

This time it isn't clear that the teacher has won the argument. Look over the lesson carefully and think about what you agree and disagree with. Dakin is clearly very impressed by Irwin's arguments, Lockwood less so.

Script and perform your own duologue between Dakin and Lockwood, discussing Irwin's teaching and his beliefs.

1. What do you find challenging about the way he teaches?

2. Do you agree with the views he expresses about truth and about poetry?

3. What about his views about tragedy versus accident?

4. Do you think he will help you to get a university place at Oxford?

Extend your learning

In drama, extreme and controversial characters are often more dramatically effective than those who are reasonable.

1. Are there examples of extreme characters in the texts you are studying?

2. What has made them behave provocatively?

3. How do other characters react and respond to them?

4. What is the audience's response?

5. What problems will the character's outrageous expressions cause for him later in the play?

7.5 Confrontation and climax: use of characters in chorus

So far we have explored characters through duologues and conversation. However, drama also involves bigger set pieces. We will look at an American drama which contains a big courtroom scene, where the reactions of all of those present will influence the audience's judgments of the principal characters, and where characters will also have an audience of their own to play up to (just as we saw Trotter and Irwin do). In the case of the famous play *The Crucible* by Nobel Prize-winning American dramatist Arthur Miller, the trial closes the penultimate scene and produces the climactic dramatic moment of the play, and the downfall of the play's flawed hero, John Proctor.

Think ahead

1. What do you understand by a witch hunt?

2. Why are courtroom scenes especially powerful places for the confrontations which bring drama to a climax?

3. Can you think of courtroom scenes in films and plays you have seen?

4. What is the role of supporting characters in large (or set piece) scenes? Think about the role of Mason and Raleigh in Sherriff's scene.

5. How will the comments of other characters influence the audience's judgment and evaluation?

 See Worksheet 5 for an exercise on judging a character in one of your own set texts.

The play is set against the background of the Salem witch trials in Massachusetts in 1692–93. Abigail Williams, a teenager, has had an affair with Proctor, but in an attempt to cover this up has accused his wife Elizabeth of witchcraft, an accusation which the highly religious community believes. In this culture, anyone who is found guilty of witchcraft is put to death unless they sign a confession. A court has been set up, presided over by Judge Danforth and Reverend Hale, a priest and witchfinder. Proctor has confessed his affair and one of the girls, Mary, has confessed that the girls are lying. Danforth, not believing them, summons Elizabeth and questions her under oath about her husband's affair, but she has denied this, in order to protect him. Ironically, this has endangered everyone, as Danforth now believes Abigail even more strongly. Abigail pretends that Mary has been possessed by the devil, who haunts her in the shape of a bird, and goes on (with the other girls) to accuse Proctor and others of devil worship, having frightened Mary into joining in. The language of the play is archaic (deliberately old–fashioned): it fits the setting of seventeenth-century New England.

Daniel Day-Lewis in a film adaptation of the play

The Crucible by Arthur Miller (1953)

PROCTOR: Elizabeth, tell the truth, Elizabeth!

DANFORTH: She has spoken. Remove her. (*Hale crosses R. following Elizabeth.*)

PROCTOR: (*Cries out.*) Elizabeth, I have confessed it!

ELIZABETH: Oh, John! (*Goes out.*)

PROCTOR: She only thought to save my name!

HALE: Excellency, it is a natural lie to tell; I beg you, stop now; before another is condemned!

DANFORTH: She spoke nothing of lechery, and this man lies!

HALE: (*He cries out in anguish.*) I believe him! I cannot turn my face from it no more. (*Pointing at Abigail.*) This girl has always struck me false! She … (*Abigail with a weird cry screams up to ceiling.*)

ABIGAIL: You will not! Begone! Begone, I say! (*Mercy and Susanna rise, looking up.*)

DANFORTH: What is it, child? (*She is transfixed—with all the girls, in complete silence, she is open-mouthed, agape at ceiling, and in great fear.*) Girls! Why do you …?

MERCY: It's on the beam!—behind the rafter!

DANFORTH: (*Looking up.*) Where!

ABIGAIL: Why …? Why do you come, yellow bird?

PROCTOR: Where's a bird? I see no bird!

ABIGAIL: (*To ceiling, in a genuine conversation with the 'bird' as though trying to talk it out of attacking her.*) My face? My

to save my name = *Proctor means that Elizabeth told a lie to save his reputation*

she spoke nothing of lechery = *she did not say that Proctor had an affair*

I cannot turn my face = *Hale cannot ignore his belief that Proctor told the truth*

Mercy and Susanna rise = *they are joining Abigail's act of pretending the devil is in the room*

	face?! But God made my face; you cannot want to tear my face. Envy is a deadly sin, Mary.
MARY:	Abby!
ABIGAIL:	(*Unperturbed, continues to 'bird.'*) Oh, Mary, this is a black art to change your shape. No, I cannot, I cannot stop my mouth; it's God's work I do ….
MARY:	Abby, I'm here!
PROCTOR:	They're pretending, Mister Danforth!
ABIGAIL:	(*Now she takes a backward step, as though the bird would swoop down momentarily.*) Oh, please, Mary!—Don't come down ….
ANN:	Her claws, she's stretching her claws!
PROCTOR:	Lies—lies—
ABIGAIL:	(*Backing further, still fixed above.*) Mary, please don't hurt me!
MARY:	(*To Danforth.*) I'm not hurting her!
DANFORTH:	Why does she see this vision?!
MARY:	(*Rises.*) She sees nothin'!
ABIGAIL:	(*As though hypnotized, mimicking the exact tone of Mary's cry.*) She sees nothin'!
MARY:	Abby, you mustn't!
ABIGAIL:	(*Now all girls join, transfixed.*) Abby, you mustn't!
MARY:	(*To all girls, frantically.*) I'm here, I'm here!
GIRLS:	I'm here, I'm here!
DANFORTH:	Mary Warren!—Draw back your spirit out of them!
MARY:	Mister Danforth …!
GIRLS:	Mister Danforth!
DANFORTH:	Have you compacted with the Devil? Have you?
MARY:	Never, never!
GIRLS:	Never, never!
DANFORTH:	(*Growing hysterical.*) Why can they only repeat you?!
PROCTOR:	Give me a whip—I'll stop it!
MARY:	They're sporting …!
GIRLS:	(*Cutting her off.*) They're sporting!
MARY:	(*Turning on them all, hysterically and stamping her feet.*) Abby, stop it!
GIRLS:	(*Stamping their feet.*) Abby, stop it!
MARY:	(*Screaming it out at top of her lungs, and raising her fists.*) Stop it!!

> **this is a black art to change your shape** = Abigail is accusing Mary of being a witch in league with the devil

GIRLS:	(*All raising their fists.*) Stop it!! (*Mary, utterly confounded, and becoming overwhelmed by Abigail—and the girls'— utter conviction, starts to whimper, hands half raised, powerless—and all girls begin whimpering exactly as she does.*)
DANFORTH:	A little while ago you were afflicted. Now it seems you afflict others; where did you find this power?
MARY:	(*Staring at Abigail.*) I … have no power.
GIRLS:	I have no power.
PROCTOR:	They're gulling you, Mister!
DANFORTH:	Why did you turn about this past two weeks? You have seen the Devil, have you not?
PROCTOR:	(*Seeing her weakening.*) Mary, Mary, God damns all liars! (*Mary utters something unintelligible, staring at Abigail who keeps watching the 'bird' above.*)
DANFORTH:	I cannot hear you. What do you say? (*Mary utters again unintelligibly.*) You will confess yourself or you will hang!
PROCTOR:	Mary, remember the angel Raphael … do that which is good and …
ABIGAIL:	(*Pointing upward.*) The wings! Her wings are spreading! Mary, please, don't, don't …! She's going to come down! She's walking the beam! Look out! She's coming down! (*All scream. Abigail dashes across the stage as though pursued, the other girls streak hysterically in and out between the men, all converging.—and as their screaming subsides only Mary Warren's is left. All watch her, struck, even horrified by this evident fit.*)
PROCTOR:	(*Leaning across the table, turning her gently by the arm.*) Mary, tell the Governor what they …
MARY:	(*Backing away.*) Don't touch me … don't touch me!
PROCTOR:	Mary!
MARY:	(*Pointing at Proctor.*) You are the Devil's man!
PARRIS:	Praise God!
PROCTOR:	Mary, how …?
MARY:	I'll not hang with you! I love God, I love God—
DANFORTH:	(*To Mary.*) He bid you do the Devil's work?
MARY:	(*Hysterically, indicating Proctor.*) He come at me by night and every day to sign, to sign, to …
DANFORTH:	Sign what?
PARRIS:	The Devil's book? He come with a book?

gulling you = *fooling you, taking you in*

MARY:	(*Hysterically, pointing at Proctor.*) My name, he want my name; I'll murder you, he says, if my wife hangs! We must go and overthrow the court, he says …!
PROCTOR:	(*Eyes follow Mary.*) Mister Hale …!
MARY:	(*Her sobs beginning.*) He wake me every night, his eyes were like coals and his fingers claw my neck, and I sign, I sign ….
HALE:	Excellency, the child's gone wild.
PROCTOR:	Mary, Mary …!
MARY:	(*Screaming at him.*) No, I love God; I go your way no more, (*Looking at Abigail.*) I love God, I bless God…. (Sobbing, she rushes to Abigail.) Abby, Abby, I'll never hurt you more! (*All watch, as Abigail reaches out and draws sobbing Mary to her, then looks up to Danforth.*)
DANFORTH:	What are you! You are combined with anti-Christ, are you not? I have seen your power, Mister, you will not deny it!
HALE:	This is not witchcraft! Those girls are frauds! You condemn an honest man!
DANFORTH:	I will have nothing from you, Mister Hale! (*To Proctor.*) Will you confess yourself befouled with hell, or do you keep that black allegiance yet? What say you?
PROCTOR:	I say … God is dead!
PARRIS:	(*Crossing L. toward door.*) Hear it, hear it!
PROCTOR:	A fire, a fire is burning! I hear the boot of Lucifer, I see his filthy face. And it is my face and yours, Danforth. For them that quail now when you know in all your black hearts that this be fraud. God damns our kind especially, and we will burn, we will burn together!
DANFORTH:	Marshal, take him and Corey with him to the jail!
HALE:	(*Crossing D.L.*) I denounce these proceedings! I quit this court! (*Hale EXITS.*)
PROCTOR:	You are pulling heaven down and raising up a whore.
DANFORTH:	(*Shocked.*) Mister Hale, Mister Hale!
CURTAIN	

we will burn together = Proctor says something evil is happening in Salem, but it is the work of human beings not of the devil. Danforth refuses to understand him

Check your understanding

1. Why do Hale and Danforth take different views about who is lying at the beginning of the scene?
2. How does this affect the audience (who know Abigail is lying)?
3. How do the stage directions indicate an atmosphere of growing hysteria?
4. Why does Abigail begin pretending to see the devil? What does she want to draw attention away from?
5. What does Abigail pretend the 'bird' is doing to her?
6. What is the effect of the girls' repetitions?
7. What does Danforth believe is happening? Why is he described as 'hysterical'?
8. List the words which show that Mary has completely broken down with fear of being accused of witchcraft.
9. Why does she make her 'confession'?
10. What is the effect on stage of the girls screaming and rushing around?
11. Where do we see Danforth 'leading the witness' by putting words into her mouth through the way he asks questions?
12. What is Mary accusing Proctor of doing?
13. Why does Proctor appeal to Hale?
14. Why do Danforth's questions not give Proctor a chance to tell the truth?
15. What does Proctor mean by 'God is dead'?
16. What does Danforth think he means?
17. What do all the exclamation marks towards the end of the scene suggest about its tone? Is anyone listening to anyone else?
18. How does Miller's language make the end of this scene especially powerful and shocking?

Pair and share

You and your partner have been sent to Salem a few months after the trials and executions have ended and have been asked to compile a report on why a miscarriage of justice has occurred. Examine the transcripts of the trial and prepare your evidence. Then, thinking about two of the following points each, argue in front of the class and explain:

1. why Abigail is guilty of perjury (lying in court)
2. why Mary changed her evidence
3. why John Proctor was misunderstood
4. why Danforth handled the situation badly.

Viewpoints

When groups become hysterical or full of prejudice, it is difficult to carry out justice effectively. Think of examples from your own knowledge or experience. Can you find evidence of trials being influenced by prejudice?

How effective is Miller's drama in re-creating this atmosphere of prejudice? How do both the words and the reactions of his characters reinforce that idea of prejudice?

Consider the following question:

How does Miller's writing make this scene so powerfully dramatic?

Use these questions to shape your response.

1. How does Miller's overall theme make this such a powerful and disturbing scene?
2. Why are Proctor's confrontation with Abigail and Danforth's with Hale both so provocative?
3. How does Miller show the cunning of Abigail's deceptions?
4. How does he demonstrate the hold Abigail has over the other girls, especially Mary?
5. What qualities in the writing make Proctor's use of language so powerful and what does it make the audience reflect on?

Extend your learning

Consider the following questions with regard to a drama text you are studying.

1. What is the contribution that the more minor characters make to the text?
2. How do contrasting characters and opinions contribute to the **tension**?
3. What is the most dramatic scene and why?
4. How does the writing involve the audience in making judgments about characters?
5. Do any of the scenes have especially effective final lines?

KEY TERMS

tension = conflict between characters, felt by the audience.

soliloquy = a verse monologue, especially in Shakespeare's plays, where a character speaks his thoughts – always to himself or herself.

7.6 Using monologue to reveal character

When we studied *Macbeth*, it was clear that part of the dramatic irony came from the fact that the audience probably knew that Macbeth would betray the King. Shakespeare's audience would have known this from history and legends—this was already a well-known story before Shakespeare wrote his play. However, they also find this out because Macbeth tells them his darker thoughts in a soliloquy. In a **soliloquy** or monologue, a character tells the truth—or at least his or her version of the truth—directly to the audience, giving us their thoughts and telling us things they have not revealed to other characters. It is a little like the empathic exercises we looked at in chapter 5 when you wrote down your thoughts. Often characters, like Osborne and Trotter, are reluctant to show their true thoughts and fears to each other and cover this up by joking. Other Shakespeare characters also reveal the truth about themselves in a soliloquy. Prince Henry, the future Henry V, tells the audience that when he was joking and playing with other characters, like Falstaff and his gang, he was concealing his true character.

Henry IV Part One **by William Shakespeare (circa 1597)**

PRINCE HENRY:

I know you all, and will awhile uphold
The unyoked humour of your idleness:
Yet herein will I imitate the sun,
Who doth permit the base contagious clouds
To smother up his beauty from the world,
That, when he please again to be himself,
Being wanted, he may be more wonder'd at,
By breaking through the foul and ugly mists
Of vapours that did seem to strangle him.
If all the year were playing holidays,

the unyoked humour of your idleness = your uncontrolled and pointless jokes

vapours = clouds or gases

To sport would be as tedious as to work;
But when they seldom come, they wish'd for come,
And nothing pleaseth but rare accidents.
So, when this loose behaviour I throw off
And pay the debt I never promised,
By how much better than my word I am,
By so much shall I falsify men's hopes;
And like bright metal on a sullen ground,
My reformation, glittering o'er my fault,
Shall show more goodly and attract more eyes
Than that which hath no foil to set it off.
I'll so offend, to make offence a skill;
Redeeming time when men think least I will.

foil = opposite. In drama a foil is a character who is the opposite of the main character, so Falstaff is the foil for Prince Henry

✎ Check your understanding

The Prince's soliloquy is made up of a series of similes and metaphors. Find the quotations which make the following comparisons.

Explanation	Quotation
The Prince is like the sun, waiting to emerge from behind the 'clouds' of his gang of unruly companions.	
We enjoy holidays much more because they don't happen as often as work days.	
So we prefer surprises to the predictable.	
When the Prince becomes a reformed character, it will be like paying back more than the money you owe.	
Or showing people's predictions were wrong.	
I'll glow more brightly surrounded by dull things, and appear more precious.	
Until then, I'll carry on behaving badly in order to make my change even more of a surprise.	

💡 Viewpoints

Do you think this is a clever way to behave? Or is it dishonest and sly? Debate the issue with your classmates, think about whether you approve of this kind of behaviour, and take a vote on the Prince. Has he found a clever way to make himself popular? Or is he just using his 'friends' for his own ambitions?

Extend your learning

Consider the following questions with regard to a text you are studying.

1. How has the writer balanced monologue, duologue, and crowd scenes or set pieces?

2. Is there a place where characters reveal their inner thoughts to the audience or to each other?

3. Is the audience aware of examples of dramatic irony which some of the characters do not understand?

4. How is tension sustained and where does it break out into confrontation or climax?

5. Where is the setting for that confrontation or climax?

We have looked at ways in which characters are revealed and their impact portrayed through their dynamic relationship with others. We have also seen the creation of dramatic tension through clashes between characters and their ideas, or ways in which characters are brought into closer relationships and understandings. We have explored ways in which elements of comedy and tragedy may be present in the same work. Proud characters will express themselves in outrageous, provocative, and often funny ways. Nevertheless, hubris (the pride which goes before a fall) often brings on nemesis (unavoidable destruction).

In the play you are studying, where have you found examples of the following?

1. Tension
2. Provocation
3. Revelation
4. Hubris
5. Nemesis

Shakespeare's play *Richard III* is set out as a tragedy on the opening page. The audience would have known that Richard was doomed to meet a violent death on the battlefield. However, this tragedy, like that of *Macbeth*, gains its power from the increasing number of those close to him that Richard murders, beginning with his own brother and culminating with his young nephews, who had a better claim to the throne than Richard himself. Rather surprisingly, nevertheless, Richard keeps part of the audience's sympathy for much of the play. This is because however much he lies to other characters, he is quite honest with the audience, sharing his feelings in the form of soliloquies and asides. He takes us into his confidence. However, by the end of the play, his murderous acts have outraged the country, and his nemesis Henry Tudor has arrived in Britain to challenge his reign. Richard has just had a dream in which the ghosts of all those he has killed appeared to curse him and tell him he will lose the next day; the ghosts then visit Henry Tudor (known as 'Richmond') and tell him he will win.

Sir Laurence Olivier stars as Richard III in the 1955 film

Richard III by William Shakespeare (circa 1592)

The Ghosts vanish

KING RICHARD III starts out of his dream

KING RICHARD III

Give me another horse: bind up my wounds.
Have mercy, Jesu!—Soft! I did but dream.
O coward conscience, how dost thou afflict me!
The lights burn blue. It is now dead midnight.
Cold fearful drops stand on my trembling flesh.
What do I fear? Myself? There's none else by:
Richard loves Richard; that is, I am I.
Is there a murderer here? No. Yes, I am:
Then fly. What, from myself? Great reason why:
Lest I revenge. What, myself upon myself?
Alack, I love myself. Wherefore? For any good
That I myself have done unto myself?
O, no! alas, I rather hate myself
For hateful deeds committed by myself!
I am a villain: yet I lie. I am not.
Fool, of thyself speak well: fool, do not flatter.
My conscience hath a thousand several tongues,
And every tongue brings in a several tale,
And every tale condemns me for a villain.
Perjury, perjury, in the high'st degree
Murder, stern murder, in the direst degree;
All several sins, all used in each degree,
Throng to the bar, crying all, Guilty! Guilty!
I shall despair. There is no creature loves me;
And if I die, no soul shall pity me:
Nay, wherefore should they, since that I myself
Find in myself no pity to myself?
Methought the souls of all that I had murder'd
Came to my tent; and every one did threat
To-morrow's vengeance on the head of Richard.

Enter RATCLIFF

RATCLIFF

My lord!

KING RICHARD III

'Zounds! who is there?

soft = quietly

fly = run away

a thousand several tongues = a thousand different tongues
brings in a several tale = brings in a different story
perjury = lying

'Zounds = a curse

RATCLIFF

Ratcliff, my lord; 'tis I. The early village-cock
Hath twice done salutation to the morn;
Your friends are up, and buckle on their armour.

KING RICHARD III

O Ratcliff, I have dream'd a fearful dream!
What thinkest thou, will our friends prove all true?

RATCLIFF

No doubt, my lord.

KING RICHARD III

O Ratcliff, I fear, I fear,—

RATCLIFF

Nay, good my lord, be not afraid of shadows.

KING RICHARD III

By the apostle Paul, shadows to-night
Have struck more terror to the soul of Richard
Than can the substance of ten thousand soldiers
Armed in proof, and led by shallow Richmond.

> *The early village-cock/Hath twice done salutation to the morn* = a cockerel has crowed twice

> *will our friends prove all true?* = will our allies stay loyal?

> *armed in proof* = fully armed

✎ Check your understanding

In the soliloquy, Richard appears to be arguing with himself. Does he really want his enemy dead, or is his true enemy himself, and what he has done?

1. As he wakes up ('starts') what is Richard dreaming about?

2. Why does he personify conscience and call it a coward?

3. What does the word 'afflict' mean?

4. How does the writing make Richard's midnight fears come to life?

5. Why can't Richard believe that he is afraid of himself?

6. Why does he contradict himself?

7. How could he revenge himself on himself?

8. Why does he imagine his conscience has so many tongues and so much to say?

9. Which words does he use which show he imagines he is on trial?

10. What do the ghosts seem to want from him?

Look at how the scene continues through the duologue with Ratcliff.

11. How does Ratcliff's way of speaking, the morning before the big battle, create more tension?

12. What is Richard really afraid of?

13. What is the meaning of Ratcliff's answer to this?

14. Why is Richard still not reassured?

15. How does this scene change the audience's reaction to Richard?

Pair and share

What will Ratcliff tell another of Richard's supporters about the King? Why might their optimism about the battle be changing? Dramatize a short scene in which Ratcliff tells a friend in a duologue about what he has seen and heard and why it disturbs him.

Now have some fun with the soliloquy itself. Although these are meant to be Richard's private thoughts, what we really see is that he is arguing with himself. Mark up your copy of the speech. Which parts should be said by Repentant Richard, and which parts by the old Reckless Richard? Reckless Richard did not believe in conscience, ghosts, or God. He thought you made your own fate through violent action. He felt no need to repent.

Dramatize the soliloquy by getting two actors to represent Richard's two voices. What effect does this have, and who wins the argument?

 Viewpoints

There is no creature loves me;
And if I die, no soul shall pity me:
Nay, wherefore should they, since that I myself
Find in myself no pity to myself?

Why has Richard stopped congratulating himself on the murders he committed to obtain and hold on to the crown?

How might the audience's view of him be changing? Do we have any pity or sympathy?

It helps to remember what Richard has done. While his early victims were other politicians who have themselves committed terrible deeds or were guilty of betrayal, the murder of the young princes is different: most in the audience lose any pity for Richard at this moment (compare with the murder of Macduff's family in *Macbeth*).

Let's look at how different students have reacted to this soliloquy.

Student A

Shakespeare has made Richard afraid of himself. He feels like the ghosts that came to him were real. He started by asking for forgiveness from God. Richard is really scared of the war and what it is going to do to him. When he says 'O coward conscience', we can see that Richard does not trust himself at that moment.

Student B

When Richard wakes up from his frightening dream of the ghosts of his victims, he is shaken and very afraid. His immediate exclamation, 'Give me another horse!' is an allusion to the final scene in which he cries out 'A horse! My kingdom for a horse'. William Shakespeare here conveys Richard as a frightened man—what we as the audience were never used to. It also shows that Richard's fear for his life now is as intense as it will be when he comes to his violent end in the battlefield.

Comments

This shows sound understanding. This student knows what has just happened and sees that Richard is perhaps his own conscience, beginning to want forgiveness from a God he has always denied exists until now. A quotation is well integrated into the sentence.

Comments

This student rightly sees this moment as the true climax of the play. Richard is already anticipating the play's tragic conclusion, and the student sees the playwright at work here, showing the audience a new side to Richard's character. There is a very strong sense of the writer's choices, always the sign of a very strong answer.

Student A

His selfish thoughts then creep into his head. He tells himself that he loves himself. This is a way of boosting his own confidence. 'Is there a murderer here? No!' This phrase is dramatic because he asks himself a question and then answers it abruptly. The 'No' came with an exclamation as if he is being defensive about what he said. This then changes his mind to telling us that there is a murderer which is him. He then makes us think he is a threat to himself. 'Lest I revenge'. This is ironic knowing Richard. He loves himself too much to bring any sort of pain upon himself. He says it in the next line that 'I love myself'. Richard has too much pride in him to think of killing himself or bringing harm to himself.

Comments

This is a good answer, showing good knowledge and understanding, and integrating some well-chosen textual support. There is appreciation of what is dramatic about the language and form of expression, and what an audience will find ironic, although there is a tendency to narrate the story instead of giving direct analysis of the effect of the writer's choices.

Student B

Richard has never known love and so when he says 'Alack I love myself' it is only an attempt to cling to any hope that he is good, at least to himself, but still that is not true. He therefore goes on to say 'I rather hate myself'. It is as if Richard dismisses all the good qualities, easily replacing them with his evil characteristics. This shows that Richard is in conflict with himself. He is confused and afraid but the truth still remains clear and he states it clearly when he says 'I am a villain'.

Comments

This is an even better answer. The choice of quotations brings out Richard's inner contradictions and there is strong understanding of why he is like this—he is someone who has never known what love is. There is appreciation of Richard's tone; the student's words 'dismisses', 'conflict', and 'states it clearly' show that for the student Richard is always fighting, even if his enemy is himself.

Student B

The conflict with his conscience is like a trial and his conscience is confessing against him, accusing him of all the crimes of his lies. Richard will not 'flatter' by trying to defend himself. It is made clear here that Richard cannot deny the truth about himself that his conscience now reveals to him. 'My conscience hath a thousand several tongues and every tongue brings in a several tale', the sins that Richard has committed are numerous and they are the most gruesome and brutal of sins. This is shown by the repetition of the word 'degree' which just emphasizes the brutality of Richard when victimizing people. The audience is moved almost to pity when Richard says with finality 'I shall despair. There is no creature that loves me.' This is the plain truth and the dramatic thing is that Richard makes it an unwavering declaration. Though the audience may be moved, to Richard it is a plain truth stated emotionlessly. It is also as if he accepts defeat now and will not care, whatever will happen to him next. He is not as resourceful as he once was and it disappoints the audience somewhat to see him like this.

Comments

This becomes a model commentary on this scene. Notice the student's excellent integration of short quotations from the text and commentary on the dramatic effect of the language. There is a constant sense of the impact on the audience, as well as detailed comment on the choice of words, their repetition, and their emotive power. The student notices that the audience might feel a pity for Richard which he never really feels for himself. There is also a very interesting final and personal response to the way Richard has deteriorated as a character and how this changes the audience's reaction. There is a very strong appreciation of three things we have emphasized in this chapter:

- the craft of the playwright and the shape of the play
- the character's journey during the drama
- changes in the audience's response to and evaluation of characters.

7.7 Confrontation

Self-recognition is just one form of turning point in drama. Whereas Richard's true nemesis is arguably himself, a more conventional way of dealing with contrasting characters and their conflict is through a central dramatic showdown. The turning point leads to a decisive shift in power or status: perhaps a character who was the underdog now emerges triumphant, or a tragic figure sees the inevitability of his destiny. Certainly there will be a decisive shift in the feelings of the audience. This moment in a play is sometimes called the reversal of fortune. In the Middle Ages, fortune was seen as a wheel, with the king on top, and someone being crushed at the bottom. The goddess Fortune is a personification of fate or destiny, so, as in tragedy, the change is inevitable, and only partly under the character's control. The turning of fortune's wheel is a decisive moment in drawing the action to its climax.

Think ahead

Look at the structure of the drama text you are studying. Can you identify a turning point?

1. Where does the wheel of fortune turn in your text?

2. Whose fortune goes down?

3. Who emerges on top?

4. Why does this happen?

5. Where do the sympathies of the audience lie?

6. Do they change too?

7. How does the change in fortune relate to the fate of the characters?

8. What does the reversal of fortune suggest about the themes of the play?

9. How has the writer dramatized this: through action, duologue, or monologue?

10. How does this prepare the audience for the play's climax?

Not everyone will agree about where the turning point lies. In *Richard III*, it could be the death of the princes (which happens offstage, like many key moments) or the moment Richard orders their deaths, or it might not come until later, perhaps in the soliloquy we've discussed. In *A Midsummer Night's Dream* it comes when Oberon and Puck bring the lovers back into their correct pairings and remove the effects of the love juice from Titania, bringing the madness of the night to an end. These are all points you can debate and discuss.

Rattigan's *The Winslow Boy* dramatizes a once-famous case about a 14-year-old naval cadet Ronnie, summarily dismissed without a fair investigation for allegedly stealing a postal order from a fellow student. In this scene from Act 3, Ronnie's sister, Catherine, is under pressure from her fiancé, John Watherstone, whose father disapproves of the family pursuing a case against the British establishment. This dramatic confrontation makes it clear to the audience the price the family are paying for their fight to prove that Ronnie was falsely accused, and it ensures that the focus of the last act will be on the relationship between Catherine, a Liberal suffragette, and Sir Robert, the Conservative lawyer defending Ronnie.

The Winslow Boy by Terence Rattigan (1946)

CATHERINE. (*Quietly.*) His innocence or guilt aren't important to me. They are to my father. Not to me. I believe he didn't do it; but I may be wrong. To prove that he didn't do it is of hardly more interest to me than the identity of the college servant, or whoever it was, who did it. All that I care about is that people should know that a Government Department has ignored a fundamental human right and that it should be forced to acknowledge it. That's all that's important to me.

JOHN. But, darling, after all those long noble words, it does really resolve itself to a question of a fourteen-year-old kid and a five bob postal order, doesn't it?

five bob postal order = the equivalent of a cheque for five shillings, a small sum of money

CATHERINE. Yes, it does.

JOHN. (*Reasonably.*) Well now, look. There's a European war blowing up, there's a coal strike on, there's a fair chance of civil war in Ireland, and there's a hundred and one other things on the horizon at the moment that I think you genuinely could call *important*. And yet, with all that on its mind, the House of Commons takes a whole day to discuss him (*Pointing to RONNIE.*) and his bally postal order. Surely you must see that's a little out of proportion –

bally postal order = trivial thing

Pause. CATHERINE *raises her head slowly.*

CATHERINE. (*With some spirit.*) All I know is, John, that if ever the time comes that the House of Commons has so much on its mind that it can't find time to discuss a Ronnie Winslow and his bally postal order, this country will be a far poorer place than it is now. (*Wearily.*) But you needn't go on, John dear. You've said quite enough. I entirely see your point of view.

JOHN. I don't know whether you realize that all this publicity you're getting is making the name of Winslow a bit of a – well –

CATHERINE. (*Steadily.*) A nation-wide laughing-stock, your father said.

JOHN. Well, that's putting it a bit steep. But people do find the case a bit ridiculous, you know. I mean, I get chaps coming up to me in the mess all the time and saying: 'I say, is it true you're going to marry the Winslow girl? You'd better be careful. You'll find yourself up in front of the House of Lords for pinching the Adjutant's bath.' Things like that. They're not awfully funny –

chaps coming up to me in the mess = *John's fellow soldiers speaking to him in the common room*

CATHERINE. That's nothing. They're singing a verse about us at the Alhambra –
Winslow one day went to heaven
And found a poor fellow in quod.
The fellow said I didn't do it,
So naturally Winslow sued God.

poor fellow in quod = *unfortunate man in prison*

JOHN. Well, darling – you see –

CATHERINE. Yes. I see. (*Quietly.*) Do you want to marry me, John?

JOHN. What?

CATHERINE. I said: Do you want to marry me?

JOHN. Well, of course I do. You know I do. We've been engaged for over a year now. Have I ever wavered before?

CATHERINE. No. Never before.

JOHN. (*Correcting himself.*) I'm not wavering now. Not a bit I'm only telling you what I think is the best course for us to take.

CATHERINE. But isn't it already too late? Even if we gave up the case, would you still want to marry – the Winslow girl?

JOHN. All that would blow over in no time.

CATHERINE. (*Slowly.*) And we'd have the allowance –

JOHN. Yes. We would.

CATHERINE. And that's so important –

the allowance = *money paid to John by his father (he can't make enough money on his officer's salary for both of them)*

JOHN. (*Quietly.*) It is, darling. I'm sorry, but you can't shame me into saying it isn't.

CATHERINE. I didn't mean to shame you –

JOHN. Oh, yes you did. I know that tone of voice.

CATHERINE. (*Humbly.*) I'm sorry.

JOHN. (*Confidently.*) Well, now – what's the answer?

CATHERINE. (*Slowly.*) I love you, John, and I want to be your wife.

JOHN. Well, then, that's all I want to know. Darling! I was sure nothing so stupid and trivial could possibly come between us.

He kisses her. She responds wearily. The telephone rings. After a pause she releases herself and picks up the receiver.

Check your understanding

Act 3 is a masterpiece of sustained dramatic tension, with the case going badly and its effect on the family becoming clear. The only character who does not contribute to the tension is Ronnie himself, who is onstage but asleep throughout most of the act.

1. What is the point of principle that Catherine believes they are defending?

2. How does John suggest that the case is not worthwhile?

3. How does Rattigan introduce the context of Britain in 1910?

4. Why does Catherine believe the case still matters?

5. What kind of jokes are people making about the Winslows?

6. Why doesn't John find them funny?

7. How does Rattigan increase the tension and slow the pace of the scene?

8. How do stage directions indicate the way John puts Catherine under pressure?

9. How does the discussion of the allowance keep up the tension between John and Catherine?

10. What indications does Rattigan give that John is wrong to be so confident that he has won the argument?

 Pair and share

Practise this duologue together. Remember that the play shows audiences a time when women, even suffragettes like Catherine, were meant to submit to men, and be dependent on them. Try performing the dialogue in two different ways:

1. Catherine takes the traditional view and still desperately wants to marry John. She is doing what she can to explain her views, but accepts that the case is lost.

2. Catherine still believes strongly in the cause and is being sarcastic towards John. She is fighting her corner because she believes the engagement is already over.

Both interpretations are possible. Which did you find more convincing and why? Could the best performance combine a little of each? Try this out.

Catherine's apparent submission proves very temporary. The telephone call is an effective dramatic device to remind the audience of the offstage drama. It brings in Sir Robert and Catherine's father, Arthur, to whom Sir Robert communicates the news of progress at last in the case. An argument in Parliament has led to the approval of the Winslows' Petition of Right.

The Winslow Boy by Terence Rattigan (1946)

SIR ROBERT. …The case of Winslow versus Rex can now therefore come to Court.

There is a pause. ARTHUR *and* CATHERINE *stare at him unbelievingly.*

(*At length.*) Well, sir. What are my instructions?

Winslow versus Rex = *Winslow against the Crown*

ARTHUR. (*Slowly.*) The decision is no longer mine, sir. You must ask my daughter.

SIR ROBERT. What are my instructions, Miss Winslow?

CATHERINE *looks down at the sleeping* RONNIE. ARTHUR *is watching her intently.* SIR ROBERT, *munching sandwiches, is also looking at her.*

CATHERINE. (*In a flat voice.*) Do you need my instructions, Sir Robert? Aren't they already on the Petition? Doesn't it say: Let Right be done?

> **the Petition** = the Petition of *Right allowing the Winslows to sue the Crown (the British state)*

JOHN *makes a move of protest towards her. She does not look at him. He turns abruptly to the door.*

JOHN. (*Furiously.*) Kate! Good night.

He goes out. SIR ROBERT, *with languid speculation, watches him go.*

SIR ROBERT. (*His mouth full.*) Well, then – we must endeavour to see that it is.

 Check your understanding

The audience should detect that there is tension up to the phone call. The confrontation between Catherine and John has not been resolved and we should not be sure about Catherine's decision until the very end of the act, making this the climax and turning point of the play. Of course, this is helped by the action offstage, which we only hear about from Sir Robert's account of the telephone call.

1. Sir Robert does not know about the tension between Catherine and John. Where do we see this?

2. How do Rattigan's stage directions indicate the emotions of the different characters here?

3. Why does Catherine repeat the words of the Petition of Right?

4. Actions speak louder than words: where do we see this in John's response?

5. Whose side are we on? Which character is the audience encouraged to sympathize with most, and why?

💡 **Viewpoints**

This is the climactic end to Act 3, and the last act sees the inevitable playing out of the last stages of the drama. Consider the different viewpoints of the case and what it means for Catherine, for John, for Sir Robert and for Ronnie. Is it worth damaging families and relationships for a point of principle?

Imagine that Ronnie is not in fact asleep during the last part of this act. What are his views now about the case and its consequences? Write his thoughts.

Extend your learning

To explore *The Winslow Boy* further, there is a superb film version directed by David Mamet, a famous contemporary US playwright. Consider the changes he makes and the reasons behind them. Are there still individual rights worth fighting for today, whatever the cost? What are they for you?

Have a class debate on the motion 'Some principles are more important than family happiness'.

The Greeks called the turning point of a play **peripeteia**. Turning points often involve a decisive shift. Consider how the mood of the audience is altered by the tone and language of the characters, and the way they perform their actions.

Identify the turning point in the play you are studying. Write an essay on it, considering these questions.

1. Does everyone agree on where it is?
2. Why do you think the turning point is at this moment?
3. How does the writing make this moment tense and dramatic?
4. How does it change the way the audience see the characters and action?
5. Was it inevitable that things would turn out this way?
6. Which issues and attitudes does it make the audience think about?
7. How does it prepare the audience for the play's climax?

7.8 Everything is connected: how plays end

We will now look at the ways in which two texts end, drawing the lines of their plots into a satisfactory conclusion. As we have seen, plays are driven by audience expectation and theatrical convention. In chapter 2 we explored the comic convention of the happy ending. Shakespeare's comedies are superbly staged in order to bring everyone together at the end and to suggest fairytale marriages which ensure characters 'live happily ever after' but there is often a bitter element here too. Not everyone is included in the 'happy ending'. What happens to Antonio at the end of *Twelfth Night*?

> **KEY TERM**
>
> **peripeteia** = in tragedy, the reversal of fortune for the tragic hero or heroine. More simply the 'turning point'.

Think ahead

1. How does the play you are studying bring characters together at the end?
2. Will the consequences be comic, tragic, or a mixture?
3. Is that accident (coincidence) or fate (destiny)?
4. Are some characters excluded from the play's resolution?
5. What do you think will become of them?

We will look at extracts from two plays. One is mainly comic, the other tragic.

Shakespeare's *Twelfth Night* was written towards the end of his great comic period and it has some darker elements. Indeed at the very end of the play, the clown will sing a song which is later repeated by the Fool in the tragedy *King Lear*. Various comic consequences have resulted from the confusion between two twins washed up on the shore of Illyria, each thinking that the other was dead. The girl, Viola, has disguised herself as a boy (Cesario). Olivia, a countess, has fallen in love with 'Cesario', to the disappointment of Duke Orsino, who loved her himself and used Cesario as a servant to deliver messages of love to her. Now the boy twin, Sebastian, has arrived, and is mistaken for 'Cesario'. Unlike his sister, he quickly agrees to marry Olivia (who is very beautiful as well as rich) and he has no trouble beating up the foolish Sir Andrew and Olivia's wicked uncle Sir Toby, who has been trying to marry her to Sir Andrew, as a way of getting money. Sir Toby and others have also played a cruel trick on Malvolio, Olivia's chief servant, convincing him that Olivia is in love with him, just for a laugh. Malvolio has ended up being locked up as a madman.

Twelfth Night by William Shakespeare (1602)

Enter SIR ANDREW

SIR ANDREW

For the love of God, a surgeon! Send one presently to Sir Toby.

OLIVIA

What's the matter?

SIR ANDREW

He has broke my head across and has given Sir Toby a bloody coxcomb too: for the love of God, your help! I had rather than forty pound I were at home.

OLIVIA

Who has done this, Sir Andrew?

SIR ANDREW

The count's gentleman, one Cesario: we took him for a coward, but he's the very devil incardinate.

DUKE ORSINO

My gentleman, Cesario?

SIR ANDREW

'Od's lifelings, here he is! You broke my head for nothing; and that that I did, I was set on to do't by Sir Toby.

presently = right away

a bloody coxcomb = a bleeding head

devil incardinate = Sir Andrew means the devil incarnate (made flesh)

'Od's lifelings = a mildly blasphemous oath

I was set on to do't = I was set up or made to do it

VIOLA

Why do you speak to me? I never hurt you:
You drew your sword upon me without cause;
But I bespoke you fair, and hurt you not.

SIR ANDREW

If a bloody coxcomb be a hurt, you have hurt me: I
think you set nothing by a bloody coxcomb.

Enter SIR TOBY BELCH and Clown

Here comes Sir Toby halting; you shall hear more:
but if he had not been in drink, he would have
tickled you othergates than he did.

DUKE ORSINO

How now, gentleman! how is't with you?

SIR TOBY BELCH

That's all one: has hurt me, and there's the end
on't. Sot, didst see Dick surgeon, sot?

CLOWN

O, he's drunk, Sir Toby, an hour agone; his eyes
were set at eight i' the morning.

SIR TOBY BELCH

Then he's a rogue, and a passy measures panyn: I
hate a drunken rogue.

OLIVIA

Away with him! Who hath made this havoc with them?

SIR ANDREW

I'll help you, Sir Toby, because we'll be dressed together.

SIR TOBY BELCH

Will you help? An ass-head and a coxcomb and a
knave, a thin-faced knave, a gull!

OLIVIA

Get him to bed, and let his hurt be look'd to.

Exeunt Clown, FABIAN, SIR TOBY BELCH, and SIR ANDREW

I bespoke you fair = I said nice things to you

halting = limping

he would have tickled you othergates = he would have beaten you (if he were not drunk)

sot = fool

passy measures panyn = this is a strange drunken insult (no one is sure what it means!)

coxcomb = (here) fool

gull = gullible fool

let his hurt be look'd to = look after his injury

Exeunt = they all go out (together or separately?)

1. Why is the 'Cesario' who Sir Andrew has just met not a 'coward' but perfectly capable of beating Sir Andrew up when he thinks he is being insulted?

2. Why is he so shocked to see 'Cesario' next to the Duke?

3. Why does Viola deny having done anything to hurt Sir Andrew?

4. How can we tell that Sir Toby is drunk and that he is angry when someone stands up to him?

5. Why is the Clown's reaction ironic?

6. Why does Sir Toby now reveal his true feelings about Sir Andrew?

7. What difference does it make if Sir Andrew and Sir Toby leave separately?

8. Although this scene is funny, why might some in the audience feel the darker elements are stronger?

So a case of mistaken identity has caused all sorts of problems, as so often happens in comedy. Shakespeare is tying up the various different strands of his plot, but he is also making it clear that although there will be a happy ending for some, it will not be so for everyone. Some characters will not get married or join the final circle of happiness, some of the jokes have got out of hand, and some of the comic characters are no longer as funny as we once thought they were. Many call this play 'bittersweet'. Let us see what happens next.

Actors playing the twins in *Twelfth Night*

Twelfth Night by William Shakespeare (1602)

Enter SEBASTIAN

SEBASTIAN

> I am sorry, madam, I have hurt your kinsman:
> But, had it been the brother of my blood,
> I must have done no less with wit and safety.
> You throw a strange regard upon me, and by that
> I do perceive it hath offended you:
> Pardon me, sweet one, even for the vows
> We made each other but so late ago.

DUKE ORSINO

> One face, one voice, one habit, and two persons,
> A natural perspective, that is and is not!

SEBASTIAN

> Antonio, O my dear Antonio!
> How have the hours rack'd and tortured me,
> Since I have lost thee!

You throw a strange regard upon me = you are looking at me in an odd way

A natural perspective = a natural mirror

rack'd = a reference to an instrument of torture

ANTONIO

Sebastian are you?

SEBASTIAN

Fear'st thou that, Antonio?

ANTONIO

How have you made division of yourself?
An apple, cleft in two, is not more twin
Than these two creatures. Which is Sebastian?

OLIVIA

Most wonderful!

SEBASTIAN

Do I stand there? I never had a brother;
Nor can there be that deity in my nature,
Of here and every where. I had a sister,
Whom the blind waves and surges have devour'd.
Of charity, what kin are you to me?
What countryman? What name? What parentage?

> ***that deity in my nature*** = *I am not a god able to be everywhere at once*

VIOLA

Of Messaline: Sebastian was my father;
Such a Sebastian was my brother too,
So went he suited to his watery tomb:
If spirits can assume both form and suit
You come to fright us.

> ***So went he suited to his watery tomb*** = *that is what he looked like when he drowned*

SEBASTIAN

A spirit I am indeed;
But am in that dimension grossly clad
Which from the womb I did participate.
Were you a woman, as the rest goes even,
I should my tears let fall upon your cheek,
And say 'Thrice-welcome, drowned Viola!'

VIOLA

My father had a mole upon his brow.

SEBASTIAN

And so had mine.

VIOLA

And died that day when Viola from her birth
Had number'd thirteen years.

SEBASTIAN

O, that record is lively in my soul!

He finished indeed his mortal act
That day that made my sister thirteen years.

VIOLA

If nothing lets to make us happy both
But this my masculine usurp'd attire,
Do not embrace me till each circumstance
Of place, time, fortune, do cohere and jump
That I am Viola: which to confirm,
I'll bring you to a captain in this town,
Where lie my maiden weeds; by whose gentle help
I was preserved to serve this noble count.
All the occurrence of my fortune since
Hath been between this lady and this lord.

do cohere and jump = *all prove together*

SEBASTIAN

[*To OLIVIA*] So comes it, lady, you have been mistook:
But nature to her bias drew in that.
You would have been contracted to a maid;
Nor are you therein, by my life, deceived,
You are betroth'd both to a maid and man.

nature to her bias drew in that = *that was things working out according to nature*

DUKE ORSINO

Be not amazed; right noble is his blood.
If this be so, as yet the glass seems true,
I shall have share in this most happy wreck.

To VIOLA

Boy, thou hast said to me a thousand times
Thou never shouldst love woman like to me.

VIOLA

And all those sayings will I overswear;
And those swearings keep as true in soul
As doth that orbed continent the fire
That severs day from night.

that orbed continent = *the sun*

DUKE ORSINO

Give me thy hand;
And let me see thee in thy woman's weeds.

thy woman's weeds = *in your woman's clothes*

VIOLA

The captain that did bring me first on shore
Hath my maid's garments: he upon some action
Is now in durance, at Malvolio's suit,
A gentleman, and follower of my lady's.

in durance = *under arrest (this is a reminder of Malvolio's existence!)*

✎ Check your understanding

1. Who is the 'sweet one' whom Sebastian is addressing?

2. Why is she lost for words?

3. Why does the Duke think that the existence of two 'Cesarios' is like a miracle?

4. Antonio's presence is important. He is the sailor who saved Sebastian's life, so he knows his true identity. Why is he also confused?

5. How will Olivia say the lines 'most wonderful'?

6. How should a director stage this scene to ensure that Viola and Sebastian see each other as late as possible?

7. Why can't the twins themselves quite believe that the scene is real?

8. How does Shakespeare use coincidence to achieve **recognition** between the twins?

9. Why does Viola now feel confident enough to admit that she is a woman?

10. What does Sebastian mean by 'nature to her bias drew in that'?

11. How does this ending ensure that both couples will live happily ever after? (You might compare it with the 'happy ending' of *The Importance of Being Earnest* in chapter 2).

12. Why does the mention of Malvolio remind the audience of a part of the play which has not ended so happily and what is the effect of this?

💬 Pair and share

What will Viola and Sebastian have to say to each other? Write a script which will dramatize their dialogue using your own words, but keeping the same optimistic and robust character Shakespeare uses here.

KEY TERM

recognition = when a character understands something about himself or herself.

💡 Viewpoints

Do we really believe that Orsino can so easily switch from loving Olivia to loving Viola?

Are we confident that Olivia, who fell in love with 'Cesario' when he was played by Viola, will really be happy with the much more masculine Sebastian?

> *And all those sayings will I overswear;*
> *And those swearings keep as true in soul*
> *As doth that orbed continent the fire*
> *That severs day from night.*

1. How does Viola's language here make sure that we believe in the poetry of this moment, even if we are not sure that it is 'realistic'?

2. What simile does she use?

3. Why does she refer to her 'soul'?

4. What does she mean by suggesting that love has more to do with the 'soul' than the body, or its gender?

5. Do you agree?

It depends how you treat comedy: romance is always close to being a fairytale and therefore not to be confused with realism. In the fairytale world, as we saw with *A Midsummer Night's Dream* in chapter 2, all is well which ends well, whatever the confusions in the middle part.

However, there are very realistic (and more cruel) aspects of the comedy in *Twelfth Night*, and they are acted out by humans, not by fairies. There is no happy ending for Sir Toby or for Malvolio.

a) Do you prefer comedy to have a fantasy element?

b) Or should it be close to real life?

c) If comedy is realistic, do we learn something from it?

Comedy which teaches us something about real life, or makes fun of things which we normally take seriously is often called satire. Satirical endings are rarely as happy as comic ones. Satire often has the effect of shocking an audience, as well as making them laugh.

Extend your learning

Answer these questions with reference to the set text which you are studying.

1. What is learned or recognized by the audience at the end of the play?
2. Is the ending happy, sad, or bittersweet?
3. Would you classify the play as comedy, tragedy, tragic-comedy, or **satire**?
4. How realistic do you find the ending?
5. Is it important for audiences to use their imagination, or should they expect an ending which is close to real life?
6. Are the 'loose ends' all tied up at the end of the play? Or are there discordant elements, which don't fit in with that sense of harmony?
7. What does the audience feel like at the end?
8. Why did the writer want to leave them with that particular feeling?

KEY TERM

satire = using comedy and irony to mock convention, provoke the audience and teach lessons about life, often by shock effects.

7.9 Recognition

We have seen that recognition is an important element at the end of a drama. Characters recognize something about themselves or about others, and realize something that perhaps we in the audience realized much earlier. However, not everyone wants to recognize what a play appears to be telling them, and not all characters share in the revelations, recognitions, and reconciliations at the end of a comedy. Characters are even less likely to achieve recognition or reconciliation at the end of a tragedy.

In a serious or tragic play, we should expect disturbing, discordant elements, and tears, not laughter. If everything is connected up and explained, it might not be in the way characters like, and they will often learn uncomfortable things about themselves.

Let us explore a well-known example from mid-twentieth-century British drama.

Priestley's *An Inspector Calls* is noticeable for having two endings. The first comes when the Inspector closes his notebook, shuts the case, and makes a powerful speech which will provoke the audience, as well as the Birling family. It makes the message to the audience very clear and obvious. The play is set in 1912, before the First World War, but was first staged in 1946, just after the Second World War. It therefore makes very clear the collapse of the class-based culture of Britain that existed before the twentieth century (as we saw in chapter 2). It clearly blames that collapse on the ways in which that culture ignored and blamed the poor, represented here by Eva Smith, who lost her jobs because of Mr Birling and Sheila Birling, became the pregnant mistress of Eric Birling, and finally was turned down by Mrs Birling's charity committee.

A scene from *An Inspector Calls*

An Inspector Calls **by J.B. Priestley (1946)**

Eric   Come on, don't just look like that. Tell me – tell me – what happened?

Inspector   (*with calm authority*) I'll tell you. She went to your mother's committee for help, after she'd done with you. Your mother refused that help.

Eric   (*nearly at breaking point*) Then – you killed her. She came to you to protect me – and you turned her away – yes, and you killed her – and the child she'd have had too – my child – your own grandchild – you killed them both – damn you, damn you –

Mrs Birling   (*very distressed now*) No – Eric – please – I didn't know – I didn't understand –

Eric   (*almost threatening her*) You don't understand anything. You never did. You never even tried – you –

Sheila   (*frightened*) Eric, don't – don't –

Birling   (*furious, intervening*) Why, you hysterical young fool – get back – or I'll –

Inspector   (*taking charge, masterfully*) Stop!

They are suddenly quiet, staring at him.

And be quiet for a moment and listen to me. I don't need to know any more. Neither do you. This girl killed herself – and died a horrible death. But each of you helped to kill her. Remember that. Never forget it. (*He looks from one to the other of them carefully.*) But then I don't think you ever will. Remember what you did, Mrs Birling. You turned her away when she most needed help. You refused her even the pitiable little bit of organized charity you had in your power to grant her. Remember what you did –

Eric   (*unhappily*) My God – I'm not likely to forget.

Inspector   Just used her for the end of a stupid drunken evening as if she was an animal, a thing, not a person. No, you won't forget. (*He looks at Sheila.*)

Sheila   (*bitterly*) I know. I had her turned out of a job. I started it.

Inspector   You helped but you didn't start it. (*Rather savagely, to Birling.*) You started it. She wanted twenty-five shillings a week instead of twenty-two and sixpence. You made her pay a heavy price for that. And now she'll make you pay a heavier price still.

Birling   (*unhappily*) Look, Inspector – I'd give thousands – yes, thousands –

Inspector   You are offering the money at the wrong time, Mr Birling. (*He makes a move as if concluding the session, possibly shutting up notebook, etc. Then surveys them sardonically.*) No, I don't think any of you will forget. Nor that young man, Croft, though he at least had some affection for her and made her happy for a time. Well, Eva Smith's gone. You can't do her any more harm. And you can't do her any good now, either. You can't even say, 'I'm sorry, Eva Smith.'

Sheila   (*who is crying quietly*) That's the worst of it.

Inspector   But just remember this. One Eva Smith has gone – but there are millions and millions and millions of Eva Smiths and John Smiths still left with us with their lives, their hopes and fears, their suffering and chance of happiness, all intertwined with our lives, and what we think and say and do. We don't live alone. We are members of one body. We are responsible for each other. And I tell you that the time will soon come when, if men will not learn that lesson, then they will be taught it in fire and blood and anguish. Good night.

This is an extremely powerful and effective piece of writing. It is full of tension and forms a strong climax to the play. All the different strands of the story are now connected, and they all condemn the Birling family for their selfishness. The Inspector becomes a mouthpiece for the writer's view on society—'we are members of one body'—which is conveyed directly in the rhetoric of the Inspector's speech.

✎ Check your understanding

1. Look at the stage directions first. How do they show the contrast between the emotions of the Birling family and those of the Inspector?

2. Do the stage directions also suggest that the older Birlings have slightly different feelings to the younger ones?

3. Why has the writer given Eric such broken sentences? What does he want the actor to show about him?

4. What does the audience see about the relationship between Eric and his mother?

5. How does the Inspector use language in order to take control? What do we notice about his sentences and the pace of his speech?

6. Why does he keep repeating the pronoun 'you' to Mrs Birling?

7. What is interesting about her reaction?

8. What does Birling not understand when the Inspector says he must 'pay'?

9. How does the Inspector underline the tragedy of Eva's death?

10. How does he use Eva's death as a metaphor?

11. Where does he use patterns of three to give his speech rhetorical power and shape?

12. What kind of future does he seem to be predicting? How does this add to the supernatural element of his character?

💡 Viewpoints

Debate and discuss the questions which follow.

1. Why do you think the Birlings are shocked and surprised by the Inspector's message?

2. What do you think were their views about society?

3. Why do you think Priestley wanted us to notice such a big difference between the older and younger Birlings?

4. Look back at chapter 3 and the way we explored conflict between generations. Is Priestley saying something about a changing world?

5. What would an audience in 1946 think about these characters from 1912?

6. Why would they criticize their attitudes?

The dramatic effectiveness of the play depends on its impact on the audience.

7. Why would the play have made such a powerful impression after the Second World War?

8. Do rich people still feel little responsibility for the poor?

9. How well would this play work today, or outside the UK?

10. Is it just a 'period piece' or can it work for today's audiences?

For further research, look at www.aninspectorcalls.com. This is a record of the Stephen Daldry production which was so successful in 1992 that it had a year on Broadway, a major revival in 2009, and finished a UK tour in 2012. Clearly audiences still find that the play has plenty to say to them.

However, the first extract is not quite the end of the play. Mr Birling phones around and proves the 'Inspector' was not a real police officer and that no suicidal young woman called Eva Smith had been brought to the hospital ('infirmary'). He tries to convince the others in his family that it makes everything all right, even though they have confessed that all the events the Inspector asked them about did really happen. What does this suggest to the audience about the 'truth' of theatre?

At the very end of the play, the phone suddenly rings. This kind of ending to a play is sometimes called a **coda** (or tail). In this case the tail has a sting.

Daldry production of *An Inspector Calls*

***An Inspector Calls* by J.B. Priestley (1946)**

Birling   (pointing to Eric and Sheila) Now look at the pair of them – the famous younger generation who know it all. And they can't even take a joke –

The telephone rings sharply. There is a moment's complete silence. Birling goes to answer it.

Yes?…Mr Birling speaking…What? – here-

But obviously the other person has rung off. He puts the telephone down slowly and looks in a panic-stricken fashion at the others.

Birling   That was the police. A girl has just died – on her way to the infirmary – after swallowing some disinfectant. And a police inspector is on his way here – to ask some – questions –

As they stare guiltily and dumbfounded, the curtain falls.

KEY TERMS

coda = tail end after the main action, like an epilogue (see chapter 2).

anti-climax = something which contrasts with the climax expected.

Extend your learning

1. Why follow the climax of the play with what at first seems an '**anti-climax**'?
2. Was the Inspector a ghost? (He is called Inspector Goole.)
3. What game did Priestley play with realism here?
4. Why did he want the play to have a fantasy element?
5. How do the stage directions show the effect of taking that fantasy away?
6. How much attention is he suggesting the Birlings would pay to a warning which was 'art' rather than 'reality'?
7. What is he suggesting to the audience about the relationship between theatre and real life?
8. How has he successfully played games with our understanding of time?

Looking at the way your own set play ends, answer the following questions.

a) Does it conclude with a climax? Or is there an element of anti-climax?
b) Is your play entirely realistic, or is there a sense of fantasy or magic?
c) We have seen that dramatists sometimes end their plays with an epilogue or coda. How does this help the audience to reflect on what they have seen?
d) What do you think is the lingering impact of the ending on the audience? What will it make them think about?
e) Does the ending fit audience expectations, or will it surprise them?
f) Will the audience feel comfortable or uncomfortable at the end of the play?

Looking back

We have looked closely at extracts from dramas of different periods to accompany your study of your set text, in order to develop your appreciation of dramatic effectiveness. This phrase refers to the impact drama makes on a live audience in the theatre. As we have seen, this depends on the structure of the text, as well as the language and humour or tension of the scenes portrayed.

To reinforce your understanding, look back at the extracts we have studied. Audience expectations and the conventions of theatre are provoked in different ways in the scenes we have studied. We are often surprised. Write notes on what you have observed about the following.

1. The ways characters and situations are introduced
2. What we learn from the ways in which characters develop and differ
3. How playing and performing in theatre can be serious as well as comic
4. How drama comes from a clash of ideas as well as a clash of characters
5. How the turning point of a drama changes the audience's sympathies
6. How confrontation builds to a climax or catastrophe
7. How resolutions do not always bring everything together
8. How audiences are encouraged to evaluate and think about the ways in which plays end

Can you apply these ideas to your own set text? Draw plot lines for your play, showing the sequence of developments in the play.

Don't just map the journey that the main character or characters have been on, although this is always useful. Map the journey the audience has made, and bring out the moments when they have been surprised.

For further advice on working with your drama text, look at the website materials.

Studying prose texts

In chapter 3, we looked at how to study prose texts by exploring the structure of the short story. Novels follow a similar structure to short stories, but on a much larger scale. Reading the class novel will look at first like the most daunting challenge of your course, and it is definitely a good idea to begin your preparation early. You will certainly notice more about the novel when you re-read it, knowing how the narrative will end, so this chapter will help you to make both a first reading and a re-reading of the prose text chosen for your course.

The emphasis in this chapter will be on language as well as structure. Once again, a lot of the work will be based on looking closely at extracts, as will much of the work you and your teachers do while you are reading your set texts. This enables you to look more closely at the techniques used by prose writers. However, you will also need your own notes to track your progress through the prose text, including:

- a brief note on what happens in each chapter
- notes on the principal characters as they are introduced
- quotations to accompany those characters—what they say and what is said about them (add the page numbers so that you can find them again)
- notes about the principal themes and ideas of the novel as they emerge: these may be based around different settings, different periods of time or the kinds of relationships which emerge.

In online chapter 10, you will find advice for re-reading set texts and improving your essay writing skills for prose.

LEARNING POINTS

- ▶ To understand and appreciate how narrative texts work through description, dialogue and development
- ▶ To analyse the significance of the narrative voice or viewpoint
- ▶ To explore prose writers' use of mystery and tension
- ▶ To explore and evaluate different kinds of narrative closure

8.1 Openings

Writers need to capture the reader's attention quickly at the beginning of a piece of prose fiction, whether it is a novel or short story. When you begin your set prose text you are at the beginning of a long journey and the writer needs to convince you that it will be an interesting one. It is common to begin a story 'in media res', which is a Latin term meaning 'in the middle of things'—in other words, to plunge the reader into the middle of some action and for them to discover the background or backstory gradually later, through narration or flashback. A reader, just like a theatre audience, likes to be plunged into the action right away. Readers like to have a sense of where the writing is set, and what kind of writing (genre) they will be reading, but they also like a sense of mystery. While they want to be introduced to interesting characters, they also want to see them doing something immediately. The explanations can always come later.

Write a short review (200 words) of a novel or short story you have read for yourself recently (not part of your course or on the syllabus). Write down what you liked about its:

▶ action

▶ characters

▶ genre

▶ setting.

Share your review with the class. What kind of stories are most popular? Action? Gothic? Fantasy? Realistic? Comic? Detective stories? Ghosts? Vampires? What kind of characters are most appealing, and why?

The novels or stories you will study in depth for the Cambridge Literature in English course may not be the same type that you read for fun or to relax, although you may notice that they have certain characteristics in common with them. Novels for study need a certain kind of depth and engagement with the real world—their main purpose cannot be simply to escape from the everyday. They also need a certain complexity both of language and ideas in order to help you to meet the assessment objectives which you know are so important to your course. They therefore need to be substantial and canonical texts, which we study either because of their influence and impact, or because of the ways in which they engage with the culture which produced them. However, we also hope that you will find them well-written and entertaining!

Edgar Allan Poe (1809–1849) was an American poet and professional writer best known for his short stories. He often wrote within the Gothic genre, producing stories of suspense and horror. He wrote at the time when the modern United States was beginning to emerge, but many of his influences were European, such as E.T.A. Hoffmann. He was drawn to write frequently about the past and with European settings, and invented the genre of the detective story. He was little known in his own time and had a troubled life, but his rich yet morbid imagination and extravagant prose style had a wide influence on later writers, especially in the horror and short story genres. He was particularly disturbed by the idea of things being buried alive, or living on after death.

Edgar Allan Poe

'The Fall of the House of Usher' (1839) is perhaps his best-known story. The narrator is visiting the home of his friend Roderick Usher. Roderick, a hyper-sensitive artist, and his sister Madeline are the last remaining children of the house of Usher and both are doomed. The narrator can already sense this as he makes his way to the house.

'The Fall of the House of Usher' by Edgar Allan Poe' (1839)

…when I again uplifted my eyes to the house itself, from its image in the pool, there grew in my mind a strange fancy – a fancy so ridiculous, indeed, that I but mention it to show the vivid force of the sensations which oppressed me. I had so worked upon my imagination as really to believe that about the whole mansion and domain there hung an atmosphere peculiar to themselves and their immediate vicinity – an atmosphere which had no affinity with the air of heaven, but which had reeked up from the decayed trees, and the gray wall, and the silent tarn – a pestilent and mystic vapour, dull, sluggish, faintly discernible, and leaden hued.

An illustration of the mansion

Shaking off from my spirit what *must* have been a dream, I scanned more narrowly the real aspect of the building. Its principal feature seemed to be that of an excessive antiquity. The discoloration of ages had been great. Minute *fungi* overspread the whole exterior, hanging in a fine tangled web-work from the eaves. Yet all this was apart from any extraordinary dilapidation. No portion of the masonry had fallen; and there appeared to be a wild inconsistency between its still perfect adaptation of parts, and the crumbling condition of the individual stones. In this there was much that reminded me of the specious totality of old wood-work which has rotted for long years in some neglected vault, with no disturbance from the breath of the external air. Beyond this indication of extensive decay, however, the fabric gave little token of instability. Perhaps the eye of a scrutinising observer might have discovered a barely perceptible fissure, which, extending from the roof of the building in front, made its way down the wall in a zigzag direction, until it became lost in the sullen waters of the tarn.

Noticing these things, I rode over a short causeway to the house. A servant in waiting took my horse and I entered the Gothic archway of the hall. A valet, of stealthy step, thence conducted me, in silence, through many dark and intricate passages in my progress to the *studio* of his master.

Check your understanding

When you begin studying a novel or short story, you should first pay attention to who is telling you the story. Here there is a first-person narrator, and it is retrospective, in other words the narrator is looking back after the events of the story. He therefore has the benefit of knowing how the story will end, and that influences the way he sees things and describes them to you.

1. Which words indicate that the narrator is lost in his own imagination when he looks at the house?

2. If the atmosphere has 'no affinity with the air of heaven' what does it resemble?

3. What is remarkable about the building itself and how does the narrator reveal that it is both aged and decayed?

4. What would you normally find in a 'neglected vault with no disturbance from the breath of the external air'?

5. Why do you think the narrator especially draws your attention to 'a barely perceptible fissure', a crack going from the roof of the house to the 'tarn' or lake? What does this suggest to you about the house?

6. The 'House of Usher' could refer either to the house itself or the family. What is the narrator suggesting that they might have in common, and how does the title of the story prove this?

7. The 'Gothic archway' suggests something old-fashioned. What other descriptive elements in the final paragraph are 'archaic', 'Gothic' or historical?

8. What kind of story do these descriptions prepare you for?

Description

 # Pair and share

After establishing the narrator's voice and the setting, the writer focuses your attention on the house and the surrounding atmosphere. Here the choice of words, or diction, is significant. Words are not just used for precise description but also to have an emotive effect on you, the reader. We are in an uncomfortable setting, almost hellish and certainly nightmarish, with an unavoidable air of decay and imminent destruction.

Comment on the **implication** of these descriptive words. What associations do they have for you? Some of the work has been done for you, so complete the table with your partner.

Adjectives	Associations
gray	gloomy
silent	
pestilent	diseased
mystic	
sluggish	
leaden	heavy, possibly poisonous
excessive	
minute	
tangled	
crumbling	
neglected	
sullen	
stealthy	secretive

KEY TERM

implication = what is not stated explicitly, the connotations of words.

Do you agree that this sounds more like the description of a graveyard than of a fine country house? We should not be surprised that when the narrator meets Usher he thinks he looks like a ghost, and that there will be a supernatural element to the way the story develops.

Once the narrator sees Roderick, he starts to wonder if he is sane. They are now in a place where anything is possible, and which seems haunted by the past. How do the servants, and the architecture of the house, prepare you for a horror story? For further reading, you might consider Bram Stoker's *Dracula*. Jonathan Harker's first meeting with the Count is rather similar in style.

How does the description seem to take us back in time, and into a nightmare world? In what ways might it be preparing us for the idea of 'the undead', and of things still moving which belong in the grave?

KEY TERM

allegory = a tale which works on two levels, often conveying a moral.

Development

 Viewpoints

The horror genre remains popular even in the world of modern industry and now technology. What are the timeless themes which horror helps us to explore?

Clearly the 'House of Usher' stands for the family as well as the physical house they live in. Both are ancient and have seen better days. Now they are decayed, crumbling and close to collapse. They seem to be rotting from within. Is this story a metaphor or **allegory**? If it means something beyond its surface meaning, is it a comment on a kind of artistic or aristocratic existence which is doomed? Is it an allegory for a diseased or poisoned imagination? Is Poe in control of his own allegory and of the voice of the narrator? Or is the story an elaborate and Gothic hoax? You will need to read on to make your mind up, but try out your ideas by debating these questions with your partner.

In allegory, everything could stand for something else. Consider how your own studied text established its opening.

1. Are we in a world that is realistic, supernatural, allegorical or imagined?

2. How does the writer establish the genre within which the story works?

3. How does this affect the reader's expectations?

Extend your learning

Read on and finish the short story. How well does the opening set up later developments, and the tragic conclusion?

8.2 Setting

Even when a story has a realistic setting, it can still be haunting and its meaning can go a long way beyond the surface narrative. As we have seen, writers use description to establish the emotional world of the story and to allow you, as the reader, to picture a place where things are more complex than they appear to be. Even a place as realistic as a school can appeal strongly to our imagination. Schools are places of intense emotions and formative experience, but time at school is very short, even if it may seem to pass slowly at the time! As a result, everything seems to have heightened significance.

All this is especially true of John Knowles's *A Separate Peace* (1959). Again the narrator is looking back, in this case to events that happened more than a decade before. As we found with Poe's short story, the title also provides a clue about the nature of the story. Here the peacefulness of the exclusive US boarding school comes from its separation, as it is a world set apart and almost denying what is happening outside. In particular, Phineas or Finny, the story's hero, refuses to accept what he is told about the Second World War, which the United States has recently joined. The war and how it will affect the fates of the boys in the story is a constant backdrop to the story, which suggests neither the war nor its damage can be avoided, even while its main focus is on the uncomfortable rivalry as well as friendship of Finny and the narrator.

The early pages of the novel need to establish the following:

- characters we care about and find interesting
- a narrative viewpoint we can share
- a realistic sense of time and place
- an understanding of context, or historical background
- a sense of anticipation and suspense, as we begin to suspect that all will not end happily.

Think ahead

1. The novel is set in 1942. What was the state of Central Europe at the time? Find out what you can about the first year of America's entry into the Second World War.

2. Adolescence is an important time in shaping our characters. Why was the Second World War such an important time in shaping the characters of different countries in the twentieth century? How did it affect the country you live in?

3. What is the relationship between real and imaginary history in the text you are studying?

4. What is the relationship between the setting of your text, and its symbolism, in other words its deeper meaning?

5. Personal relationships, and especially the loss of innocence, can also be an allegory for larger themes of loyalty and betrayal. Why is a school a good setting for such stories of growing up (sometimes called bildungsroman)?

A Separate Peace by John Knowles (1959)

We walked along through the shining afternoon to the river. "I don't really believe we bombed Central Europe, do you?" said Finny thoughtfully. The dormitories we passed were massive and almost anonymous behind their thick layers of ivy, big, old-looking leaves you would have thought stayed there winter and summer, permanent hanging gardens in New Hampshire. Between the buildings, elms curved so high that you ceased to remember their height until you looked above the familiar trunks and the lowest umbrellas of leaves and took in the lofty complex they held high above, branches and branches of branches, a world of branches with an infinity of leaves. They too seemed permanent and never-changing, an untouched, unreachable world high in space, like the ornamental towers and spires of a great church, too high to be enjoyed, too high for anything, great and remote and never useful. "No, I don't think I believe it either", I answered.

Far ahead of us four boys, looking like white flags on the endless green playing fields, crossed toward the tennis courts. To the right of them the gym meditated behind its gray walls, the high, wide, oval-topped windows shining back at the sun. Beyond the

gym and the fields began the woods, our, the Devon School's woods, which in my imagination were the beginning of the great northern forests. I thought that, from the Devon Woods, trees reached in an unbroken, widening corridor so far to the north that no one had ever seen the other end, somewhere up in the far unorganized tips of Canada. We seemed to be playing on the tame fringe of the last and greatest wilderness. I never found out whether this is so and perhaps it is.

✎ Check your understanding

1. What does the opening of this extract establish about Finny's character?

2. Why do you think the narrator does not argue with him?

3. 'Devon School' is in New Hampshire, part of New England. What does the narrator notice about the setting of the school?

4. How does he make that setting appear to be timeless?

5. Which season is it?

6. How does the narrator make the buildings and woods seem more alive than the boys?

7. What does the narrator imagine about the woods beyond the school?

8. How does this fantasy contribute to the boys' sense of where they are?

Pair and share

The setting is created through the writer's choice of words, especially verbs and adjectives. With your partner, copy the table below and fill in the boxes, which ask you to comment on the effect of the writer's choices.

Adjectives	Effect
almost anonymous	
permanent	
lofty	
untouched	
unreachable	
Personification	**Effect**
the gym meditated behind its gray walls,	
Similes	**Effect**
like the ornamental towers and spires of a great church	
like white flags on the endless green	
Metaphors	
trees reached in an unbroken, widening corridor	**Effect**
which in my imagination were the beginning of the great northern forests	
playing on the tame fringe of the last and greatest wilderness	

You will see that imagery is as important in descriptive prose as in poetry. It does not just set the scene but creates a tone for the narrative voice, establishes genre and influences the mood of the reader. All of these drive your personal response and affect how you see the world of the text.

1. Discuss with your partner the effect of all those descriptions taken together. What does it suggest about the isolated world of Devon School? Why doesn't war seem to touch it?

2. What might be the effect of that sense of height and space on the boys themselves?

3. A particular tree plays an important part in the novel, and is the first thing the narrator notices when he goes back to Devon. Consider the phrase 'branches and branches of branches, a world of branches with an infinity of leaves'. What does the writing make you think about the trees and woods and what they represent here?

4. Look again at the metaphors at the end of this passage and what you have written about them. What do they suggest about the relationship between the school and the outside world? Has the school really tamed the 'great wilderness' beyond?

5. How do your conclusions about the nature of the school, its grounds and its effect on the boys link to the title of the novel, *A Separate Peace*?

 See Worksheet 4 for more on narrative and the natural world.

Viewpoints

The two texts we have looked at so far have first-person narrators. They are, however, both narrators who admit to having very vivid imaginations. What are the advantages and disadvantages of such a narrative voice?

The narrator of *A Separate Peace*, Gene, sounds here as if he is recording his thoughts during that summer of 1942, when he spent so much time with Phineas. However, the beginning of the novel shows us that he is remembering events ten years later. He is certainly an imaginative narrator; does that mean he is also an 'unreliable' narrator? Consider the effect of the last words of the passage:

'I never found out whether this is so and perhaps it is.'

What does this suggest about Gene's attitude to facts and fantasy? In what ways does this make him an interesting but dangerous storyteller?

Draw up a table of the advantages and disadvantages of first-person narration.

Think ahead

We have just seen how the previous passage gives Gene's viewpoint or perspective. The thoughts, reflections, experiences and judgments on other people are all Gene's. What is the effect of seeing events through the eyes of a particular character? Are their judgments always reliable? Review the different forms of prose narrative. Which one of the following does your set text use?

▶ A first-person narrator

▶ An omniscient narrator (someone who knows everything and stands outside the narrative)

▶ The viewpoints of various different characters (often called a limited viewpoint)

How reliable are the narrators or viewpoints? How sympathetic do you find the person who tells or 'sees' the story? Do you find it easy to put yourself in their place? How would you describe their voice? Do they take you inside the story, because it happened to them? Or do they remain slightly outside the story, as if looking in? What are the benefits of a detached narrative? Or one which shows complete involvement?

Narrative (story-telling) depends on memory, which also raises the question of reliability, and the border between reality and fantasy. How does your text handle the passing of time, and does that make you ask questions about the reliability of the narrator? What are the limits and limitations of the viewpoint which you are presented with?

Write a paragraph about the narrator or narrators of your set text and evaluate their characteristics and the ways in which they involve you, as the reader, in the events of the story.

8.3 Viewpoint

The choice of narrator and narrating voice needs to be the first choice a novelist or short story writer makes. Henry James, a great writer born in the USA, but who lived most of his life in Europe, described first-person narration as 'barbaric' and avoided it in his short stories and novels. However, his technique of narrative is very different from the 'omniscient narrator' of eighteenth-century novelists, who knows all the thoughts as well as actions of his characters and passes judgment on them. From the time of Jane Austen, a new style of narrative emerged, sometimes called the 'indirect free style' or third-person limited narrative. The story is told in the third person, but with particular access to the viewpoints of particular characters at particular times. Sometimes the narrative is mainly from one person's viewpoint, but it is a limited one—there are key things this person does not know (for example, Elizabeth Bennet does not know Mr Darcy loves her, and Emma does not know that most of her schemes are going to go wrong). However, there are also advantages in seeing the same events from more than one viewpoint.

Henry James

Henry James, in the prefaces to his novels, was one of the great theorists about the art of fiction, as well as a great writer. The novel *Washington Square* takes its name from a fashionable address in New York. Like most of James's novels, the focus is on high society, and in this case the family who live at this expensive address. Doctor Sloper is a widower and a wealthy and fashionable doctor. Highly intelligent, witty and judgmental, he is popular and successful among the rich. His one failure was his inability to save the life of his beautiful and clever wife; he has been left with just one daughter, Catherine, who is neither beautiful nor clever, but will inherit a very large sum of money.

When a handsome young man, Morris Townsend, appears on the scene and begins to get close to Catherine, the Doctor is immediately suspicious. He can't imagine what Morris sees in Catherine other than the money, although Morris tells Catherine that he loves her and she certainly loves him. Their romance is also encouraged by Aunt Penniman, who reads a lot of romantic fiction. The tension of the novel comes partly from our suspicion that the Doctor is right about Morris's intentions, and partly from our feeling that even if he is right it would be wrong for him to interfere. We also know more about each character's private thoughts than they do about each other, which is the great advantage of this kind of narration.

In the passage, Morris has been invited to dinner so that the Doctor can meet him for the first time. Up to now, he has been seeing Catherine with Aunt Penniman as chaperone, but the Doctor is determined to find out what he is like.

Washington Square by Henry James (1880)

He came very soon again, and Mrs Penniman had of course great pleasure in executing this mission. Morris Townsend accepted her invitation with equal good grace, and the dinner took place a few days later. The Doctor had said to himself, justly enough, that they must not have the young man alone; this would partake too much of the nature of encouragement. So two or three other persons were invited; but Morris Townsend, though he was by no means the ostensible, was the real occasion of the feast. There is every reason to suppose that he desired to make a good impression; and if he fell short of this result, it was not for want of a good deal of intelligent effort. The Doctor talked to him very little during dinner; but he observed him attentively, and after the ladies had gone out he pushed him the wine and asked him several questions. Morris was not a young man who needed to be pressed, and he found quite enough encouragement in the superior quality of the claret. The Doctor's wine was admirable, and it may be communicated to the reader that while he sipped it Morris reflected that a cellarful of good liquor – there was evidently a cellarful here – would be a most attractive idiosyncrasy in a father-in-law. The Doctor was struck with his appreciative guest; he saw that he was not a commonplace young man. 'He has ability,' said Catherine's father, 'decided ability; he has a very good head if he chooses to use it. And he is uncommonly well turned out; quite the sort of figure that pleases the ladies; but I don't think I like him.' The Doctor, however, kept his reflexions to himself, and talked to his visitors about foreign lands, concerning which Morris

An actor playing Morris Townsend from a film adaptation of the novel

offered him more information than he was ready, as he mentally phrased it, to swallow. Doctor Slope had travelled but little, and he took the liberty of not believing everything that his talkative guest narrated. He prided himself on being something of a physiognomist; and while the young man, chatting with easy assurance, puffed his cigar and filled his glass again, the Doctor sat with his eyes quietly fixed on his bright, expressive face. 'He has the assurance of the devil himself!' said Morris's host; 'I don't think I ever saw such assurance. And his powers of invention are most remarkable. He is very knowing; they were not so knowing as that in my time. And a good head, did I say? I should think so – after a bottle of Madeira, and a bottle and a half of claret!'

After dinner Morris Townsend went and stood before Catherine, who was standing before the fire in her red satin gown.

'He doesn't like me – he doesn't like me at all,' said the young man.

Check your understanding

1. The first three sentences are each from a different viewpoint. Consider the attitudes towards Morris's invitation to Washington Square of (a) Aunt Penniman; (b) Morris; (c) the Doctor.

2. What is the real (as opposed to 'ostensible') reason why Morris has been invited?

3. Why does Henry James tell us from the beginning that Morris did not 'make a good impression', and whose viewpoint is he giving us?

4. What are the two things the Doctor does to trap Morris into beginning to show his true character?

5. We are also given Morris's viewpoint, especially on the quality of Doctor Sloper's wine. What does this reveal to us about his character?

6. We are also told what the Doctor thinks to himself about Morris, although he does not say any of this out loud. How does he weigh up the strengths and weaknesses of his character?

7. We are told that the Doctor does not entirely believe Morris's stories about his travels, and prides himself on being a 'physiognomist', in other words someone who can judge people on their physical appearance. This is a useful quality in a doctor, but how fair do you think he is being to Morris?

8. Can you find evidence that the Doctor might be jealous of Morris?

9. Why do you think the Doctor makes several different references to Morris's 'good head'? What are the different things these might relate to?

10. How do Morris's comments afterwards to Catherine, which the Doctor does not hear, show us that he is both sensitive and intelligent?

 See Worksheet 3 for more on how writers can show us events of the past.

 # Pair and share

Why might a man like Morris be a very dangerous husband for a young woman like Catherine, who is painfully shy, unintelligent, not very beautiful and rich? Do you think the Doctor is right to interfere and express his disapproval?

With a partner, draw up a list of Morris's good qualities – and then analyse why each of them might be a danger to Catherine.

Prepare to interview Doctor Sloper in the hot seat. Ask questions which will find out why he is so opposed to Morris and what he intends to do about it. How will he prevent the marriage without damaging his relationship with Catherine?

Perform your interview as a dialogue.

Viewpoints

The strength of James's style of narrative is that we know more about what characters are thinking than they ever know about each other. The tension in the novel comes because we know less about Morris's thoughts than those of other characters. The Doctor's thoughts are ironic and intelligent; those of Aunt Penniman frivolous and stupid; and those of Catherine painfully represent her shyness and capacity to be hurt. We get some indications in this passage of Morris's thoughts and nature.

1. Where is the evidence here that he is a bounty-hunter, in search of a rich wife who can allow him the lifestyle he wants but can't afford?

2. His intelligence clearly makes him a formidable enemy to the Doctor, and the novel will be about their battle of wits. Who do you think will win, and what will be the cost?

3. Where do we see who he has recruited to his side?

4. We don't have Catherine's viewpoint here. What might be her thoughts?

Write up a diary entry for Catherine. Remember that she is influenced a little by her Aunt's romantic fantasies, and has little of the Doctor's analytical ability. However, she is honest and she does not play games. She has also fallen for Morris's charms and trusts him completely. Why would she be very worried about this dinner?

Language links

It is a fact that the Doctor is very wealthy. The quality of his cellar of wine and his address alone promise Morris enough money to live the lifestyle of a man about town. In the past, marriages were often arranged, and social classes defended their privileges by keeping out outsiders. The real-life elements of James's writing are the reason why we believe in his characters, and the inner workings of their minds.

How does viewpoint allow us different ways of interpreting the same facts and details? Are there limitations to the Doctor's factual and scientific approach to people and relationships?

Debate the proposition that 'fiction can reveal more about what people are like than facts'. Consider what you have learned about the past from history books, biographies and fiction. What extra elements are brought in by fictional accounts of the past? What are the risks of relying too much on fictional reading?

Extend your learning

How does your own set text handle factual and real-life elements to the story? Do you find the historical aspect of the story convincing and realistic? How has the story engaged your interest in what has happened in the past?

Write an essay on how past events are presented to you in the opening chapters of your novel. Think about:

● the way the narrator presents past events

● how realistic the setting and description are

● how a sense of anticipation or mystery is created.

8.4 Mysteries

Think ahead

We can see that the viewpoint, as well as the setting, of a narrative can involve and interest the reader and make them curious about what happens next. We are interested in experiences and places very different from our own, and the writing helps to engage our imagination, so that we can picture the scene and begin to share the feelings of the characters. A sense of mystery helps to keep the reader turning the pages.

In your own set text:

1. What has remained unexplained after the initial chapters?
2. What do you want to find out more about?
3. Can you begin to predict what will happen?
4. Are there clues in the text and its narrative voice?
5. How does your text handle memory and the passing of time?

Charlotte Brontë's *Jane Eyre* created a sensation when first published in 1848. The sensation was caused by the honesty and passion of the narrative voice and viewpoint of Jane, mistreated as a girl and having to work as a governess but in love with the charismatic yet mysterious Mr Rochester. It also surprised readers that such a passionate and extraordinary narrative should emerge from someone who had grown up in a remote Yorkshire parsonage. Now Haworth is a place of literary pilgrimage from admirers all over the world of Charlotte and her sisters, Emily and Anne.

Haworth Parsonage where the Brontë sisters grew up

Jane is forthright in expressing her opinions and desire for a better life and is a strong match for the forceful Rochester. Rochester is troubled by something in his past, and someone trapped in the attic of Thornfield Hall, who has emerged twice now to attack those in the house. This 'madwoman' has just attacked a visitor called Mr Mason. In this passage, Jane is continuing to puzzle out the nature of this mystery.

Jane Eyre by Charlotte Brontë (1847)

Amidst all this, I had to listen as well as watch: to listen for the movements of the wild beast or fiend in yonder side-den. But since Mr Rochester's visit it seemed spellbound: all the night I heard but three sounds at three long intervals – a sharp creak, a momentary renewal of the snarling, canine noise, and a deep human groan.

Then my own thoughts worried me. What crime was this, that lived incarnate in this sequestered mansion, and could neither be expelled nor subdued by the owner? – what mystery, that broke out, now in fire and now in blood, at the deadest hours of night? What creature was it, that, masked in an ordinary woman's face and shape, uttered the voice, now of a mocking demon, and anon of a carrion-seeking bird of prey?

And this man I bent over – this commonplace, quiet stranger – how had he become involved in the web of horror? and why had the fury flown at him? What made him seek this quarter of the house at an untimely season, when he should have been asleep in bed? I had heard Mr Rochester assign him an apartment below – what brought him here? And why, now, was he so tame under the violence of treachery done him? Why did he so quietly submit to the concealment Mr Rochester enforced? Why *did* Mr Rochester enforce this concealment? His guest had been outraged, his own life on a former occasion had been hideously plotted against; and both attempts he smothered in secrecy and sank in oblivion! Lastly, I saw Mr Mason was submissive to Mr Rochester; that the impetuous will of the

A scene from a film adaptation of *Jane Eyre*

latter held complete sway over the inertness of the former; the few words which had passed between them assured me of this. It was evident that in their former intercourse, the passive disposition of the one had been habitually influenced by the active energy of the other; whence then had arisen Mr Rochester's dismay when he heard of Mr Mason's arrival? Why had the mere name of this unresisting individual – whom his word now sufficed to control like a child – fallen on him, a few hours since, as a thunderbolt might fall on an oak?

Oh! I could not forget his look and his paleness when he whispered: 'Jane, I have got a blow – I have got a blow, Jane.' I could not forget how the arm had trembled which he rested on my shoulder: and it was no light matter which could thus bow the resolute spirit and thrill the vigorous frame of Fairfax Rochester.

✎ Check your understanding

1. What does Jane think is the nature of the creature in the attic? Find quotations which describe it. Do they describe something animal, human or supernatural?

2. Where does Jane link the mystery to crimes in the past?

3. Which adjectives place Thornfield Hall in the tradition of the haunted house which we have already explored earlier in this chapter?

4. What do her adjectives suggest that she thinks about Mason?

5. Who does she think is behind the cover-up (or 'concealment') of what has just happened?

6. You have probably heard of the 'rule of three' (or 'tricolon'). Find examples of lists of three in the questions which Jane asks herself.

7. What is the effect on the reader of this succession of questions?

8. She notices that Mason is easily dominated by Rochester. Which words suggest the power of Rochester?

9. Which words show Rochester's determination to cover up this mystery?

10. Despite Rochester's strength, the news of Mason's coming seemed to knock him down 'as a thunderbolt might fall on an oak'. What does this suggest about Rochester's character?

11. The last paragraph shows how much Jane loves him: what does she normally admire about Rochester?

12. How does she reveal the powerful effect of his dependence on her at this moment?

💬 Pair and share

The power of this passage comes from two sources: the tension of the unsolved mystery and our growing awareness of how the relationship of Jane and Rochester is becoming more powerful when under pressure.

How does this passage reveal to the reader the risks and dangers of a relationship with Rochester for Jane? Why does this only deepen her love for him?

Perhaps Jane suspects the truth, but does not want to admit it to herself because she loves Rochester so much. She is much happier asking questions than providing answers. Her viewpoint is a deliberately limited one. Now see if you can get her to reveal more of her feelings.

Prepare an interview with Jane. What does she really think is going on in the attic? Why isn't she more suspicious about Rochester? What are her suspicions about Mason? Try to get her to provide answers to her own questions.

💡 Viewpoints

Mason clearly knows something about Rochester's past, and wanted to contact the creature in the attic. As a detective, take a more objective view of this passage. Jane herself asks:

'What crime was this, that lived incarnate in this sequestered mansion… ?'

What is the living crime that is hidden away in the attic of this remote house, and who knows about it? Explore the evidence in the passage, collect quotations to make your case and present your conclusions to the jury. Who do you think is guilty of a crime, the woman in the attic or Rochester himself?

It is natural and understandable for human beings to want to solve mysteries and find certainties, and readers often want to do this when reading literary texts. However, in 1817 the poet John Keats wrote about what he called Negative Capability, which he defined as:

"…when a man is capable of being in uncertainties, mysteries, doubts, without any irritable reaching after fact and reason."

This would not be a good quality in a detective, whose job it is to find evidence and details which would fit a hypothesis. Sometimes being a student or critic of literature is like being a detective: you need to collect evidence, especially in the form of quotations, to fit your argument or hypothesis about a text. However, in the matter of interpretation, sometimes the literary critic needs negative capability: we will not always find the answers or solve all the mysteries, and we can make mistakes by searching too hard.

Now look back at the quotations you have collected. They may show evidence of Rochester's guilt, but they also show how Jane is suppressing this because of the power of her love for him. What are the effects of hiding the truth and what might be the impact of revealing the mystery? Discuss your own response to this with your partner and then share with others in your class.

John Keats

Extend your learning

1. How does your own set text handle mysteries and their solution?

2. How reliable have you found the narrators and how limited are their viewpoints?

3. Are there mysteries in your text which are not likely to be solved? What are the different possible reactions of readers?

8.5 Irony

Think ahead

One theme of this chapter has been unreliable narrators and limited viewpoints. Another has been mysteries and different ways of interpreting them, and the descriptive passages of prose narratives. We have learned that a lot depends on the point of view of the narrator who is describing what we 'see'. We will now look at the function of irony and surprise in narrative. They can act similarly to 'turning points' in the drama which we looked at in the previous chapter. They are moments when we, or the characters, begin to see things very differently.

In prose, these surprises have a particular impact not just on the characters but also the ways in which their viewpoints (what they see and their thoughts and feelings) are presented to us.

1. Can you identify such a turning point in your own set text?
2. Does it involve a character seeing things differently?
3. Or does it involve the reader seeing the character in a different way?
4. What is the nature of the revelation?
5. Do things change in the book as a result?

In the famous extract which follows, written by the nineteenth-century novelist Jane Austen whom we have already encountered in chapter 5, the character of Catherine Morland, a girl of 17, has been invited by the clever and handsome Henry Tilney to stay at his family home, Northanger Abbey. Catherine has read a lot of Gothic fiction and strongly believes in the supernatural, so she quickly puts together a fantasy, based on false evidence, that Henry's father (General Tilney) murdered his mother. In this passage, Henry catches her doing her 'detective work' and she is surprised into revealing her fantasies. The other characters mentioned are Henry's older brother Frederick and younger sister Eleanor, and Isabella, Catherine's friend who encouraged her reading of fantasy and tendency to exaggerate, confusing her sense of what is real and what is fiction. The passage begins at what Catherine thinks is a 'forbidden door' (see chapter 5 for another example of this convention in Gothic fiction).

Northanger Abbey by Jane Austen (1803)

It was done; and Catherine found herself alone in the gallery before the clocks had ceased to strike. It was no time for thought; she hurried on, slipped with the least possible noise through the folding doors, and without stopping to look or breathe, rushed forward to the one in question. The lock yielded to her hand, and, luckily, with no sullen sound that could alarm a human being. On tiptoe she entered; the room was before her; but it was some minutes before she could advance another step. She beheld what fixed her to the spot and agitated every feature. She saw a large, well–proportioned apartment, an handsome dimity bed, arranged as unoccupied with an housemaid's care, a bright Bath stove, mahogany wardrobes, and neatly painted chairs, on which the warm beams of a western sun gaily poured through two sash windows! Catherine had expected to have her feelings worked, and worked they were. Astonishment and doubt first seized them; and a shortly

dimity = a lightweight cotton fabric

succeeding ray of common sense added some bitter emotions of shame. She could not be mistaken as to the room; but how grossly mistaken in everything else! — in Miss Tilney's meaning, in her own calculation! This apartment, to which she had given a date so ancient, a position so awful, proved to be one end of what the general's father had built. There were two other doors in the chamber, leading probably into dressing–closets; but she had no inclination to open either. Would the veil in which Mrs. Tilney had last walked, or the volume in which she had last read, remain to tell what nothing else was allowed to whisper? No: whatever might have been the general's crimes, he had certainly too much wit to let them sue for detection. She was sick of exploring, and desired but to be safe in her own room, with her own heart only privy to its folly; and she was on the point of retreating as softly as she had entered, when the sound of footsteps, she could hardly tell where, made her pause and tremble. To be found there, even by a servant, would be unpleasant; but by the general (and he seemed always at hand when least wanted), much worse! She listened — the sound had ceased; and resolving not to lose a moment, she passed through and closed the door. At that instant a door underneath was hastily opened; someone seemed with swift steps to ascend the stairs, by the head of which she had yet to pass before she could gain the gallery. She had no power to move. With a feeling of terror not very definable, she fixed her eyes on the staircase, and in a few moments it gave Henry to her view. "Mr. Tilney!" she exclaimed in a voice of more than common astonishment. He looked astonished too. "Good God!" she continued, not attending to his address. "How came you here? How came you up that staircase?"

She is referring to an earlier conversation with Eleanor.

he had too much wit ... = the General was too clever to leave obvious clues

"How came I up that staircase!" he replied, greatly surprised. "Because it is my nearest way from the stable–yard to my own chamber; and why should I not come up it?"

Catherine recollected herself, blushed deeply, and could say no more. He seemed to be looking in her countenance for that explanation which her lips did not afford. She moved on towards the gallery. "And may I not, in my turn," said he, as he pushed back the folding doors, "ask how you came here? This passage is at least as extraordinary a road from the breakfast–parlour to your apartment, as that staircase can be from the stables to mine."

"I have been," said Catherine, looking down, "to see your mother's room."

"My mother's room! Is there anything extraordinary to be seen there?"

"No, nothing at all. I thought you did not mean to come back till tomorrow."

"I did not expect to be able to return sooner, when I went away; but three hours ago I had the pleasure of finding nothing to detain me. You look pale. I am afraid I alarmed you by running so fast up those stairs. Perhaps you did not know — you were not aware of their leading from the offices in common use?"

"No, I was not. You have had a very fine day for your ride."

"Very; and does Eleanor leave you to find your way into all the rooms in the house by yourself?"

"Oh! No; she showed me over the greatest part on Saturday — and we were coming here to these rooms — but only" — dropping her voice — "your father was with us."

"And that prevented you," said Henry, earnestly regarding her. "Have you looked into all the rooms in that passage?"

"No, I only wanted to see — Is not it very late? I must go and dress."

"It is only a quarter past four" showing his watch — "and you are not now in Bath. No theatre, no rooms to prepare for. Half an hour at Northanger must be enough."

She could not contradict it, and therefore suffered herself to be detained, though her dread of further questions made her, for the first time in their acquaintance, wish to leave him. They walked slowly up the gallery. "Have you had any letter from Bath since I saw you?"

"No, and I am very much surprised. Isabella promised so faithfully to write directly."

"Promised so faithfully! A faithful promise! That puzzles me. I have heard of a faithful performance. But a faithful promise — the fidelity of promising! It is a power little worth knowing, however, since it can deceive and pain you. My mother's room is very commodious, is it not? Large and cheerful–looking, and the dressing–closets so well disposed! It always strikes me as the most comfortable apartment in the house, and I rather wonder that Eleanor should not take it for her own. She sent you to look at it, I suppose?"

"No."

"It has been your own doing entirely?" Catherine said nothing. After a short silence, during which he had closely observed her, he added, "As there is nothing in the room in itself to raise curiosity, this must have proceeded from a sentiment of respect for my mother's character, as described by Eleanor, which does honour to her memory. The world, I believe, never saw a better woman. But it is not often that virtue can boast an interest such as this. The domestic, unpretending merits of a person never known do not often create that kind of fervent, venerating tenderness which would prompt a visit like yours. Eleanor, I suppose, has talked of her a great deal?"

"Yes, a great deal. That is — no, not much, but what she did say was very interesting. Her dying so suddenly" (slowly, and with hesitation it was spoken), "and you — none of you being at home — and your father, I thought — perhaps had not been very fond of her."

"And from these circumstances," he replied (his quick eye fixed on hers), "you infer perhaps the probability of some negligence — some" — (involuntarily she shook her head) — "or it may be — of something still less pardonable." She raised her eyes towards him more fully than she had ever done before. "My mother's illness," he continued, "the seizure which ended in her death, was sudden. The malady itself, one from which she had often suffered, a bilious fever — its cause therefore constitutional. On the third day, in short, as soon as she could be prevailed on, a physician attended her, a very respectable man, and one in whom she had always placed great confidence. Upon his opinion of her danger, two others were called in the next day, and remained in almost constant attendance for four and twenty hours. On the fifth day she died. During the progress of her disorder, Frederick and I (we were both at home) saw her repeatedly; and from our own observation can bear witness to her having received every possible attention which could spring from the affection of those about her, or which her situation in life could command. Poor Eleanor was absent, and at such a distance as to return only to see her mother in her coffin."

"But your father," said Catherine, "was he afflicted?"

"For a time, greatly so. You have erred in supposing him not attached to her. He loved her, I am persuaded, as well as it was possible for him to — we have not all, you know, the same tenderness of disposition — and I will not pretend to say that while she lived, she might not often have had much to bear, but though his temper injured her, his judgment never did. His value of her was sincere; and, if not permanently, he was truly afflicted by her death."

"I am very glad of it," said Catherine; "it would have been very shocking!"

"If I understand you rightly, you had formed a surmise of such horror as I have hardly words to — Dear Miss Morland, consider the dreadful nature of the suspicions you have entertained. What have you been judging from? Remember the country and the age in which we live. Remember that we are English, that we are Christians. Consult your own understanding, your own sense of the probable, your own observation of what is passing around you. Does our education prepare us for such atrocities? Do our laws connive at them? Could they be perpetrated without being known, in a country like this, where social and literary intercourse is on such a footing, where every man is surrounded by a neighbourhood of voluntary spies, and where roads and newspapers lay everything open? Dearest Miss Morland, what ideas have you been admitting?"

They had reached the end of the gallery, and with tears of shame she ran off to her own room.

✎ Check your understanding

1. Which word in the first sentence suggests that something terrible is about to happen?

2. Which verbs in the second sentence suggest Catherine's nervousness?

3. How does the writer create suspense as the 'forbidden door' is opened?

4. Why does the room turn out to be a surprise for Catherine?

5. Which phrases suggest that she is already beginning to get embarrassed?

6. How does she explain to herself what has happened?

7. Why is she in a hurry to get back to her own room?

8. Whose footsteps does she think she hears?

9. Who actually catches her in the room and why is this so embarrassing for Catherine?

10. What does Henry seem to think about the room?

11. Why is he curious about Catherine's reasons for being in the room?

12. How does she try to change the subject?

13. What is peculiar about the way Catherine speaks about Henry's father and mother?

14. Why does she not want Henry to ask her any more questions?

15. Henry likes language to be exact. When Henry talks about Isabella why does he make fun of the idea of a 'faithful promise'? Why is that term a tautology or form of exaggeration?

16. Which phrases suggest he is testing her when he does ask her questions?

17. What fact does Catherine exaggerate when speaking about the death of Henry's mother, Mrs Tilney?

18. How does Henry's language make clear the facts of his mother's death?

19. What does he mean by 'we have not all, you know, the same tenderness of disposition'? What does he imply about his father's temper?

20. Why does Henry say that the crimes which Catherine has imagined could never happen in England?

Pair and share

This is a text which clearly divides into two parts, the first made up entirely of description, from Catherine's (rather biased) viewpoint, and the second of dialogue. We will explore the ways in which description is influenced by viewpoint and the drama of the dialogue.

The comic effect of the first part of the text depends on a series of contrasts. Together, search for and find the matching quotations to bring out these contrasts (the first is done for you):

Gothic fiction (Catherine's imagination)	Reality
'without stopping to look or breathe, rushed forward', she rushed at the door	But it opened 'with no sullen sound that could alarm a human being'
She saw something which 'fixed her to the spot and agitated every feature'	But it was …
In her anxiety, Catherine expected 'to have her feelings worked'	But the feelings she actually felt were …
She expected a Gothic torture chamber with 'a date so ancient, a position so awful'	Instead she realizes it is …
She thinks the General has covered up his crimes and then is frightened as 'the sound of footsteps, she could hardly tell where, made her pause and tremble'	It turns out to be …
She is astonished and asks Henry 'How came you up that staircase?'	He replies very matter-of-factly that it is …

What is the effect of these contrasts and what do they suggest about Catherine's viewpoint?

Now dramatize the dialogue and prepare a performance in pairs to share with your partners. Remember that Catherine is a rather innocent teenage girl, and Henry a well-educated man in his twenties, who enjoys reading Gothic fiction too, but has seen enough of the world to be rather clearer about the difference between fact and fiction.

1. Have you noticed changes in Catherine's feelings and emotions?

2. Where do they occur and how are they expressed through her language?

3. Try two different readings of Henry's role in the duologue: one in which he appears to be very angry, and one in which he appears to be very amused. Which worked better?

4. Now try a reading in which he appears to Catherine to be angry, but is actually quite amused.

5. Why would this last reading fit the atmosphere of the extract best?

💬 Pair and share

As we have seen, drama depends upon conflict and tension which leads to a climax. What has created the tension between Catherine and Henry? (Remember there may be more than one answer!) Where is the climax of the passage?

As in drama there is also irony: this is when the reader (or audience) knows more than the characters do, especially when they read the text (or see the play) for a second time, aware of how things will end.

1. Looking over the description again, where can the reader tell that Catherine does not fully believe her own fantasies even before Henry points out her errors?

2. Looking over the dialogue again, how can we tell that Henry isn't being entirely serious even when he seems to be telling Catherine off?

3. Can you and your partner find the clues that show Henry and Catherine are already deeply in love, even if they don't admit it?

4. What do the conventions of romantic comedy suggest will happen once the jokes, misunderstanding and ironies are over? (Check chapter 2!)

💡 Viewpoints

When Henry speaks about England, it is with the confidence of a nineteenth-century English gentleman, sure of his rational judgment and of his nation's powerful place in the world as it was at that time. What is he suggesting about the kinds of worlds portrayed in a lot of fiction at that time? What is the writer suggesting about fantasy and realism in fiction?

- Do you prefer writing which is fantastic, or writing which is realistic?

- What are the advantages and disadvantages of both kinds of writing?

- In what ways do readers' expectations differ, depending on whether the text uses realism or other conventions such as fantasy, the Gothic or science fiction?

Actors play Catherine Morland and Henry Tilney in a 2007 adaptation

Language links

If you are also studying the Cambridge First Language English course, you will know it makes a very clear distinction between descriptive writing (which must be, or appear to be, non-fiction) and narrative writing, which must be a story.

1. How do the literature texts which you have read deliberately blur this distinction?
2. How are the descriptive passages in the text related to the character of the narrator?
3. How do literature texts blur fact and fiction?

With this in mind, choose one of the following writing activities:

Write a story of your own in which a character discovers that they have made a very embarrassing mistake.

OR

Describe the experience of looking around a place which you know you should not be in.

Extend your learning

How does your own set text handle irony? Are there situations and emotions the characters experience which the reader knows are based on a mistake?

Characterization

Think ahead

This chapter has focused less on character than you might have expected. Although we take an interest in characters from the very beginning of a piece of prose fiction, and they can often keep us involved in the story, there is a danger in writing too much about characters when preparing for your exams. We need to beware of treating characters as if they were real people, and writing their diaries or dramatizing their stories as if they had a life outside the text we are studying. Although this kind of exercise can be fun, and the idea of the empathic response comes out of it, we always need to be aware that a character is a construct. Their thoughts, and especially their language, are the creation of the writer. It is therefore better to think about characterization, the way writers present characters, rather than the characters themselves.

Similarly we should beware of thinking about characters as simply good or evil. Nor can we always easily label characters as heroes or villains. Sometimes we call the main character of a novel or play the hero or heroine, even if he or she isn't always particularly heroic. For example, it would not be wrong to call Catherine Morland the heroine of *Northanger Abbey*, even though the brave things she does are rather different from what she imagines she is doing when she enters the 'forbidden room'.

It is better to think about characters as sympathetic (if it is easy for the reader to share their feelings) or unsympathetic (if we see them from outside, so we don't really share their feelings, or find it hard to side with them).

1. Which characters in your text are sympathetic?
2. Which are unsympathetic?

8.6 Surprise

In this extract from a Pulitzer Prize-winning novel by the Canadian writer Carol Shields, a nasty surprise awaits a fairly nasty character—you may feel he gets what he deserves. The passage is told from the viewpoint of his new bride, who may also surprise you by her thoughts and feelings. The story is set in Europe in the twentieth century, between the two World Wars, and Harold and his bride Daisy are on their honeymoon in France.

The Stone Diaries by Carol Shields (1993)

He manages in the space of an hour to rent an immense car, a Delage Torpedo, black as a hearse with square rear windows like wide startled eyes. Grasping the steering wheel, he seems momentarily revived, singing loudly and tunelessly, as if a great danger had passed, though his tongue whispers of gin: Daisy, Daisy, give me your answer true. I'm half crazy all for the love of you. He shoots out through the Paris suburbs and into the countryside, honking at people crossing the road, at cows and chickens, at the pale empty air of France. They hurtle down endless rural avenues of trees, past fields of ravishing poppies and golden gorse, and eventually, after hours and hours, they reach the mountains.

She keeps pleading with him to stop, whimpering, then shouting that he oughtn't to be driving this wildly and drinking wine at the same time, that he is putting their lives in danger. He almost groans with the pleasure of what he is hearing, his darling scolding bride who is bent so sweetly on reform.

They stop, finally, at the sleepy Alpine town of Corps, their tires grinding to a halt on the packed gravel, and register at the Hotel de la Poste. A hunched-looking porter carries their valises up two flights of narrow stairs to an austere room with a sloping ceiling and a single window which is heavily curtained.

Daisy lies down, exhausted, on the rather lumpy bed. Her georgette dress, creased and stained, spreads out beneath her. She can't imagine what she's doing in this dim, musty room, and yet she feels she's been here

Delage Torpedo = a French luxury saloon car

hearse = a vehicle for carrying a coffin at funerals

"Daisy, Daisy…" = a poplar song at the time the story is set

valises = suitcases

georgette = a thin silk dress material

before, that all the surfaces and crevasses are familiar, part of the scenery sketched into an apocryphal journal. Sleep beckons powerfully, but she resists, looking around at the walls for some hopeful sign. There is a kind of flower-patterned paper, she sees, that lends the room a shabby, rosy charm. This, too, seems familiar. It is seven o'clock in the evening. She is lying on her back in a hotel room in the middle of France. The world is rolling over her, over and over. Her young husband, this stranger, has flung open the window, then pushed back the shutters, and now the sun shines brightly into the room.

apocryphal = invented

And there he is, perched on the window sill, balanced there, a big fleshy shadow blocking the sunlight. In one hand he grasps a wine bottle from which he takes occasional gulps; in his other is a handful of centimes which he is tossing out the window to a group of children who have gathered on the cobbled square. He is laughing, a crazy cackling one-note sound.

centimes = French coins of small value

She can hear the musical ringing of the coins as they strike the stone, and the children's sharp singing cries. A part of her consciousness drifts toward sleep where she will be safe, but she stares sternly at the ceiling, the soiled plaster, waiting.

At that moment she feels a helpless sneeze coming on – her old allergy to feather pillows. The sneeze is loud, powerful, sudden, an explosion that closes her throat and forces her eyes shut for a fraction of a second. When she opens them again, Harold is no longer on the window sill. All she sees is an empty rectangle of glaring light. A splinter of time passes, too small and quiet to register in the brain; she blinks back her disbelief, and then hears a bang, a crashing sound like a melon splitting, a wet injurious noise followed by the screaming of children and the sound of people running in the street.

She remembers that she lay flat on the bed for a least a minute before she got up to investigate.

✎ Check your understanding

1. Which tense is used throughout and what is the effect of this?

2. Whose viewpoint do we share and how do you know this?

3. Which details make Harold's behaviour while driving appear especially dangerous?

4. How does he react to Daisy's fears?

5. What seems strange and slightly sinister about the hotel which they arrive at?

6. What does the description suggest that Daisy feels like?

7. What is odd, even supernatural, about the bedroom?

8. How does their behaviour on reaching the room highlight the differences between the husband and his wife?

9. What does the description of Harold at the window-sill reveal about his wife's feelings?

10. What do you think are Daisy's emotions as she leans back on the bed?

11. What appears to be the effect of her sneeze?

12. What is sinister about the writer's description of the accident?

13. What is surprising about Daisy's reaction?

14. What do you think she feels about Harold's death?

Pair and share

The power of the writing depends not just on its shock and surprise effect, but also on the ways in which, when we look back, the tragedy seems to be inevitable and something Daisy almost predicted. Re-read the passage with a friend, exploring all the hints of something bad which is about to happen.

Then fill in the table, commenting on the effects of the writer's choice of details. Notice how often the writer uses the technique of simile. The first quotation and comment is done for you, but afterwards you will need to supply the explanation of the effect on the reader which best fits the quotation.

Quotation	Effect
black as a hearse	A dark colour and a simile which reminds us of death give the reader a premonition of disaster to come
windows like wide startled eyes	
as if a great danger had passed	
I'm half crazy	
he is putting their lives in danger	
almost groans with the pleasure	
A hunched-looking porter	
this dim, musty room	
she feels she's been here before	
looking around at the walls for some hopeful sign	
This, too, seems familiar	
The world is rolling over her, over and over	
Her young husband, this stranger	
a big fleshy shadow blocking the sunlight	
he grasps a wine bottle from which he takes occasional gulps	
a crazy cackling one-note sound	
she stares sternly at the ceiling, the soiled plaster, waiting	
an explosion that closes her throat	
an empty rectangle of glaring light	
a crashing sound like a melon splitting	
a wet injurious noise	
the screaming of children and the sound of people running	
she lay flat on the bed for a least a minute before she got up to investigate	

Now discuss the questions which follow and reach agreed conclusions, which you can report back to the class.

1. What do you think the language you have explored reveals about Daisy's attitude to Harold, and her likely feelings about his death?

2. How do these phrases suggest ideas of déjà vu or the supernatural?

3. Do you think Harold's fate is inevitable? Do you feel he deserves it?

4. Why is Daisy a more complex character than Harold, and what elements in the characterization make Harold rather 'flat'?

5. Who does the writer encourage the reader to sympathize with, and how?

💡 Viewpoints

Many of the effects of the writing depend on the contrast between the beautiful descriptions of the French landscape and evening sunlight, and Daisy's horror at Harold's behaviour and the shock of his sudden death. How many examples of this contrast can you find?

What is the effect on the reader of this contrast?

What does it also suggest about Daisy's likely response to Harold's death?

Explore the reactions of two students:

Student A

I wondered if something was going wrong because Daisy feels like she had been here before. But then the story mentioned that she laid in her bed and then she started to see her husband at the window pane but she stood up Harold was no longer in the window she just see the rectangular window and flashback. She remember that when lay flat on the bed for at least a minute before she got up to investigate. I knew it something was going wrong.

Comment

This is a response showing basic narrative understanding. The student understands and retells the story but does not use quotation or comment on the language. It is essential to move away from paraphrase (just saying what happens) to analysis (exploring the writer's use of language) to get into the higher bands.

Student B

In the hotel room the writer clearly conveys the tension in their relationship. Daisy is so fed up with her husband that she was more worried and intrigued with some things in her bedroom than her husband's situation of being totally drunk...in the ending she shows that Daisy was not so worried about Harold and what might have happened to him: "She blinks back her disbelief" "She lay flat on the bed for at least a minute before she got up to investigate" And to build up the feeling that things would go wrong, the author makes use of short, emotionless and direct sentences.

Writing techniques

Use a highlighter pen to pick out key phrases in the text when re-reading it, in order to identify the phrases you will want to quote and comment on in your answer. This will also help you to think about and plan your response before you begin writing.

Comment

This is a stronger response: this student does use quotation and begins to comment on language, but the quotations and comments are not well integrated within the sentences, nor does the student look far beyond the surface meaning of the words.

Your task:

What advice would you give these two students in order to help them improve?

Write your own reaction to the final three paragraphs of the original, making sure you incorporate short quotations within your sentences in order to show:

● Daisy's anger with Harold
● her reaction to the moment when she sneezes and he falls
● the coolness of her response to the accident.

Why do you think Daisy does not seem to blame herself for Harold's death? Do you think she is right not to feel guilty?

8.7 Sympathy

Think ahead

In contrast, it would be useful to look at a character we are encouraged to feel sympathetic towards, and who has a good experience rather than a bad one. George Eliot (1819–80) was one of the great successors to Jane Austen and Charles Dickens. Like Austen, she concentrated her writing on small, largely rural communities, but like Dickens, she drew her characters from a wide social range. Silas Marner, a weaver, has moved to the village of Raveloe after being accused of theft and thrown out of a religious community (Lantern Yard). The true thief was his best friend, who also stole the girl Silas loved. In the circumstances, it is not surprising that once he is in Raveloe Silas keeps away from his neighbours and concentrates on building up a stock of gold. He is very short-sighted and is prone to fits ('catalepsy' or a form of epilepsy), and does not know what has happened just before losing consciousness, which superstitious people have believed to be a sign that he is bad or 'half-crazy'. One winter his gold is stolen, forcing him to meet his neighbours in the Rainbow Inn and he finds them surprisingly sympathetic. He soon has a surprise gift he does not expect.

Extend your learning

Consider the following questions in response to the set text you are studying.

1. Where do surprises and shocks occur in the narrative which you did not expect?

2. When you look back, were there hints that something like this would happen?

3. Who do you blame or feel sorry for when bad things happen in your text?

4. How has the writer manipulated your feelings to make you feel more sorry for some characters rather than others?

George Eliot

Silas Marner by George Eliot (1861)

This morning he had been told by some of his neighbours that it was New Year's Eve, and that he must sit up and hear the old year rung out and the new rung in, because that was good luck, and might bring his money back again. This was only a friendly Raveloe-way of jesting with the half-crazy oddities of a miser, but it had perhaps helped to throw Silas into a more than usually excited state. Since the on-coming of twilight he had opened his door again and again, though only to shut it immediately at seeing all distance veiled by the falling snow. But the last time he opened it the snow had ceased, and the clouds were parting here and there. He stood and listened, and gazed for a long while—there was really something on the road coming towards him then, but he caught no sign of it; and the stillness and the wide trackless snow seemed to narrow his solitude, and touched his yearning with the chill of despair. He went in again, and put his right hand on the latch of the door to close it—but he did not close it: he was arrested, as he had been already since his loss, by the invisible wand of catalepsy, and stood like a graven image, with wide but sightless eyes, holding open his door, powerless to resist either the good or the evil that might enter there.

When Marner's sensibility returned, he continued the action which had been arrested, and closed his door, unaware of the chasm in his consciousness, unaware of any intermediate change, except that the light had grown dim, and that he was chilled and faint. He thought he had been too long standing at the door and looking out. Turning towards the hearth, where the two logs had fallen apart, and sent forth only a red uncertain glimmer, he seated himself on his fireside chair, and was stooping to push his logs together, when, to his blurred vision, it seemed as if there were gold on the floor in front of the hearth. Gold!—his own gold—brought back to him as mysteriously as it had been taken away! He felt his heart begin to beat violently, and for a few moments he was unable to stretch out his hand and grasp the restored treasure. The heap of gold seemed to glow and get larger beneath his agitated gaze. He leaned forward at last, and stretched forth his hand; but instead of the hard coin with the familiar resisting outline, his fingers encountered soft warm curls. In utter amazement, Silas fell on his knees and bent his head low to examine the marvel: it was a sleeping child—a round, fair thing, with soft yellow rings all over its head. Could this be his little sister come back to him in a dream—his little sister whom he had carried about in his arms for a year before she died, when he was a small boy without shoes or stockings? That was the first thought that darted across Silas's blank wonderment. *Was* it a dream? He rose to his feet again, pushed his logs together, and, throwing on some dried leaves and sticks, raised a flame; but the flame did not disperse the vision—it only lit up more distinctly the little round form of the child, and its shabby clothing. It was very much like his little sister. Silas sank into his chair powerless, under the double presence of an inexplicable surprise and a hurrying influx of memories. How and when had the child come in without his knowledge? He had never been beyond the door. But along with that question, and almost thrusting it away, there was a vision of the old home and the old streets leading to Lantern Yard—and within that vision another, of the thoughts which had been present with him in those far-off scenes. The thoughts were strange to him now, like old friendships impossible to revive; and yet he had a dreamy feeling that this child was somehow a message come to him from that far-off life: it stirred fibres that had never been moved in Raveloe—old quiverings of tenderness—old impressions of awe at the presentiment of some Power presiding over his life; for his imagination had not yet extricated itself from the sense of mystery in the child's sudden presence, and had formed no conjectures of ordinary natural means by which the event could have been brought about.

But there was a cry on the hearth: the child had awaked, and Marner stooped to lift it on his knee. It clung round his neck, and burst louder and louder into that mingling of inarticulate cries with "mammy" by which little children express the bewilderment of waking. Silas pressed it to him, and almost unconsciously uttered sounds of hushing tenderness, while he bethought himself that some of his porridge, which had got cool by the dying fire, would do to feed the child with if it were only warmed up a little.

Check your understanding

1. How does Eliot make sure we share Silas's point of view and appreciate the exact moment when this incident happens?
2. Why is the New Year such an appropriate moment for this change in his life?
3. Why does he keep opening his door?
4. What is significant about the snow stopping and the clouds parting?
5. Which details bring out Silas's sense of his own solitude as he looks out of the door?
6. What has happened during the moments of Silas's 'catalepsy'?
7. How can Silas tell that some time has passed?
8. In what ways does the sleeping child seem to resemble his lost gold?
9. How is the child very different from the gold?
10. Who does it remind Silas of?
11. Why is he unsure what is a dream and what is real?
12. Why does the child remind him of emotions which he has buried ever since he had to leave Lantern Yard?
13. Which words bring out a sense of mystery or the miraculous?
14. How does the last paragraph bring both Marner and the reader back to reality?

 # Pair and share

Explore through discussion the implications of language. We infer (or make inferences) when the writer has implied more than the surface meaning of the language. This is especially often the case in descriptive writing. Why do you think the writer set the scene in winter, surrounded by snow, on New Year's Eve?

Here the descriptions set not only the physical scene but also a certain emotional mood. George Eliot wants the reader to feel a sense of renewal and hope. She wants you to see that the arrival of the child will bring renewal and healing to Silas, in ways that accumulating money never could. Silas will need help to bring up the girl, Eppie, and that will involve him once again in the whole community of Raveloe, which, as he found in the Rainbow Inn, is surprisingly helpful and supportive. How do the following descriptions imply a special kind of atmosphere, and a hope which is almost miraculous? Where does choice of words imply some kind of magic, or the arrival of something special brought into Silas's winter world?

Quotation	Comment
he must sit up and hear the old year rung out and the new rung in	This image of the bells, ringing to celebrate the new year, implies a change that might await Silas, which the Raveloe community wants him to enjoy
only a friendly Raveloe-way of jesting	They were only joking, but the irony is that a real change will occur
the snow had ceased, and the clouds were parting here and there	
the stillness and the wide trackless snow seemed to narrow his solitude	
the invisible wand of catalepsy	
stood like a graven image	
powerless to resist either the good or the evil that might enter	

Quotation	Comment
a red uncertain glimmer	
to his blurred vision, it seemed as if there were gold	
The heap of gold seemed to glow and get larger beneath his agitated gaze	

Your comments will reflect the idea that something very special is happening to Silas. We know that there is a rational explanation: Eppie is Godfrey Cass's child, abandoned by her dying mother Mollie; we know about what happened to Silas's gold too. The carelessness of the wealthy but dysfunctional Cass family lies behind the apparently mysterious events in Raveloe, which shows Eliot's clear social message about the true nature of community. However, for Silas everything is touched with the miraculous, and the event stirs up his memories of the religious community he used to belong to in Lantern Yard.

Before we look together at the last two paragraphs, it is important to work through the passage in sections, so that we see the writer's purpose in presenting Silas's limited and short-sighted viewpoint.

We see:

- Silas's excitement and hope that his gold will be miraculously returned
- his recovery from his cataleptic trance and discovery that the 'gold' is actually a child
- his dreams and visions that his life has been blessed by God
- the reality of the child and her needs, and how Silas begins to break out of his isolation and help her.

How does the writer's use of language make the discovery of the child both dramatic and revealing? This is clearly an emotional and exciting moment, but the language also encourages us to read symbolism into Silas's discovery. The writer uses a lot of contrast between coldness and warmth. Where do you find descriptions of coldness and cold colours? Where do these contrast with warmth? Where does Eliot contrast hardness and softness?

There are several key descriptions which need analytical comment. Discuss these together and work out your responses. You need to reflect not on the literal meaning, but the connotations of words. What is implied by calling the coins 'hard' and 'resisting'? In what ways is the child different?

Quotation	Comment
When Marner's sensibility returned, he continued the action which had been arrested	How does this suggest that Silas's actions are not under his control, as if he is being manipulated?
the chasm in his consciousness	What else has Silas not noticed for many years?
to his blurred vision, it seemed as if there were gold	Think this time about the implications of Silas having 'blurred' vision. What has made his vision of anything other than gold confused?
instead of the hard coin with the familiar resisting outline, his fingers encountered soft warm curls	What does this suggest about the difference between money and human love?
a round, fair thing, with soft yellow rings all over its head	How does the language present the child as an image of innocence and hope?
Silas fell on his knees and bent his head low to examine the marvel	What kind of miracle does Silas appear to be worshipping? What kind of implications does this have in the English winter, and in the Christmas season?

Silas himself, because of his upbringing and background, sees this as a miracle, or a present from God. The irony is that as readers we know the rational explanation and the more human and sordid circumstances which have led Eppie to be abandoned, albeit with very happy consequences.

The writer's choice of words (diction or lexis) is full of references to dreams or miracles. Highlight these and similar words in the second paragraph:

> vision/mysteriously/treasure/amazement/marvel/ dream/inexplicable/message/awe/mystery/no … ordinary means

What other kinds of experience could this kind of language refer to? Silas at one point thinks he has seen a vision of his lost sister returned to life from the dead, and at another he sees the religious community of faith which he used to be a part of and feels the stirrings of the kind of religious experience he used to believe in when at Lantern Yard.

Not only does the diction suggest the miraculous, but the syntax, the length and structure of the sentences, also shows the transformation in Silas's mood. We have seen the importance of syntax in poetry; it is even more important in prose, where there is no regular beat to give the rhythm. The rhythm of sentences comes from their structure and gives you the emotions and excitement of the person whose viewpoint we share.

With your partner, mark out the sentence breaks in the second paragraph in one colour. Where are the sentences longer? Where do they get shorter? Where do you find that Silas asks himself a lot of questions? How long is the final sentence? Use another colour to highlight commas and dashes. Where do these pauses within sentences show Silas's agitation and excited, questioning emotions? What can you tell about his state of mind and heightened feelings from the language used to describe what he sees, or thinks he sees?

💡 Viewpoints

In Silas's dreams or visions, his past life seems to be literally flashing past him. The sentence below needs particular exploration:

> The thoughts were strange to him now, like old friendships impossible to revive; and yet he had a dreamy feeling that this child was somehow a message come to him from that far-off life: it stirred fibres that had never been moved in Raveloe—old quiverings of tenderness—old impressions of awe at the presentiment of some Power presiding over his life; for his imagination had not yet extricated itself from the sense of mystery in the child's sudden presence, and had formed no conjectures of ordinary natural means by which the event could have been brought about.

It is a long and difficult sentence so it needs breaking down. Here Eliot uses semi-colons and colons to both split up and connect different parts of Silas's thoughts. Why is this a much more controlled form of punctuation than lots of commas? A colon precedes an explanation. How does Eliot explain Silas's idea that the child is a message to him from his past life? What is the emotional effect of the use of dashes and repetitions: ' – old quiverings of tenderness – old impressions of awe'? How do these descriptions combine physical and spiritual feelings?

Silas feels he is in the presence of a miracle, a gift from a higher 'Power'. However, Eliot makes it clear that this is his point of view, and the narrator does not necessarily share it. Where do you find two 'negatives' in the sentence? These 'nots and nos' suggest that Silas is feeling so positive that he can't think of any more rational explanation.

1. How does Eliot's description of the child's cry and of its needs bring the reader back down to earth?

2. How practical is Silas's response to the need to bring up the child?

3. How does this prevent the passage from being falsely sentimental or over emotional?

🔗 Language links

Revise the use of semi-colons and colons and examine the ways in which they can make your own use of language more effective. A colon precedes an explanation: it is therefore a useful way of showing that ideas are connected; semi-colons provide a pause as controlled as a full stop, while also making a clear link between this clause and the one preceding it.

💡 Viewpoints

You will have noticed that the last two passages both have hints of mystery or the supernatural, and confuse dream and reality in order to present events which are so surprising that they seem almost a miracle.

- Why do you think writers like to play with hints of the supernatural or mysterious?

- Do you believe in them?

- Or do you think the events in novels should have a rational explanation?

- Have you seen similar treatment of the supernatural in the text you are reading?

Debate these issues in class. Are stories more convincing and more powerful when more realistic? How far should we allow writers a touch of magic?

Form teams to argue for and against the motion that: 'Writers of fiction will interest us more if they stick to events we know are realistic.'

You should have two prepared speeches on each side, a chairman to keep order, a floor debate with formal questions directed to the speakers and a summing-up by each side, answering points made by opponents and from the floor. Give the proposition the first and the last word. Then take a vote.

Remember that a good debating speech is based around arguments supported by examples and discussion of what they show (rather like a good literary essay). It is not just a matter of demolishing the opposition's arguments, but also having good ones of your own.

There is no clear right or wrong side (the best speakers are likely to win the argument); different readers have different tastes and writers often want both sides to be satisfied.

Writing techniques

To write about this passage, consider the writer's purpose and the reader's response. You should consider how Silas's character is communicated through his point of view, so that we understand what this moment means to him, but we should also consider our own response and viewpoint and how they are influenced by the kind of techniques which we have seen the writer use.

Look back at the passage of *Silas Marner*, perhaps informed by what you know of the novel.

1. How has George Eliot combined magic and **realism** in this powerful moment?

2. Has she managed to make it tender without making it too sentimental or unbelievable?

3. How has she made sure we understand the way Silas feels, and how important this moment is for him?

KEY TERM

realism = when a text closely corresponds to real-life events. Magic realism is when a text combines aspects of reality and fantasy.

Extend your learning

Choose the most dramatic moment from your own set text. The extract should be about a page of text. Analyse how the writing works in that extract by devising a series of 'check your understanding' questions, then highlight a series of quotations, following them with comment on the effect of the writing. Think about the importance of that moment for the rest of the text. Share your ideas with a friend, and you are now ready to write. If you include ideas which move outside the extract and say what it reveals about a character or about other parts of the text, then you could use this extract for coursework.

How does the writer make this moment so dramatic and revealing?

Write an essay of 800–1,000 words in response.

8.8 Closure

Think ahead

A sense of the miraculous, or its opposite, the horrific, can help a prose text to achieve its closure. We tend to expect some form of justice, or appropriate ending for the characters. We have already seen that we have expectations of closure from the dramatic genres of comedy and tragedy, which can resurface in prose fiction. However, prose fiction can often also be open-ended ('resist closure'), perhaps because the writer plans a sequel, or perhaps because he or she wants to leave the reader with a sense of mystery, be true to the messiness of real life (rather than the tidier endings of fiction) or leave the reader to make up their own minds about the ending.

Miss Prism, played by Margaret Rutherford

Do you feel that characters get the ending they appear to deserve? Consider these two quotations by two great comic dramatists, one of whom we have already met earlier in this book:

'The good ended happily, and the bad unhappily. That is what Fiction means.' Miss Prism, *The Importance of Being Earnest*, Oscar Wilde (1854–1900)

'The bad end unhappily, the good unluckily. That is what tragedy means.' Player King, *Rosencrantz and Guildenstern Are Dead*, Tom Stoppard (1937–)

1. Does your novel have the neatness of the kind of fiction Wilde's Miss Prism is talking about?

2. Or the kind of tragic justice Stoppard's Player King describes?

3. Which characters survive and what do you feel about the journey they have been on and what they have learned?

4. Do you feel that characters get their 'just deserts', in other words, the kind of ending they deserve?

5. What remains a mystery or uncertain at the end of your set text?

This is an extract from R.L. Stevenson's *The Strange Case of Dr Jekyll and Mr Hyde*. Utterson's narrative, and that of his friend Dr Lanyon, leave many questions unanswered and we need a third account of events, 'Henry Jekyll's Full Statement of the Case', in order to achieve full understanding of that character's double life and the price he has paid for it. We already know that Jekyll had found it increasingly difficult to control his transformation into the murderous Hyde, and that Hyde has been found dead, dressed in Jekyll's clothes. Lanyon's narrative told the story of seeing Hyde turn himself into Jekyll by taking a drug, suggesting that they really are the same person.

Throughout the chapter, we have explored the ways in which writers use viewpoint to present characters and their feelings. Here we see a character who is so divided he has become two people, the calm and respected Dr Jekyll and the 'Ape-like' and criminal Mr Hyde. Stevenson is suggesting that many of us may have a monstrous **alter ego**, waiting for the opportunity to break out. Here, at the end of the novel, Dr Jekyll confesses what has become of him.

> **KEY TERM**
>
> **alter ego** = double or alternative identity.

The Strange Case of Dr Jekyll and Mr Hyde by R.L. Stevenson (1886)

I was stepping leisurely across the court after breakfast, drinking the chill of the air with pleasure, when I was seized again with those indescribable sensations that heralded the change; and I had but the time to gain the shelter of my cabinet, before I was once again raging and freezing with the passions of Hyde. It took on this occasion a double dose to recall me to myself; and alas! six hours after, as I sat looking sadly in the fire, the pangs returned, and the drug had to be re-administered. In short, from that day forth it seemed only by a great effort as of gymnastics, and only under the immediate stimulation of the drug, that I was able to wear the countenance of Jekyll. At all hours of the day and night, I would be taken with the premonitory shudder; above all, if I slept, or even dozed for a moment in my chair, it was always as Hyde that I awakened. Under the strain of this continually impending doom and by the sleeplessness to which I now condemned myself, ay, even beyond what I had thought possible to man, I became, in my own person, a creature eaten up and emptied by fever, languidly weak both in body and mind, and solely occupied by one thought: the horror of my other self. But when I slept, or when the virtue of the medicine wore off, I would leap almost without transition (for the pangs of transformation grew daily less marked) into the possession of a fancy brimming with images of terror, a soul boiling with causeless hatreds, and a body that seemed not strong enough to contain the raging energies of life. The powers of Hyde seemed to have grown with the sickliness of Jekyll. And certainly the hate that now divided them was equal on each side. With Jekyll, it was a thing of vital instinct. He had now seen the full deformity of that creature that shared with him some of the phenomena of consciousness, and was co-heir with him to death: and beyond these links of community, which in themselves made the most poignant part of his distress, he thought of Hyde, for all his energy of life, as of something not only hellish but inorganic. This was the shocking thing; that the slime of the pit seemed to utter cries and voices; that the amorphous dust gesticulated and sinned; that what was dead, and had no shape, should usurp the offices of life. And this again, that that insurgent horror was knit to him closer than a wife, closer than an eye; lay caged in his flesh, where he heard it mutter and felt it struggle to be born; and at every hour of weakness, and in the confidence of slumber, prevailed against him, and deposed him out of life.

This is a difficult passage, partly because it conveys difficult ideas, so we will pause and have a closer look.

1. Which words in the first sentence portray the calm Jekyll?

2. Which word shows the terror he feels at becoming Hyde?

3. Which details show that the drug is no longer working and it is becoming hard for him to hold onto this Jekyll identity and not involuntarily become Hyde?

4. What is the effect of this realization on Jekyll's health and happiness?

5. Which descriptions bring out the kind of emotions he feels as Hyde?

6. In what ways are Jeykll and Hyde still the same person, whatever the drug does to transform their appearance?

7. Which words show clearly the hatred and horror which Jekyll feels at the thought of Hyde?

Now read on and see how this passage develops. It examines what Hyde feels about Jekyll: remember that Jekyll is writing, so this shows the interesting ways in which he is both different from, and the same man as Hyde. Although they have different appearances and different emotions, they share the same consciousness. Hyde wants to take over Jekyll completely, and wants to stop playing a subordinate role.

The Strange Case of Dr Jekyll and Mr Hyde by R.L. Stevenson (1886)

The hatred of Hyde for Jekyll was of a different order. His terror of the gallows drove him continually to commit temporary suicide, and return to his subordinate station of a part instead of a person; but he loathed the necessity, he loathed the despondency into which Jekyll was now fallen, and he resented the dislike with which he was himself regarded. Hence the ape-like tricks that he would play me, scrawling in my own hand blasphemies on the pages of my books, burning the letters and destroying the portrait of my father; and indeed, had it not been for his fear of death, he would long ago have ruined himself in order to involve me in the ruin. But his love of me is wonderful; I go further: I, who sicken and freeze at the mere thought of him, when I recall the abjection and passion of this attachment, and when I know how he fears my power to cut him off by suicide, I find it in my heart to pity him.

It is useless, and the time awfully fails me, to prolong this description; no one has ever suffered such torments, let that suffice; and yet even to these, habit brought -- no, not alleviation -- but a certain callousness of soul, a certain acquiescence of despair; and my punishment might have gone on for years, but for the last calamity which has now fallen, and which has finally severed me from my own face and nature. My provision of the salt, which had never been renewed since the date of the first experiment, began to run low. I sent out for a fresh supply and mixed the draught; the ebullition followed, and the first change of colour, not the second; I drank it and it was without efficiency. You will learn from Poole how I have had London ransacked; it was in vain; and I am now persuaded that my first supply was impure, and that it was that unknown impurity which lent efficacy to the draught.

About a week has passed, and I am now finishing this statement under the influence of the last of the old powders. This, then, is the last time, short of a miracle, that Henry Jekyll can think his own thoughts or see his own face (now how sadly altered!) in the glass. Nor must I delay too long to bring my writing to an end; for if my narrative has hitherto escaped destruction, it has been by a combination of great prudence and great good luck. Should the throes of change take me in the act of writing it, Hyde will tear it in pieces; but if some time shall have elapsed after I have laid it by, his wonderful selfishness and circumscription to the moment will probably save it once again from the action of his ape-like spite. And indeed the doom that is closing on us both has already changed and crushed him. Half an hour from now, when I shall again and forever re-indue that hated personality, I know how I shall sit shuddering and weeping in my chair, or continue, with the most strained and fearstruck ecstasy of listening, to pace up and down this room (my last earthly refuge) and give ear to every sound of menace. Will Hyde die upon the scaffold? or will he find courage to release himself at the last moment? God knows; I am careless; this is my true hour of death, and what is to follow concerns another than myself. Here then, as I lay down the pen and proceed to seal up my confession, I bring the life of that unhappy Henry Jekyll to an end.

✎ Check your understanding

1. What does Hyde hate about Jekyll?

2. How does he try to get his revenge on him?

3. Why is Hyde nevertheless afraid of going too far in his hatred of Jekyll?

4. Why does Jekyll feel 'pity' for Hyde?

5. Jekyll says that he has got used to the miseries of his double life: what is the problem which has brought on the final catastrophe?

6. What does he now think caused the formula in the drug he created to work?

7. What does the change in Jekyll's face and feelings show the reader about the success or failure of Jekyll's attempt to keep his own identity and that of Hyde completely separate?

8. Why will he now have to bring the experiment to an end through his own death?

9. Why is he worried if the manuscript will survive?

10. Hyde's dead body was found in Jekyll's clothes. What does this suggest about how closely linked the two identities really are?

💬 Pair and share

We have seen how the language that surrounded Silas Marner in the previous extract is full of implications of the miraculous. In his confession Jekyll surrounds himself with the language of tragedy. Look together at the text and highlight the terms which show his sense of fate or doom.

1. How often does Jekyll use the first-person pronoun ('I')? What does this suggest about how self-obsessed he is? Why is he now so isolated?

2. How often does Jekyll use the third-person pronoun ('he')? Who does this invariably refer to? What does this suggest about his fear about the 'other' (who is really a part of himself)?

3. Can you find the one moment when he refers to 'us'? Why is this so revealing?

Look back at the definitions of tragedy we explored in chapter 7. Is Jekyll a tragic figure, or is he entirely to blame for his own fate? With your partner's help, draw up reasons for and against sympathizing with Jekyll. We can call this the evaluation of a character. Of course, characters can have more than one side to them; that's especially true of Henry Jekyll!

Viewpoints

Looking back to *The Importance of Being Earnest*, you will have noticed how the 'double life', questions about whether your identity can be split and divided or whether you are a whole person (both body and soul) greatly troubled nineteenth-century writers.

1. Why do you think this was the case?

2. What would have been the influence of discoveries in science (for example, evolution) and technology?

3. How might greater social mobility and the effect of urbanization have influenced these worries?

4. Notice that Hyde is referred to as 'ape-like'. How might evolutionary theory and fear about other races have influenced these European obsessions with threats to the 'purity' of humanity?

5. Why might religious anxiety have been a factor?

6. Do these anxieties relate to declining belief in an after-life or the supernatural?

7. Do we have similar concerns today (for example, over the creation of online 'avatars')?

Debate these questions with your classmates. Using the debate format we used earlier, argue for or against the proposition:

Human beings only have one life, and need to make up their mind about how to live it.

 Look up the following terms in the glossary and revise their meanings: tragedy, revelation, irony, convention.

 See the following worksheets on the website:

Worksheet 6: Character evaluation

Worksheet 7: Character timeline

8.9 Reader response

Think ahead

We call the kind of ending we expect 'closure'. It gives a fate to the characters which they seem to deserve. Not all writers want their texts to have this kind of ending, where most of the loose ends are tied up. Increasingly in the later twentieth century and in more recent novels as well as plays, narratives are said to resist closure. Which is true of your set text? Did you feel happy and satisfied with the way your text ended? Or did you want something more? Either way, you can see that the text is written in a way which will stimulate 'personal response'.

Writers want their readers to respond to characters and situations, and want to work on your emotions. This is not just in order to sell more books: books often have a purpose which goes beyond the reader's engagement and entertainment. Why do you read books? How have they informed your understanding of the world and what you feel about it?

Harper Lee (1926–2016) wrote *To Kill a Mockingbird* at the beginning of the 1960s. Although it looks back to an earlier time, the time of her childhood in the American South before the Second World War, the themes of racism and injustice which it portrays so powerfully captured the mood of the time when the novel was published. It has since been studied in most American high schools and in secondary schools all over the world. Look up an online biography of Martin Luther King in order to appreciate the issues of racial segregation and discrimination in the Southern states of America at this time.

In this scene from the 1962 film, Atticus Finch and Tom Robinson are seen in the courtroom

How does your own set text achieve closure not only for individual characters, but also for the themes of the novel? How does it help the reader to reflect on their response to those themes?

In the following passage, the narrative viewpoint is that of Scout, a young girl, as it has been throughout the novel. The life of her brother Jem has been saved by their neighbour, the mysterious Boo Radley. Boo has been confined to his house by his parents throughout the book up to this point, and the children have been afraid of him. Now Scout realizes that Boo was their friend and protector. This passage is part of the novel's epilogue (the part that comes after the main action is over). Scout realizes that her father, Atticus, was right, and that you can only understand another person if you are able to adopt their viewpoint. Scout is standing on Boo's front porch. As she looks back at the houses belonging to all her neighbours, she slips back in time. In her imagination, she sees things as Boo would, describing the events of the novel from his viewpoint (confined to his house) rather than hers. In the process, we see how she has grown up, and her view of the world has matured.

To Kill a Mockingbird by Harper Lee (1960)

Neighbours bring food with death and flowers with sickness and little things in between. Boo was our neighbour. He gave us two soap dolls, a broken watch and chain, a pair of good-luck pennies, and our lives. But neighbours give in return. We never put back into the tree what we took out of it: we had given him nothing, and it made me sad.

I turned to go home. Street lights winked down the street all the way to town. There were Miss Maudie's, Miss Stephanie's – there was our house, I could see the porch swing – Miss Rachel's house was beyond us, plainly visible. I could even see Mrs Dubose's.

I looked behind me. To the left of the brown door was a long shuttered window. I walked to it, stood in front of it, and turned around. In daylight, I thought, you could see to the post office corner.

Daylight…in my mind, the night faded. It was daytime and the neighbourhood was busy. Miss Stephanie Crawford crossed the street to tell the latest to Miss Rachel. Miss Maudie bent over her azaleas. It was summertime, and two children scampered down the sidewalk towards a man approaching in the distance. The man waved, and the children raced each other to him.

It was still summertime, and the children came closer. A boy trudged down the sidewalk dragging a fishing-pole behind him. A man stood waiting with his hands on his hips. Summertime, and his children played in the front yard with their friend, enacting a strange little drama of their own invention.

It was fall, and his children fought on the sidewalk in front of Mrs Dubose's. The boy helped his sister to her feet, and they made their way home. Fall, and his children trotted to and fro around the corner, the day's woes and triumphs on their faces. They stopped at an oak tree, delighted, puzzled, apprehensive.

Winter, and his children shivered at the front gate, silhouetted against a blazing house. Winter, and a man walked into the street, dropped his glasses, and shot a dog.

Summer and he watched his children's heart break. Autumn again, and Boo's children needed him.

Atticus was right. One time he said you never really know a man until you stand in his shoes and walk around in them. Just standing on the Radley porch was enough.

✎ Check your understanding

1. In the first paragraph, why does Scout feel sad about her relationship with Boo now she realizes that he was the person who left presents in the tree?

2. In the second paragraph, why is Scout so interested in the view from Boo's house across to those of her neighbours, and across to her own house?

3. In the third paragraph, why does she go back to stand outside Boo's shuttered window?

4. How can we tell that she goes back in time, in her imagination?

5. Who do you think the children are, who she now looks at from Boo's point of view?

6. Why does Boo call them 'his' children?

7. Why might the children be 'puzzled' by what is left for them in the tree?

8. How does the whole passage support Atticus's claim that you can only understand another person if you can 'stand in his shoes'?

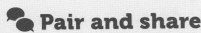

Pair and share

1. How have you come to understand the ways in which characters in the text you have studied think?

2. Decide on a character with whom you have empathized while reading your text. How did the writer encourage you to understand their point of view? Has it been through first-person narrative, the portrayal of their thoughts and feelings or through the things they have said?

3. Using your notes on characters, find quotations from the text to show ways in which you have come to understand characters very different from yourself.

4. Take different characters from your partner, and then share your notes and quotations. Do you agree about your experience of the novel or do you disagree?

5. It is possible to take very different views about characters. Which characters is it possible to see from more than one point of view?

6. How successful is the time shift in the extract here? How does the novel you have studied present the passing of time?

Draw up a timeline for a wall display, tracking the key events of the novel, and the key developments for the main character. Use this as a visual aid, to chart the progress of your novel, its characters and your understanding of them.

 # Viewpoints

In this passage, we see that Scout has grown up, and it also adds to what we have already seen to be the fate of the other main characters. However, Harper Lee achieves closure not just for the characters of the text but also for her principal theme. Empathy is the ability to adopt the point of view of other people, or as Atticus puts it, standing in other people's shoes and walking around in them.

1. Why is empathy an important quality in combating prejudice and unfairness?

2. Why is empathy also an important quality in law and the administration of justice?

3. Why would empathy be a key characteristic of a writer?

4. How can empathy help the literature student to understand characters and their choices?

The passage makes it clear that Harper Lee writes with a purpose and that Scout has grown up. Indeed her voice and the techniques used to convey her thoughts are probably not now those of the young girl, but more like those of an older woman looking back, and finding words to describe the feelings of her younger self.

How does your text encourage you, as a reader, to look back over the events of the novel? Does the writing help you to make sense of what you have seen described? Does the novel still have something to say to readers today?

Extend your learning

Apply these ideas to the way in which the writer achieves, or resists, closure in your own text.

To what extent has the writing helped you to see the novel as a whole and to appreciate the writer's purpose in telling you this story?

- Base your answer on the close reading of a passage at or close to the end of the book.

- Use this to look back at events, characters and themes of the rest of the text.

- Consider both the writer's purpose and the reader's reaction at the end of the novel.

Looking back

In completing the class novel, or short stories, you have finished the biggest task in your Cambridge Literature in English course. Well done! The last pages here have encouraged you to look back and reflect on what you have read. You will need to re-read the text and revise it as you move closer to your exams. Looking back at this chapter, reflect both on the prose text you have read and what you have learned.

Think about how your reading has extended your understanding of the following points.

1. The ways in which writers capture your attention
2. How writers use the conventions of different genres of prose (for example, mystery, romance, science fiction)
3. The importance of the setting in establishing the atmosphere of the text
4. Why the narrative voice and viewpoint are significant
5. How prose writers use allegory and symbolism
6. The importance of interesting and realistic characterization
7. The way writers use shock effects and mystery
8. How to explore time shifts during the course of a narrative
9. The extent to which novels reflect real-life events
10. The ways in which writers contrast the human and natural worlds
11. The function of irony and suspense, and how they create turning points and revelation in works of fiction
12. How writers create sympathetic and unsympathetic characters
13. The ways in which description takes the reader beyond surface meaning
14. The impact of revelation and closure on the reader's evaluation of character
15. How prose texts encourage different kinds of empathy from their readers

You can apply any of these ideas to the structure and expression of your own set text, either basing your answer around a single extract, or using several examples from different parts of the text to analyse ways in which the text and the reader's understanding of it develop.

For further advice about preparing coursework essays, and revising your set texts, look at the website materials.

 Explore Worksheet 8, narrator checklist.

Studying poetry

9

Your Cambridge Literature in English poetry selection will either be a selection of texts from various different poets from different cultures and ages, or it will be a selection of the work of an individual poet. You will not need to compare poems in the exam. However, there may be a question which asks you about more than one poem, or which asks you to look at a theme or technique common to more than one poem, and to make a choice about which poem you write on.

You will need to read the poems very closely. Poems will need line-by-line annotation, with close attention to rhythm, imagery and the choice of words: you should work with a copy of each poem which you can mark up, as you were shown to do in chapter 4. For these reasons, you might choose to read the poems relatively late in your course, when you have developed good close reading skills.

All the questions on the exam paper will include a copy of the poems they refer to, and you should make the close study of individual poems the principal focus of your writing. When interpreting or evaluating a poem, what is distinctive and different is usually more interesting than what makes it similar to other poems you have read.

Above all, remember that structure, language and form should guide your response to poetry as much as their subject matter or narrative.

LEARNING POINTS

▶ To understand the ways in which poets use form and structure to shape their writing

▶ To explore the impact of the poet's choices of words (diction) and sentence structure (syntax)

▶ To appreciate in detail the ways in which **rhythm** shapes the music of poetry (tone)

▶ To respond in individual ways to poets' use of imagery to affect the reader's thoughts and feelings (mood)

KEY TERM

rhythm = the musical patterns of stress formed by the beat of a line of poetry.

9.1 Poetic voice

Think ahead

John Keats (1795–1821) belonged to the second generation of English Romantic poets, and grew up in London. Never wealthy or privileged, he was determined, after a brief medical training, to be 'among the great English poets'. His letters show his passionate commitment to literature and its importance, what he called 'the holiness of the heart's affections and the truth of the imagination'. In a short literary career, before his death from tuberculosis, he wrote many poems, but is especially famous for the great odes he wrote in the summer of 1819. In love with a young neighbour, Fanny Brawne, he had made an intense study of Shakespeare, Milton and Dante and was gaining greater confidence in his own poetic voice just as he realised he would die of the same illness as his brother, whom he had nursed.

What else can you add to the notes above, from your own internet research about Keats's life, his work, famous lines that he wrote, and critical opinions about his writing? In a group of four, construct a presentation, including illustrations or slides if you wish, in which you each take one of the following tasks or roles:

1. The biographer, presenting interesting aspects of his life: what made him an unusual and interesting man?

2. The literature professor exploring his famous works and a few well-known lines from them: what were his favourite themes?

3. The historian, presenting facts about Keats's world: in what ways were his interests typical of people of his age?

4. The critic: use quotations to show what people said about Keats's work, both in his own lifetime and since. Why has Keats had a strong influence on other poets in the century since his death?

🔗 Language links

Activities like this can also form part of a Speaking and Listening assessment if you are studying Cambridge First Language English. Make sure that you turn the presentation into an argument, by addressing an overall question, and that after the mini-presentation you debate the question as a group and reach an agreement. Your question could be:

What are the key factors which make Keats such a well-known and significant poet?

Later in this chapter, we will look at different ways of tackling either the selection or the set poet, in order to combine close reading with contextual understanding. However, here we will focus above all on form, structure and language.

Poetic form

Look closely at the formal qualities of the poem which follows, paying careful attention to:

- stanza form
- rhyme
- rhythm
- sound patterns
- syntax.

Then look more closely at word level, and broaden your thinking to consider the impact of the whole poem. The rhythms are especially interesting. See if you can mark up the stress patterns of the verse, as you learned to do in chapter 4.

Put a stress mark over each vowel, either long (/) for a stressed syllable, which the beat falls on, or short (x) for a weak or unstressed syllable. Use the length of vowel sounds and the emphasis on individual words to guide you, and remember that poetry should not sound very different from the rhythms of standard speech.

The grave of John Keats

'Ode on Melancholy' by John Keats (1819)

I

No, no, go not to Lethe, neither twist
Wolf's-bane, tight-rooted, for its poisonous wine;
Nor suffer thy pale forehead to be kiss'd
By nightshade, ruby grape of Proserpine;
Make not your rosary of yew-berries,
Nor let the beetle, nor the death-moth be
Your mournful Psyche, nor the downy owl
A partner in your sorrow's mysteries;
For shade to shade will come too drowsily,
And drown the wakeful anguish of the soul.

Lethe = river of forgetfulness in classical underworld
Wolf's-bane = aconite, a herbal remedy for depression
nightshade = another herbal remedy which can be poisonous
Proserpine = the queen of the underworld
rosary = necklace of prayer beads
death-moth = moth with markings resembling a human skull
Psyche = goddess of the soul, sometimes represented by a butterfly

II

But when the melancholy fit shall fall
Sudden from heaven like a weeping cloud,
That fosters the droop-headed flowers all,
And hides the green hill in an April shroud;
Then glut thy sorrow on a morning rose,
Or on the rainbow of the salt sand-wave,
Or on the wealth of globed peonies;
Or if thy mistress some rich anger shows,
Emprison her soft hand, and let her rave,
And feed deep, deep upon her peerless eyes.

> *fosters* = helps to grow
> *April shroud* = alludes to rain clouds in the rainy month in England
> *rainbow of the salt sand-wave* = sun glinting on waves of sand
> *globed peonies* = large flowers with strong scents

III

She dwells with Beauty—Beauty that must die;
And Joy, whose hand is ever at his lips
Bidding adieu; and aching Pleasure nigh,
Turning to poison while the bee-mouth sips:
Ay, in the very temple of Delight
Veil'd Melancholy has her sovran shrine,
Though seen of none save him whose strenuous tongue
Can burst Joy's grape against his palate fine;
His soul shalt taste the sadness of her might,
And be among her cloudy trophies hung.

> *Beauty... Joy... Pleasure... Delight* = all personifications, like Melancholy
> *adieu* = goodbye
> *sovran* = sovereign, royal

✎ Check your understanding

An ode is a poem of praise, for a person or object, and is a traditional classical form. Keats and other English Romantic poets wanted to express their own emotions and their love of nature more directly, but saw no clash between romantic feelings and classical forms, and all wrote in traditional metres and poetic forms. Here, a complex stanza form is used, combining units of four and six lines into a ten-line stanza. Each stanza makes up a single sentence which makes up a stage of an argument about 'Melancholy'; this is not only the subject of the poem, but also the person addressed and praised. Nowadays, we might describe melancholy as depression, but Keats praises this mood, saying it is closely linked to the ability to experience 'Joy' and 'Beauty'. Answer the following questions to help you make sense of each stanza.

1. What is surprising about the first line, in what is meant to be a poem of praise?

2. Where do the strong stresses fall in the first line?

3. Lethe is the river of forgetfulness, and wolf's bane was a traditional herbal remedy or drug for 'melancholy'. Where else does Keats suggest you should not try drugs which will make you forget what makes you feel sad?

4. Keats seems to be suggesting that you should not try to shut out sadness, but he also suggests you should not turn it into a badge. What are the symbols of the night or of insomnia which he mentions?

5. Where does he suggest that we might be better off staying awake, even if it causes us pain, than trying to sleep and forget our sorrows?

6. In the second stanza, Keats suggests that the 'melancholy fit' is like a force of nature; what does he compare it to?

7. What does this suggest about sadness?

8. In the second part of this stanza, what does he say we should go and look at, in order to understand our feelings of sadness?

9. Find the words which suggest that he sees all of these as good, and not sad, things.

10. Melancholy is personified in this poem as a goddess. Why does Keats suggest that she lives alongside Beauty and Joy?

11. What does he suggest happens to our happiness which turns it into sadness?

12. Keats uses a metaphor taken from producing wine for a 'palate fine' in order to explain how things need to be lost or destroyed in order to produce our pleasures. Which words does he use which appeal to our senses?

13. Why do you think the goddess Melancholy is portrayed as 'veiled'?

14. He imagines her as living in a shrine surrounded by 'cloudy trophies'. Why does she win, even when we are most happy?

15. How would you characterize Keats's attitude to Melancholy, and why does he suggest we should praise or celebrate it?

 ## Pair and share

Once you have marked up the poem and appreciated how its rhythms work, practise reading it aloud with your partner. You will find that this works best if one of you reads the first four lines of each stanza, and the other the next six.

You will find that your reading will make more sense if you go through the following steps.

1. Use a colour to highlight the verbs which give movement and meaning to the verse. In the first stanza, these are: 'go not', 'twist', 'suffer', 'kiss'd', 'make', 'nor let', 'will come' and 'drown'. These are the words to aim for in your reading in order to make your sense clear.

2. Use a different colour to highlight adjectives, such as 'ruby' and 'downy'. These give a visual aspect, or colour to your reading.

3. Next underline the sound effects which bring out the 'sensuous' qualities of the verse, all the effects which appeal to our senses. Look out for patterns of repeated initial letters (alliteration) and soft 's' sounds (**sibilance**); these will give a musical quality or tone to your reading.

4. Pause briefly at the end of each line to bring out the rhyme, but make sure the sense carries forward through the verse until you reach the semi-colon or full stop.

5. Short words with long vowel sounds (for example, 'wine', 'owl', 'soul') get more stress and emphasis than longer words with shorter sounds.

6. Repeat the process of marking up the verse for the other two stanzas and then perform your version out loud for another pair.

 Use a copy of the poem printed from the website to mark up stress patterns and highlight rhymes.

KEY TERM

sibilance = lots of 's' sounds.

Viewpoints

When Keats's poems were first published, they caused some controversy. Some thought he had pushed Romanticism too far, and were embarrassed by his blatant emphasis on personal feelings, the imagination and an appeal to our senses. There were even some who thought his poetry was 'unhealthy'. Defend the poet against this charge and argue why his attitude to depression might actually be a helpful one, even for readers today.

Extend your learning

There are five other famous 1819 odes by Keats, a little longer than this one: 'To a Nightingale', 'On a Grecian Urn', 'On Indolence', 'To Psyche' and 'To Autumn'. You might enjoy reading all of them, and they are easy to find online. The first two are especially recommended, and the second has the famous lines:

"Beauty is Truth, Truth Beauty" – that is all

Ye know on earth, and all ye need to know'.

How successfully does Keats combine his love of beauty with his search for truth?

To find out more about this poem, have a look at the British Library website: https://www.bl.uk/romantics-and-victorians/articles/an-introduction-to-ode-on-melancholy. This useful website includes original manuscripts of poems and will tell you more about Romanticism and other poets of the period. A short selection of Keats's letters will also tell you a lot about his life, his reading and his ideas.

9.2 Imagery

Think ahead

Poets often seem 'much possessed by death'. This is not just because of personal circumstances. Poets also want their work to be immortal, and to survive what Shakespeare describes in 'Sonnet 60' as 'the cruel hand of time'.

1. How might elegies celebrate life as well as death?
2. Which other elegies have you already read?
3. What kind of immortality might poetry celebrate?
4. How does rhythm help poets to express their feelings about life and death?

Emily Dickinson (1830–86) was an American poet, who lived almost her entire life in seclusion in her family home in Amherst, Massachusetts. She shares the preoccupations of nineteenth-century English poets with elegy, and with religious faith and doubt, and her poetry also expresses private and personal emotions. Very few of her poems were published in her lifetime, however, she wrote prolifically and with a strong sense of audience. Her poems do not use conventional punctuation, and are full of symbolism, so are not to be read literally, or confined to a single meaning. You should be able to enjoy working out your own interpretations; her poems are not necessarily autobiographical, but they share her personal concerns with the nature of life and death, and with the natural world. Read the poem out to yourself, or around the class. Can you pick up its regular rhythm?

Emily Dickinson

'Because I Could Not Stop for Death' by Emily Dickinson (1862)

Because I could not stop for Death –
He kindly stopped for me –
The Carriage held but just Ourselves
And Immortality.

We slowly drove – He knew no haste
And I had put away
My labor and my leisure too,
For his Civility –

We passed the School, where Children strove
At Recess – in the Ring –
We passed the Fields of Gazing Grain –
We passed the Setting Sun –

Recess = break time at school

Or rather – He passed Us –
The Dews drew quivering and chill –
For only Gossamer, my Gown –
My Tippet – only Tulle –

A *tippet* is a scarf; *gossamer* and *tulle* are very light fabrics

We paused before a House that seemed
A Swelling of the Ground –
The Roof was scarcely visible –
The Cornice – in the Ground –

Cornice = ornamental moulding at the top of a building

Since then – 'tis Centuries – and yet
Feels shorter than the Day
I first surmised the Horses' Heads
Were toward Eternity –

✎ Check your understanding

1. Mark up the strong stresses on your own copy of the poem and note the regularity of the rhythm.

2. How does Dickinson use alternating rhythms and rhymes?

3. How does Dickinson alternate feminine and masculine voices?

4. Who do you think are the feminine and masculine characters in this poem?

5. What is the effect of using so many capital letters?

6. What sort of character does Death have in this poem and what is surprising about this?

7. What does the poet abandon in order to ride with him?

8. What do they see on their journey?

9. Why does she feel cold?

10. What kind of house do they pause at in the penultimate stanza?

11. Where do they go next, and what is surprising about the final stanza?

12. Why is it important that the poem does not end with a full stop?

Pair and share

You should have been able to establish that the poet imagines that she is on a journey with Death, and that the other characters or sights in the poem may also be personifications or symbols. However, thanks to the rhythm of the poem, the tone is quite a bright one, very different from the bleaker aspects of melancholy in Keats's poem. What do you think the poem might mean?

With your partner, look at the poem's rhythms. Where do the strong stresses fall? Which are the masculine lines and rhythms? What is the effect of this degree of finality or closure?

What do you think is the effect of the punctuation? Hyphens link words and ideas, while dashes separate them. Which do you think Dickinson is using? Does this contradict the ways in which the rhythms of the poem suggest closure?

Having looked at the rhythms and patterns of the poem, it is now necessary to interpret its images. The poet is on a journey, and the stanzas show what she sees along the way in a series of pictures or images.

Imagery embraces personifications and metaphors, and can be characterized as the 'slide show' or pictures which we see while reading the poem. In discussion with your partner, try to visualize the images which follow, before interpreting them. Imagine you are in an art gallery, imagining why the artist has chosen these images and what they suggest to you. The first three are done for you to give you some guidance. Together, work out your own answers to the other images, using the questions provided as prompts.

Image	Interpretation
The Carriage held but just Ourselves And Immortality	The carriage might be the journey of life, while the personification of Immortality suggests that while the poet's body is mortal and hand-in-hand with death, perhaps an immortal soul is on the journey with them.
And I had put away My labor and my leisure too, For his Civility	Death is a gentleman, and the ride is a gentle one. The poet has given up both work and pleasure for him; it is almost as if they are married.
We passed the School, where Children strove At Recess – in the Ring –	Early in the journey they go past a school full of children, suggesting they are leaving childish things behind. The 'striving' suggests competition among the children. Perhaps the poet sees this as something childish which she has left behind, or something innocent which she has now grown out of.
We passed the Fields of Gazing Grain – We passed the Setting Sun	What do these symbolize? Why does the grain 'gaze'?
The Dews drew quivering and chill	The dew of evening is also alive; what does it represent?
For only Gossamer, my Gown – My Tippet – only Tulle	What kind of dress does she seem to be wearing? What point is she making by being ill-equipped for this journey?
The Roof was scarcely visible – The Cornice – in the Ground	The house is made up of a series of apparent contradictions? Is it really a house or a home? Why do they 'pause before it' instead of 'pass'? Where do they go next?
Since then – 'tis Centuries – and yet Feels shorter than the Day	What does this very abstract image suggest about the time frame of the journey? Does it take place in what we think of as 'real time'? If you imagined it in a series of pictures, what setting or time period would you give them?

the Horses' Heads Were toward Eternity	This is a difficult image to picture. What kind of horses are these and why are they hard to control? What might Eternity look like?

Did it help to visualize the words and what they might describe? If so find a series of images on the internet which might illustrate and support a reading of the poem. These can be projected to support a dramatic reading of the poem, as students read different stanzas aloud.

The imagery of poems allows them to be interpreted in the same way as we might interpret art. Like art these images can represent things in life-like ways, but are just as likely to be allegorical, metaphorical or abstract. Poems are like multi-media experiences: we see these poems, but they are also accompanied by music, in the form of rhythm.

The nature of the images make this journey by carriage alongside Death much more like a dream journey than anything real. How do dreams relate to real life and our real thoughts and feelings?

Put together an illustrated reading of the poem. One partner should concentrate on finding the images, and the other on a rhythmic reading of the poem's music. Do imagery and music match? Or is there a creative tension between them? Are those tensions resolved by the ending, or does the tone of the ending 'resist closure'? Discuss these questions as a class.

Viewpoints

I first surmised the Horses' Heads

Were toward Eternity –

What kind of experience or discovery might the poem illustrate? What has 'the poet' discovered about her journey through life? Notice that she says she made this discovery long ago, but it seems like less than a day.

We know Dickinson chose to live a secluded life, never marrying or leaving the family home and devoting herself to poetry.

1. In what ways might the poem dramatize life choices?
2. Does the poem express pessimism about the inevitability of death and the brief nature of life?
3. Or does it celebrate immortality and suggest that death is nothing to be feared?

Find evidence for each interpretation above, by choosing quotations.

You will see that poems often have more than one meaning, and that they gain their meaning from the effect of the words on the individual reader.

Poems do not necessarily tell a literal story, or have a single theme. The poems in this chapter are much more complex, and even contradictory than those in chapter 4. For many of them, your own interpretation is as valid as someone else's, as long as you can support it with close attention to the language and images of the text.

Extend your learning

What would be Death's account of the ride described in the poem? Write a poem of your own using similar rhythmic patterns to portray the ride, seeing the journey from Death's point of view. What would the poet look like to him? Why has he chosen her?

9.3 Different cultures

Think ahead

We now move from Dickinson's small world of nineteenth-century Massachusetts, to the post-colonial era of the twentieth century. How have opportunities for women changed?

Find out what you can about the poet Sujata Bhatt (1956–), who has lived in India, the USA, the UK and Germany.

Start with the following website, where you can find information on her work:

http://www.carcanet.co.uk/cgi-bin/indexer?owner_id=51

You will find an interview with her at:

http://www.carcanet.co.uk/cgi-bin/scribe?showdoc=4;doctype=interview

In the poem which follows Bhatt compares the ancient classical gods with the gods of India. What do you understand by the term 'pantheism'? What difference might it make to believe that everything is sacred? What does that suggest about the place of human beings in the world?

A statute of a Hindu goddess

'A Different History' by Sujata Bhatt (1988)

Great Pan is not dead;
he simply emigrated
      to India.
Here, the gods roam freely,
disguised as snakes or monkeys;
every tree is sacred
and it is a sin
to be rude to a book.
It is a sin to shove a book aside
         with your foot,
a sin to slam books down
      hard on a table,
a sin to toss one carelessly
      across a room.
You must learn how to turn the pages gently
without disturbing Sarasvati,
without offending the tree
from whose wood the paper was made.

    Which language
    has not been the oppressor's tongue?
    Which language

Pan = the Ancient Greek god of nature, part-man, part-goat; he was also very musical, playing 'pan-pipes', and was worshipped through music and dance.

Sarasvati = the Hindu goddess of the arts.

truly meant to murder someone?
And how does it happen
that after the torture,
after the soul has been cropped
with a long scythe swooping out
of the conqueror's face –
the unborn grandchildren
grow to love that strange language.

Sarasvati, the Hindu goddess of the arts

Check your understanding

Bhatt makes a number of complex points in this poem through a series of very striking images.

1. What does the word 'emigrated' suggest about different beliefs in different parts of the world?
2. Why do you think the poet chose to concentrate on the mischievous god Pan?
3. What is the effect of using the present tense?
4. How does the poet notice that the attitude to nature is different in India?
5. How is the attitude to books and the written word different?
6. What is the relationship between books, gods and the natural world?
7. Why does she move on to consider the relationship between language and oppression?
8. How might the history of colonization link language to murder and torture?
9. What seems to happen to the soul of people who are colonized?
10. What happens to the torturer's language for future generations?
11. Does this explain why Bhatt is writing in English here (some of her poems also use Gujarati, her mother tongue)?
12. Why does the poem not end with a question mark?

Pair and share

This poem does not have a regular rhythm. However, a strong rhythmic effect is created by the short lines, and by the writer's choice of line endings. Why are some lines long and others short? Why are some indented far from the margin? Where are we encouraged to pause? Why?

In pairs, use a copy printed from the website to mark up the poem, thinking about where the lines encourage us to read slowly, and where we are encouraged to read more quickly and make more links and connections between images or ideas. How would you read the poem aloud? What is the effect of giving each new sentence a new speaker? Divide the poem up between you and decide on the pace at which you will read it.

What is the effect of the repetition which gives the poem part of its structure? Explore the effect of:

1. the three references to 'a sin'

2. the two mentions of 'without'

3. the two questions

4. the two uses of the word 'after'.

Why is the final sentence so long, and why does it eventually break free from all of these patterns?

Find images of Indian gods which combine the features of men and animals to illustrate a slide show accompanying this poem.

What does the poem remind you about books and how they are made? Research the process of making paper, and remember books are made out of what was a living thing. Can you find images to accompany this?

There are disturbing images of how language is abused and used for abuse in the second half of the poem. How has the language of colonizers been used to suppress native tongues and their speakers? What happens to the 'soul' if you are not allowed to express your thoughts and feelings in your native tongue? Why might writers nevertheless choose to write in English?

Find images which will support what the poem suggests to you about books and language, and how attitudes towards them have changed as a result of history.

Now present a dramatic reading of the poem, in pairs or groups, illustrated by pictures.

 Viewpoints

In monotheistic religions, certain books are sacred because they are the revealed word of God. In pantheistic cultures, there is a different reason for seeing books as sacred. What is it?

Think about how the poet links the first and second halves of this poem. What do they have in common? How do they contrast? A key adjective like 'gently' can help you to contrast the mood and imagery of the two halves of the poem. Notice how ideas can be linked by their differences as well as their similarities.

Why does Bhatt call the poem 'A Different History'? In what ways does she help you to read history in a different way?

The images in the second half of the poem are disturbing and painful ones. They describe some languages conquering and other languages being oppressed. Language is used to 'crop' a people's soul and limit their ability to express themselves. Which languages do you know which are 'conqueror' languages, and which ones have been restricted? Is language change now a process which is less oppressive or restricting? How does knowledge of a world language help you to express yourself?

🔗 Language links

Debate the importance of being able to communicate in English. Has the dominance of English as a world language done more harm than good?

In poetry, as we have seen, different interpretations are possible, and a personal response is the best way to interpret a poem, grounded in exploration of language, structure and form. How have the music and the choice of words and images given this poem a particular tone? What mood does it communicate to you? Does it seem angry, full of wonder or quite reassuring? What does it suggest to you about violence and how it is overcome through respect?

Tone is how the writer fills the poem with expression, and mood is the emotional world of the poem. Note how tone and mood can help you to shape an interpretation.

9.4 Interpretation

Think ahead

Of course, poets do not need to dramatize versions of themselves, or present personal ideas in all of their poems. They can also tell stories or dramatize the stories of others. Poetry is usually lyrical, but it is often dramatic. Its reliance on images can also allow it to convey snapshots of things poets have seen, or people they have met. The words and images of poems can be like a website, or social network, communicating things the poet has seen, thought, or felt to others.

We live in a world of global travel. How many different countries have you and your classmates travelled to? Use a map of the world to pinpoint locations you and others know about. What stories can you tell about places you have seen? How has travel to different parts of the world made you aware of different histories and different cultures?

The English poet Carol Rumens (1944–) writes a weekly blog called Poem of the Week for the online edition of *The Guardian* newspaper, which can be found at this link:

http://www.guardian.co.uk/books/series/poemoftheweek

In the poem which follows, Rumens describes something she saw on a visit to Morocco. It describes children at work weaving an Islamic carpet by hand on a frame-loom. What kind of images might this carpet have on it? What is the role of the carpet in Islamic worship? What images do we usually have of child labour? These children are at work in a madrasa, so their work forms part of their religious education.

Moroccan children working at a loom

Extend your learning

Look at ways in which both Dickinson and Bhatt are explaining why they write. For Dickinson, writing is a way of conveying an idea which goes on a journey beyond life and death towards immortality. For Bhatt, the written word is sacred, and alive; it embodies a respect for nature and for all life, even a history which is often an oppressive and violent word. For her, you cannot blame the language itself for its history and she encourages a gentle respect for the word.

Write an essay on the question below, which will conclude with an interpretation of each poem, but which grounds them in analysis of language and form. Look at how the question encourages you:

- to explore the writer's choices
- to analyse their effect on the reader
- to evaluate different responses and ways of interpreting the text.

How do Dickinson and Bhatt convey different ideas of the poet's need to express a personal vision of the world?

As this could be a coursework essay, write up to 1,200 words.

'Carpet-weavers, Morocco' by Carol Rumens (1994)

Their children are at the loom of another world.
Their braids are oiled and black, their dresses bright.
Their assorted heights would make a melodious chime.

They watch their flickering knots like television.
As the garden of Islam grows, the bench will be raised.
Then they will lace the dark-rose veins of the tree-tops.

The carpet will travel in the merchant's truck.
It will be spread by the servants of the mosque.
Deep and soft, it will give when heaped with prayer.

The children are hard at work in the school of days.
From their fingers the colours of all-that-will-be fly
And freeze into the frame of all-that-was.

✎ Check your understanding

1. Why does the poet describe the creation of the carpet as making 'another world'?

2. What details make the children look well cared for and proud of their work?

3. What does the sight of their different heights remind her of?

4. Why does she suggest that the story they are weaving into the carpet is like television for them?

5. As the carpet gets bigger, what do they need to do to the children's working bench?

6. What kind of images are on the carpet?

7. Who will buy the carpet from the merchant?

8. Why will the carpet make a good surface for prayer?

9. What kind of 'school' do the children attend?

10. Why are the patterns they are making patterns of the future?

11. Why is the framework which surrounds the carpet a symbol for the past which surrounds the children?

12. What is the poet suggesting about the very traditional life which these children live?

Pair and share

It is a mistake to treat all poems in the same way and to have a template or checklist for analysis of poems. Some poems are very rhythmic, some are strongly visual and some are a combination of the two. Which is most important in this poem: its imagery or its music?

A focus on the visual suits this poem's colourful subject; highlight all the references to colour. Can you find references to the other senses? How do these accompany the strong visual appearance of the carpet?

There are sound effects in this poem; look for examples of alliteration. Discuss the ways in which the alliteration in the first, third and final stanzas supports the sensuous qualities of sight, touch and movement. Why is there less alliteration in the second stanza? What does the poet concentrate on conveying here?

We have to imagine what the carpet looks like from the images we are given. What impression of the carpet do you gain from the following images?

Image	Your impression
'garden of Islam grows'	
'the dark-rose veins of the tree-tops'	
'the colours of all-that-will-be'	
'another world'	

How do the descriptions help you to picture the 'other world' which the carpet portrays? Why is it portrayed as a 'garden'? Think of the different connotations of the word 'garden'.

For the children, creating the carpet is like watching a television show, seeing a story unfold, or a school lesson about what to expect in future days. How do these metaphors work?

As the children are involved in activity, the poet uses a number of verbs to convey their actions. With your partner, highlight the verbs in your copy of the poem and discuss the following questions.

- Which words show the delicacy of their work and which words show their speed?

- What is the effect of the contrast between 'fly' in the penultimate line and 'freeze' in the final line?

- What else do we apply the word 'freeze' to?

- Why does it fit well with the reference to the 'frame' which surrounds the carpet as it is being made?

- What makes this an especially effective last line?

A Moroccan carpet

Viewpoints

Is the poem really about the carpet, about the children, or about something else? You have choices when interpreting a poem. On the surface the poem gives a vivid, colourful, lively and sensuous image of a particular moment the poet has observed on her travels. That might be enough to make it a fine poem. However, perhaps we can go beyond surface meanings and explore the implications that could be less immediate.

To do this, we will need a different, less literal way of reading some of the descriptions. If you forget the literal image of the carpet-weaving for a moment, what connotations are suggested by the following images?

Image	Connotations
'at the loom of another world'	
'the garden of Islam grows'	
'it will give when heaped with prayer'	
'the school of days'	
'the colours of all-that-will-be'	
'the frame of all-that-was'	

Do you agree that these phrases suggest a different, more spiritual reading of the poem? Islamic art replaces the representation of the human form with symbolism conveyed through geometrical and natural patterns. Can you see something similar happening in this poem?

How are the children transformed by the vision of what they are working on? How does their work and the 'school of days' determine their future? And what is the past, or tradition, which provides them with a framework?

The poet uses words to tell the story of the children's lives and their beliefs and destiny, just as the carpet is intended to tell stories about paradise and the after-life. How do the patterns and forms of the poem themselves show respect for the culture which is portrayed?

It is especially important to ensure that your different readings of a poem, both the literal, descriptive reading and the deeper, more symbolic interpretation, fit the final lines of a poem. You should have noticed that all the poems we have looked at in this chapter have especially memorable final lines. Think about the different ways you can interpret these final lines, and the ways in which they encourage you to evaluate the 'other world' portrayed:

From their fingers the colours of all-that-will-be fly

And freeze into the frame of all-that-was.

What is the effect of the enjambment between the lines? This run-on between the lines makes connections, as well as showing the speed of the children's work. How do the hyphens also make connections? In what ways might these point to a symbolic interpretation of the action of weaving? Do other patterns in the poem support this idea, such as the poet's use of alliteration, which you can also hear in these lines?

Consider how you might interpret the act of stopping the movement in a freeze-frame. How does the punctuation of the poem illustrate this idea? What has happened to the colours and activity of the children, and how does their future fit the patterns of the past?

Do you agree with this kind of reading of the poem? Sometimes students can be sceptical when discussing deeper meanings, and may think that the poet surely wouldn't have meant all this. Certainly we need to be careful about reading meanings which are not there. However, why might a poem not have words as carefully woven as the images in a carpet? Could the images have meanings the poet never intended? Once the work is complete, interpretation is the task of the reader. Like the people praying on the carpet in the mosque, they can ignore what the patterns suggest to them, or make as much meaning as they can, building associations with the words of the text.

Writing techniques

When exploring a poem beyond its surface meaning it is better not to be too definite. You will still be rewarded, even if the marker disagrees with your interpretation, especially if you use phrases like 'this could suggest …' or 'this might resemble …'.

Extend your learning

Write an essay of 800–1,000 words on the following question in order to explore the ways in which the last two poems use the poet's craft to make interesting observations about cultural diversity and mutual respect.

How do both Bhatt and Rumens portray images derived from different religions and different cultures in order to show the reader how the world is changing?

Explore the ways in which different systems of belief and ways of life are conveyed, and how both poets use images of the past to illustrate visions of the future.

This is a good moment to apply your learning to other poems you are studying. Look at the techniques we have explored so far, and list poems you have studied which illustrate them.

Poems addressed to particular people	
Poems with a very distinct rhythm or music	
Poems which use personification	
Poems which tell a story (narrative)	
Patterns of repetition within a poem	
Distinctive use of imagery or visual elements	
Poems which work at more than one level	
Memorable final lines	

9.5 Sonnets

Injured First World War soldiers

Think ahead

The next poem takes us back to the past and to traditions in English poetry. In particular, it makes use of the elegiac tradition. An elegy is a poem written to commemorate someone or something that has passed away or been lost. The poem is also a sonnet, a short but complex verse form used a great deal by many poets in the English tradition, most notably William Shakespeare. Wilfred Owen (1893–1918) was a young man very like John Keats in some ways. Determined to do good for other people, he also desired to be a great poet, but was not from a wealthy or privileged background. He became an officer in the First World War, fighting in France. He found his voice as a poet while in hospital recovering from what we would now call post-traumatic stress. He felt it was important to use the traditional forms of poetry at their most powerful to make people aware of the true horrors of war. Nevertheless, his sense of duty was strong and he returned to the Western Front, where he won a medal for bravery but was killed just a week before the end of the war. To understand the poem, it is important to remember that so many died in this war that it was not possible to bring all the bodies home, and often there were no remains to bury, or no time for a funeral.

'Anthem for Doomed Youth' by Wilfred Owen (1917)

What passing-bells for these who die as cattle?
Only the monstrous anger of the guns.
Only the stuttering rifles' rapid rattle
Can patter out their hasty orisons.
No mockeries now for them; no prayers nor bells.
Nor any voice of mourning save the choirs,—
The shrill, demented choirs of wailing shells;
And bugles calling for them from sad shires.

What candles may be held to speed them all?
Not in the hands of boys, but in their eyes
Shall shine the holy glimmers of good-byes.
The pallor of girls' brows shall be their pall;
Their flowers the tenderness of patient minds,
And each slow dusk a drawing-down of blinds.

passing bells = bells tolled before a funeral
patter = saying something quickly
bugles = military trumpets or cornets

speed = send off, especially after death
pall = cloth placed over a coffin
blinds = window shades traditionally pulled down after bereavement

Check your understanding

Sonnets are fourteen-line poems divided into eight-line and six-line sections, called the **octave** and **sestet**. This pattern also influences the choice of rhyming pattern, and the final two lines often rhyme (a couplet). The structure allows for a slight shift in subject matter or perspective after the first eight lines, often called the '**volta**' or turn. The octave may be divided into two quatrains, and the sestet into two tercets. The form was originally used for love poetry, but since the seventeenth century has also addressed public and political concerns. It is just long enough to construct a complex argument, but short enough to be easily remembered.

1. 'Passing-bells' are rung at church funerals. Why does the poet suggest that men who die in war won't get such a funeral?

2. Find the simile in the first line. What makes it shocking?

3. Who is personified in the second line and what is the effect of the choice of adjective?

4. Where is the alliteration in the third line and how does it relate to the choice of adjective?

5. 'Orisons' are formal prayers. What kind of prayers are muttered for these men?

6. There are three negatives in line 5. Why does the poet claim that formal funerals would be 'mockeries' for these men?

7. The imagery of the church service is continued in the seventh line: who sings in the choir?

8. Bugles are military trumpets used to sound the 'Last Post'. The 'shires' are the English countryside. What kind of music will commemorate these men?

9. How does the poet's focus change in the sestet and what is the new element he introduces?

10. We have moved away from music to human acts of mourning. Why is there no time for formal mourning ('candles') on the frontline?

11. Why does Owen call the soldiers 'boys'?

12. Where does he say we can see a 'holy glimmer'?

13. A 'pall' is a cloth placed over a coffin. Where does he say we can see the funeral honours?

14. Find the long vowel sounds which slow down the verse in the final line. How does this recreate the actions of remembrance and mourning?

KEY TERMS

sonnet = a 14-line poem, often following a set pattern of rhymes.

octave = eight-line section of verse, especially in a sonnet.

sestet = six-line section of verse, especially in a sonnet.

volta = the turning point, usually after line 8 of a sonnet.

 # Pair and share

It was traditional to draw down the blinds in your window when you discovered a member of your family had been killed. Owen's own mother received the telegram about her son's death on the same day that others were celebrating the news of the end of the war.

What is the emotional effect of this poem? Does it make you angry? Does it honour the dead? What does it say about mechanical warfare? How does its tone change in the final stanza?

You are a reporter who has been asked to interview Wilfred Owen's mother about his life, his death and his poetry. How should he be remembered? Script a dialogue of the interview and act this out for the class.

Viewpoints

Owen wanted his readers to feel that 'the poetry is in the pity', in other words, that they needed to make an emotional connection with the experience of being a frontline soldier, with the horrors of war and death in action, and the traumatic impact of these on those who witnessed them.

1. How successful is he in conveying the reality of war in the octave?

2. How does he movingly connect you with human mourning in the sestet?

Nowadays, church services and days of remembrance are used to commemorate the dead of the Great War with anthems, prayers, bells and choirs. What would Owen think of this? How does the poem suggest we should remember? Discuss these questions, and debate with your class whether it is right to commemorate wars and how we should do this.

Extend your learning

Do other poems in your selection address war or mourning? Or are they more concerned with other themes, such as man and nature or family relationships? Can you find other examples of elegies or sonnets?

Owen clearly felt it was important that readers knew what being under attack was really like. Compare the importance of setting in the poems you are studying.

1. How do the poets you are reading convey a sense of place, whether in the natural or man-made world?

2. What do places symbolize or represent to them?

3. How do the poets you are studying use form?

4. Are sonnet or stanza form important to them?

5. How does form give structure and expression to their writing?

6. How can you link poems in your set selection by theme?

7. How do the poems show contrasts in attitude or mood towards that theme?

8. How have poets used different forms and styles to express similar themes?

Draw up one table which links poems by theme and subject, and another which brings out differences in style and form. For example, formal structure/free verse, and imagery/sound patterns.

9.6 Poetry and history

Think ahead

Set poems may be chosen from an anthology, or you may study a selection of poems from one poet.

When you study an individual poet, you have a better opportunity to relate the poems to their historical and biographical contexts, as we have just done with Wilfred Owen. You can look more closely at the poet's individual choices of subject, form, theme and expression in each poem, because you know that poet and his or her body of work better, and so you can see both what makes an individual poem different and explore links to the poet's preoccupations and style.

The next poem, for example, is another elegy for lost youth, this time by the Victorian poet Thomas Hardy. He is writing about a young soldier who has died in a colonial war in Southern Africa (which had only just begun). In those days, soldiers' bodies were not sent back to their home countries, and unless they were officers, their graves were unmarked.

Thomas Hardy

'Drummer Hodge' by Thomas Hardy (1899)

They throw in Drummer Hodge, to rest
Uncoffined – just as found:
His landmark is a kopje-crest
That breaks the veldt around:
And foreign constellations west
Each night above his mound.

Young Hodge the drummer never knew –
Fresh from his Wessex home –
The meaning of the broad Karoo,
The bush, the dusty loam,
And why uprose to nightly view
Strange stars amid the gloam.

Yet portion of that unknown plain
Will Hodge for ever be;
His homely Northern breast and brain
Grow to some Southern tree,
And strange-eyed constellations reign
His stars eternally.

kopje = (Afrikaans) a small hill
veldt = (Afrikaans) plain
Wessex = the term for the South-Western counties of England where Hardy set most of his novels, stories and verse
the broad Karoo = a large desert region of South Africa
gloam = (rare) the period of twilight just after sunset

A South African veldt

Writing techniques

Read each poem you study on its own; you will need extensive notes for revision. However, you will become sensitive to similarities of theme and expression, and develop the ability to interpret that poet's work. Essay questions will offer you opportunities to say what is characteristic about aspects of style or tone in the poem you are asked to focus on.

✏ Check your understanding

This poem is striking for its simple structure and its unusual choice of words. Use these questions to help you to appreciate the effect of both of these.

1. How many rhymes does Hardy use in each stanza?
2. How does the rhythm alternate? Count the number of stresses in each line.
3. How does this maintain the simplicity of the poem?
4. Why does Hardy choose such a simple, monosyllabic name as 'Hodge'?
5. What is the effect of Hardy's choice of the verb 'thrown' in the first line?
6. Why does the unusual compound adjective 'uncoffined' make you pause to think in the second line?
7. Why does Hardy use Afrikaans words in the first stanza?
8. Even the stars are 'foreign' as this is a southern hemisphere sky. Why does Hardy use 'west' as a verb?
9. How does Hardy repeat this reference to the stars in the second and third stanzas?
10. What kind of eternity do those stars represent?
11. 'Uprose' and 'gloam' are rare words. What kind of light and effect does Hardy want to describe here?
12. How does Hardy describe Hodge's transformation into part of this beautiful but strange landscape?
13. What is the effect of the choice of the adjective 'homely' in this context?
14. Where do you think the strong stresses fall in the final line?
15. Why are the stars now 'his'?

💬 Pair and share

You have seen how the poem depends on its contrasts between the 'homely' boy drummer (most drummers were teenagers) and the strange landscape where he ended up. Think about how the poem illustrates the following subjects which we know Hardy was preoccupied with:

1. death and what kind of after-life human beings might have
2. time and its passing
3. fate and its strange twists and turns
4. tragedy and consolation
5. the importance of home
6. regions and people at the margins, rather than the centre of things
7. the relationship between man and nature
8. the contrast between our human concerns and eternity.

Find and share other poems by Hardy or other war poems (including others in this book) which you can compare with this poem.

This elegy is striking for its simplicity and the way in which it is a poem about an imaginary individual but might easily stand for universal experience. A sensitive reading of the poem needs to bring out the individuality of its names and places and the patterns and rhythms which give it simplicity and inevitability.

Read the poem aloud, sharing alternate lines between you and your partner. How does this help to bring out the effect of alternating longer and shorter lines as well as different rhymes? Why does this structure fit the mood and purpose of the poem so well?

Remember that the form of the elegy is meant to express mourning and loss but also consolation. The whole poem could be described as a search for meaning in Hodge's death. Where does Hardy seem to find this meaning?

Contrast the first two lines and the last two lines. Why is their tone so different? How do they help to create a very different mood for the first and third stanzas?

Viewpoints

We have looked at other poems about young men going off to fight in foreign lands in chapter 4. Look back at those poems.

1. What is different about Hardy's attitude to war and to his subject?
2. Why do you think he chooses not to express an opinion on the rights and wrongs of war?
3. Why do you think he chose to write about a particular, named young man?
4. Hardy employs tact when dealing with the reasons for the war and who to blame for Hodge's death. Why is his tact so sensitive and well-judged?

Looking back, we view these wars in South Africa very differently from the way they would have been seen at the time. What is it about Hardy's way of writing poetry which ensures that it still has meaning long after different histories and ways of looking at the world have changed our ideas?

Consider:

How much attention do we really need to pay to history and biography when reading poetry?

Look back at the poems we have explored in this book so far. History can help us to understand why poems were written, but why do we still read them? Discuss the question with your teacher and classmates, and then look back at your set poems and consider the ways in which they have been crafted. Does the meaning of the poem change over time? Is meaning purely what the writer intended, or do readers make their own meaning out of a text?

There is a superb lesson on this poem in Alan Bennett's play *The History Boys*. We have already seen how the playwright presented Mr Irwin's unusual teaching in chapter 5. Here, a rival teacher, Mr Hector, asks a student if he has any thoughts after a reading of 'Drummer Hodge'.

Mr Hector's students, in 2006 film version of *The History Boys*

The History Boys by Alan Bennett (2004)

POSNER: I wondered, sir, if this "Portion of that unknown plain/ Will Hodge for ever be" is like Rupert Brooke, sir, "There's some corner of a foreign field…" "In that rich earth a richer dust concealed…"

HECTOR: It is. It is. It's the same thought…though Hardy's is better, I think…more…more, well down to earth. Quite literally, yes, down to earth.

Anything about his name?

POSNER: Hodge?

HECTOR: Mmm – the important thing is that he has a name. Say Hardy is writing about the Zulu Wars or later the Boer War possibly, these were the first campaigns when soldiers…or common soldiers…were commemorated, the names of the dead recorded and inscribed on war

Posner is quoting from Rupert Brooke's famous poem 'The Soldier' (1915)

memorials. Before this, soldiers…private soldiers anyway, were all unknown soldiers, and so far from being revered there was a firm in the nineteenth century, in Yorkshire of course, which swept up their bones from the battlefields of Europe in order to grind them into fertilizer.

So, thrown into a common grave though he may be, he is still Hodge the drummer. Lost boy though he is on the other side of the world, he still has a name.

POSNER: How old was he?

HECTOR: If he's a drummer he would be a young soldier, younger than you probably.

POSNER: No. Hardy.

HECTOR: Oh, how old was Hardy? When he wrote this, about sixty. My age, I suppose.

Saddish life, though not unappreciated.

'Uncoffined' is a typical Hardy usage.

A compound adjective, formed by putting 'un-' in front of the noun. Or verb, of course.

Un-kissed. Un-rejoicing. Un-confessed. Un-embraced. It's a turn of phrase he has bequeathed to Larkin, who liked Hardy, apparently.

He does the same.

Unspent. Unfingermarked.

And with both of them it brings a sense of not sharing, of being out of it.

Whether because of diffidence or shyness, but a holding back. Not being in the swim. Can you see that?

POSNER: Yes, sir. I felt that a bit.

HECTOR: The best moments in reading are when you come across something – a thought, a feeling, a way of looking at things – which you had thought special and particular to you. Now here it is, set down by someone else, a person you have never met, someone who is long dead. And it is as if a hand had come out and taken yours.

Philip Larkin (1922–85) was a fine English poet of the twentieth century

Extend your learning

1. How effective are Posner's comparisons? What point does Hector make out of them?

2. How does Hector use historical circumstances to help to bring the poem to life?

3. How does he show his interest in Hardy's language and what it reveals?

4. How does his last speech here highlight personal response and the role of the reader in making meaning?

Does Hector help you to see what the poem means for him? How does he try to define Hardy's sense of the elegiac and melancholy? Does he help to resolve the debate about how much history and biography we need to interpret poetry? Or about the relationship between poetry and immortality?

9.7 Modern poetry

Think ahead

Other poets address the elegiac in different ways, by remembering people and events from their past, or particular moods and feelings. Tennyson's 'Tears, Idle Tears' and Emily Brontë's 'Cold in the Earth' express less specific feelings of loss or melancholy. Even poems about nature address the relationship between our memories and what could easily be lost, or become extinct if we did not remember it. Sometimes poets notice that nature has a continuity and permanence that we lack. It renews itself afresh, like in Philip Larkin's 'Trees', and can remind us of our own mortality or give us a glimpse of the possibility of renewal, rebirth or immortality.

As we get used to the themes which are common to the poems we study, and the various forms in which poets express them, we appreciate that poets share a tradition. Modern poets are often renewing that tradition, sometimes in modern forms and sometimes in very old ones, and applying it to the everyday events of their own lives. Poets today are more likely to write about the quotidian, the day to day, than big grand imaginative themes, but they apply the art of memory to these, by working in similar ways to the poets of the past.

In our last section, we will apply the same tools of analysis to some more recent poems, drawing on the two Cambridge anthologies, *Songs of Ourselves*. You may have needed more help with the language, structure and forms of older poems, but this has given you a toolkit to help you to make sense of more modern poems.

When you study modern poems, you will find fewer study guides and online help. That is actually a good thing: the meaning of a poem is what you make of it for yourself, and not what others say about it. Relate your personal response to the words of the poem, and to its language, structure and form, and your interpretation will be a valid one.

The modern poems you study are likely to be relatively short lyrics. By a lyrical poem, we mean one that you could imagine being set to music: it will have musical qualities (such as sound effects and patterns); will convey the emotions and viewpoint of an individual speaker (the **persona**); and will relate to a particular moment. We sometimes talk about persona (from the Greek word for mask) because the 'I' in a poem is not necessarily identical with the biographical poet. It is more like when someone sings a song: they are performing.

Other forms of poem may be narrative (telling a story) or dramatic (with more than one speaker or imagining a particular situation or audience). These poems are, of course, closer to other genres you have studied, but the lyrical poem takes you back to the original form of literature, which is one person speaking about 'their' feelings. For convenience, we call this person 'the poet' and when we read a lyric, we ask how the poet conveys feelings to us. By this, we mean the language and techniques they use to communicate their feelings to you, and encourage you to share them, through sympathy (what Owen calls 'pity') or empathy.

We will look at a number of poems about memory, loss, nature and the passing of time, all traditional lyrical subjects, but here presented in individual and modern ways.

KEY TERM

persona = The person who speaks in a poem; we often call this the poet, but that doesn't mean the poem is autobiographical.

'One Art' by Elizabeth Bishop (1911–79)

The art of losing isn't hard to master;
so many things seem filled with the intent
to be lost that their loss is no disaster.

intent = desire or purpose

Lose something every day. Accept the fluster
of lost door keys, the hour badly spent.
The art of losing isn't hard to master.

fluster = fuss or hassle

Then practice losing farther, losing faster:
places, and names, and where it was you meant
to travel. None of these will bring disaster.

I lost my mother's watch. And look! my last, or
next-to-last, of three loved houses went.
The art of losing isn't hard to master.

I lost two cities, lovely ones. And, vaster,
some realms I owned, two rivers, a continent.
I miss them, but it wasn't a disaster.

– Even losing you (the joking voice, a gesture
I love) I shan't have lied. It's evident
the art of losing's not too hard to master
though it may look like (*Write* it!) like disaster.

Check your understanding

In this poem, the US poet Elizabeth Bishop reinvents a traditional verse form, the **villanelle**. A villanelle needs to have five tercets followed by a quatrain, and the first and third lines of the first stanza are repeated alternatively in each tercet until both are repeated in the final stanza. In what ways does this resemble the way a song lyric works? Bishop manages to keep the shape of this form, while writing in a very direct way and making small variations in many of the repeated lines.

1. What does the word 'intent' mean? In what ways might many things in our lives today intend to be lost?

2. What is the first example of loss and what are its consequences?

3. How does the poet introduce each example and make us think about it?

4. Give examples of how each instance of loss gets bigger and more serious.

5. What do you think she means by 'losing' a house or a city? How has this changed your understanding of what 'losing' means?

6. Why is the third house described as 'next-to-last' and what is the effect of this?

7. Who or what is the biggest loss of all?

8. What does this reveal about who the poem is addressed to?

9. What do the lines in brackets tell us about this person?

10. What is the effect of introducing brackets again in the final line of the poem?

KEY TERMS

villanelle = poem which alternates repetition of words at the end of each stanza and then unites both sets of words in the last two lines.

hyperbole = exaggeration for rhetorical effect.

 Viewpoints

There are two quite different ways of reading this poem. You could read it at face value, and see the poet as showing bravery and resilience in the face of loss, or you could read it as a bitter and reluctant acceptance of the inevitable. Its exaggerations (**hyperbole**) and interjections (in brackets) could be read as undermining the surface meaning. Clearly the poem is addressed to someone the poet has loved and lost. Take turns with a partner in reading this poem aloud, reading it as a letter to someone who has left you. First try 'resilience and resignation' and then try 'sarcasm and bitterness'.

Which tone seems best to you? Is it possible to mix the two? Present your findings, and your agreed reading of the poem, to the rest of the class.

Modern poems are often ambivalent or ambiguous: these words suggest that they can be read and interpreted in more than one way. Remember that your reading is valid if you can make it fit the words, images and tone of the poem.

The British poet Philip Larkin wrote poems which often appear satirical or bitter but have a deeper underlying romanticism or resignation. Birdsong was frequently used by Romantic poets, and by Larkin's favourite poet (Thomas Hardy) as a metaphor for the lyrical voice. In this case, the bird is a small one, a thrush, common in English gardens.

'Coming' by Philip Larkin (1922–85)

On longer evenings,
Light, chill and yellow,
Bathes the serene
Foreheads of houses.
A thrush sings,
Laurel-surrounded
In the deep bare garden,
Its fresh-peeled voice
Astonishing the brickwork.
It will be spring soon,
It will be spring soon –
And I, whose childhood
Is a forgotten boredom,
Feel like a child
Who comes on a scene
Of adult reconciling,
And can understand nothing
But the unusual laughter,
And starts to be happy.

serene = calm or noble
Laurel-surrounded = surrounded by the leaves of a hedge

A song thrush

218

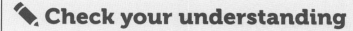

Check your understanding

1. Poems, like prose, are written in sentences. Find the verb in the first sentence and then the noun which is the subject of the sentence.
2. How would you describe the mood of that evening?
3. Laurel leaves were traditionally used to crown a successful poet ('laureate'). How does this image turn the thrush into a grander figure?
4. Who hears the bird's voice (apart from the poet)?
5. What is the effect of linking 'bare' to 'brickwork' through alliteration?
6. What is the effect of repeating the lines in the poem about spring?
7. What does spring represent and why might the bird sing about it?
8. How do you think about the poet when he describes his childhood as 'forgotten boredom'?
9. Why do you think he wants to portray himself as innocent, like a child?
10. In what ways might spring resemble 'adult reconciling'?

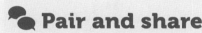

Pair and share

Reconciliation involves people coming together. What else is 'coming' in the poem? Why did the poet give it this title?

In pairs, script an interview with this poet. What makes him happy and what makes him sad? Interview him about this poem and its meaning, asking about individual lines and images and what they meant to him. Remember that if you are the poet, you don't necessarily want to give a straight answer, but leave plenty for your readers to work out! Remember, too, that the persona is not the same as the personality of the poet: you were not necessarily writing about your own feelings or experience, but imagining a situation and expressing it lyrically.

'You will Know When You Get There' is another poem with an intriguing title. The New Zealand poet Allan Curnow used it as the title of his collection, as well as the title of this poem. Like 'Coming' it suggests journeys and destination. This is a poem with a very strong sense of place, and it is less suburban than Philip Larkin's garden. It describes a fishing port. The poet's lyric should perhaps be read like a painting, as it pictures a particular scene and moment, sky, sea, shore and just a few people.

'You will Know When You Get There' by Allen Curnow (1911–2001)

Nobody comes up from the seas as late as this
in the day and the season, and nobody else goes down

the last steep kilometre, wet-metalled where
a shower passed shredding the light which keeps

pouring out of its tank in the sky, through summits,
trees, vapours thickening and thinning. Too

credibly by half celestial, the dammed
reservoir up there keeps emptying while the light lasts

over the sea, where it 'gathers the gold against
it'. The light is bits of crushed rock randomly

glinting underfoot, wetted by the short
shower, and down you go and so in its way does

the sun which gets there first. Boys, two of them,
turn campfirelit faces, a hesitancy to speak

is a hesitancy of the earth rolling back and away
behind this man going down to the sea with a bag

to pick mussels, having an arrangement with the tide,
the ocean to be shallowed three point seven metres,

one hour's light to be left, and there's the excrescent
moon sponging off the last of it. A door

slams, a heavy wave, a door, the sea-floor shudders.
Down you go alone, so late, into the surge-black fissure.

wet-metalled = pathway shines as it is wet
celestial = from the skies or heavens
dammed = there is a dam creating a reservoir of water
glinting = shining
mussels = shellfish which cling to rocks by sea
excrescent = superfluous (think about the shape of the moon)
fissure = gap or hole

A harbour

✎ Check your understanding

1. Why is this not a time for fishermen?
2. What do we know about the person going down 'the last steep kilometre'?
3. What is the weather like?
4. What is the sky compared to?
5. What is the effect of the light as the sun sets?
6. Where can the person in the poem ('you') see the sun's rays 'glinting'?
7. What do you think is the effect on his mood of the last rays of light and the sunset?
8. What is the man going down to the sea to do?
9. What is the effect of the description of the boys watching him?
10. Why would the moon be 'sponging' off the light?
11. Why does the man have 'an arrangement with the tide'?
12. Which effects make the last lines of the poem dark?
13. What is the effect of the punctuation in the final stanza?
14. What is the effect of the way the final line is printed?

Viewpoints

This is a poem which depends for its effect on two key elements of lyrical poetry: tone and mood. The tone is the music of the poem itself, and the mood is the feeling it gives you, as a reader. Discuss and list the adjectives you would use to describe its tone. Think about the colours and images of the poem, like a picture, and then imagine the music that might accompany it. What does it make the reader think about?

In your group, prepare a reading of this poem accompanied by your choice of music and visual images. You can use a slide show presentation to do this. Choose music and images which will illustrate the poem and convey its mood to listeners and viewers. Bring out the ways in which the words of the poem appeal to our senses of sight and sound, so that we can see the scene, hear the scene and feel the sun setting and the movement from light to darkness.

At the end of the presentation answer these questions.

1. The title of the poem is either a description or a riddle. How does the whole poem relate to its title?

2. Who is addressed in the title?

3. If the poem is an allegory, what is it an allegory for?

Our final poem is similarly riddling, but it may help you to decide what you understand by the previous text. This poem by the Lancashire poet, John Cassidy, also paints a particular scene and asks you to interpret it. Curnow addressed his poem to 'you' and addresses the 'mussel picker' in the same way. Cassidy tells us in his title that he is writing about his sons, but we don't see them close-up, only 'departing' as they walk away from the poet towards the sea. We need not assume any kind of 'backstory' to this poem, any more than to Curnow's. The poet is like a painter, describing a particular moment and what it seemed to mean to him at the time. However, the language of the poem makes it a memorable and moving moment, and perhaps a significant one. These adjectives are all used in Cambridge Literature in English examination questions on poetry, and their purpose is two-fold. First, they ask you to identify the emotional effect of a lyrical poem, and its effect on your mood. Secondly, it asks you how this is achieved through the poet's language and techniques. Only then should you interpret the poem and decide what it means to you. This way, you will address all the assessment objectives for the subject, and achieve a deeper understanding of the text.

'Sons, Departing' by John Cassidy (1928–)

They walked away between tall hedges,
their heads just clear and blond
with sunlight, the hedges' dark sides
sickly with drifts of flowers.

They were facing the sea and miles
of empty air; the sky had high
torn clouds, the sea its irregular
runs and spatters of white.

They did not look back; the steadiness
of their retreating footfalls lapsed
in a long diminuendo; their line
was straight as the clipped privets.

They looked at four sliding gulls
a long way up, scattering down frail
complaints; the fickle wind filled in
with sounds of town and distance.

They became sunlit points; in a broad
haphazard world the certain focus.
Against the random patterns of the sea
their walk was one-dimensional, and final.

spatters = deliberate spots, like paint
diminuendo = musical term for getting gradually quieter
privets = hedges often found next to paths
complaints = could be a lamenting poem or song

Two men walking away

✎ Check your understanding

1. Why do the boys' heads contrast with the hedges?
2. How does the sky look to the poet?
3. How does he use language to capture the look and sounds of the sea?
4. A 'diminuendo' is a musical term and it describes the slowly decreasing sound of the boys' footsteps. Why does the poet notice that they do not look back towards him?
5. 'Privets' are hedges; how does the description of the hedges add to the sense of growing distance between the poet and the boys?
6. How does the poet capture the sounds of being by the sea in the fourth stanza?
7. How do the boys continue to show contrast, this time with the sea, in the final stanza?
8. What do you think the poet means by describing them as 'the certain focus' in a 'haphazard world'?
9. Which other words make the boys sound very sure and certain about where they are going?
10. What is the effect of the final line, and how does it make you think about growing up?
11. How does the poem as a whole capture a parent's feelings about their children?
12. What do the descriptions of the poem suggest about the world the boys are walking towards?

Pair and share

Discuss what this poem has in common with Curnow's poem 'You will Know When You Get There'.

Consider the similarities of:

- setting
- atmosphere
- imagery
- description of two boys
- description of going down to the sea
- sound effects
- the impact of the final lines.

Then consider what makes each poem different and distinct. Do they have the same mood? Do they have the same attitude to the sea? Is the imagery of sunlight similar or different? What do they suggest about the different poets' attitudes to time and age?

Viewpoints

You are now ready to write on your own about a single poem, and to answer an exam-style question. Write about 500-750 words in answer to the following question:

How does the poet movingly convey the significance of this moment for him?

Looking back

This chapter has demonstrated models of how to study poetry from different periods and in different styles. The emphasis has been on close reading, but also on relating poems to their historical and cultural contexts and exploring ways to link and compare different poems within the set selections in order to make your study more interesting and to help you to construct longer coursework essays.

Review your learning by testing yourself with the following questions.

1. What is a lyrical poem?
2. What do you understand by elegy and the elegiac?
3. What is alternating rhyme?
4. What is the persona a poet uses in poetry?
5. What do you understand by the term 'ode'?
6. What do you understand by stanza form?
7. Why are so many poems in the present tense?
8. What is the name for a four-line stanza?
9. What are the different parts which make up a sonnet?
10. What is the name for lots of 's' sounds?
11. Which techniques do we group together and call imagery?
12. What do you understand by a poem's syntax?
13. How does punctuation affect the ways in which you read poems?
14. Which word do we use to express the poet's choice of words?

15. Why are the words of a poem especially charged with connotations?

16. Which subjects were especially attractive to nineteenth-century poets?

17. Which beliefs and interests did the Romantic poets share?

18. What is the role of tone and mood in shaping your interpretation of a poem?

19. How much is the interpretation of a poem controlled by the writer's choices and how much by a reader's response?

20. Why are the last lines of a poem worth especially close attention?

You will find more advice on how to read and analyse unseen poetry on the website.

Last words

'Sons, Departing' tells us that the boys' journey will go on. The voyage you began when you started your Cambridge Literature in English course also continues; as we have seen, plays, novels and poems continue to fascinate and provoke long after they were written, because debate about their meaning continues.

The emphasis of this book has been the development of your own reading skills by encouraging you to ask the right questions. Your writing skills have developed as you have learned how to answer questions, and show that you are meeting the aims of the course.

As exams get closer, you will want more specific guidance on writing essays and preparing and revising for examination.

On the accompanying website you will find extension units aimed at taking your skills to a higher level. Your teachers can print out or display on a whiteboard the sections of online chapters 10, 11 and 12 which are relevant to your own studies, and work on them with you.

They are chapter 10 (guidance for extended essays, especially for Coursework), chapter 11 (an extension chapter for students studying Paper 4, unseen texts) and chapter 12 (a revision chapter, giving examples of how to respond to different types of exam question).

Index